PHILIP JODIDIO

Nomadic

Architecture on the move | Architektur in Bewegung | L'architecture mobile

HOMES

TASCHEN

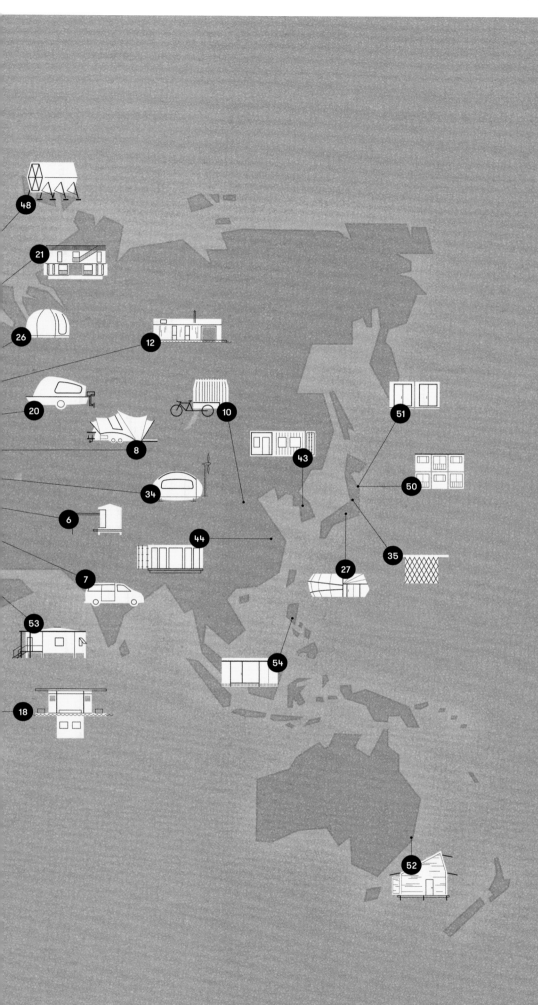

We are all Nomads

Adah gave birth to Jabal, who became
the ancestor of those who live in tents and herd livestock
Genesis 4:20

It should be no surprise that the word "nomad" has ancient origins. It comes from the Latin *nomad* via the Greek word *nomás*, which refers to pasturing flocks, or *némein* meaning to pasture, or to graze. Nomadic hunting and gathering, following seasonally available wild plants and game, is by far the oldest human subsistence method. In fact, until 10 000 years ago, all modern humans were hunter-gatherers. Put even more simply, humans were nomads for 99 percent of the period of their known existence on earth. Though nomadic lifestyles in the traditional meaning of the word are gradually disappearing, many groups, such as reindeer herders in the tundra regions of the north, still practice nomadism, following their animals according to the season. Most nomadic groups follow a fixed annual or seasonal pattern of movements and settlements. Nomadic peoples usually travelled by animal, canoe, or on foot, but even in remote regions of the world, technology and motorized transport have made inroads. Forms of transhumance, the seasonal movement of people with their livestock, certainly imply an existence of constant movement, albeit between two usually fixed points, reached in spring and fall.

For obvious reasons tents, whose existence is known to go back to the early Iron Age (8th century B.C. in Central Europe), have usually been the preferred type of "home" for nomadic peoples, in the image of examples such as the *tipi* of the North American Plains Indians, whose history may go back 4000 years, or the *yurt* used by nomads in the steppe regions of Central Asia for at least 3000 years. The military use of tents, for example the leather structures of the Roman army, is also ancient.

Gypsies and Voortrekkers

And yet it would be an error to limit the idea of nomadic lifestyles to our more distant ancestors. Peoples such as the Romani (or gypsies) have travelled Europe since medieval times, if not before. Their presence is in any case attested to in 1322 in Crete. Of different origins, Irish Travellers are also a nomadic people of whom more than 22 000 were identified in the 2006 census of the Irish Republic. Travelling first in covered wagons or caravans, Romani peoples bring to mind more "modern" forms of population movement such as the conquest of the American West, first carried forward with "wagon trains" or groups of covered wagons that carried belongings and served as shelter. The Trekboers and Voortrekkers in South Africa were nomadic pastoralists who spread north and east from Cape Town in the 17th and 18th centuries. They also employed a form of covered wagon in their travels.

On the Road

Surely due to this history of the conquest of the Far West, Americans to this day have retained a higher rate of movement between places of residence than most other people in the world. As it happens, in 2016, the percentage of Americans moving over a one-year period fell to an all time low in the United States to 11.2 percent, according to the US Census Bureau. And yet, to imagine in a nation of 325 million people that no less than 35 million moved in a single year is to appreciate a profound aspect of American culture. This might be called the culture of the road, celebrated by such figures as Jack Kerouac (*On the Road*, 1951) or, in a different mode, Ken Kesey, the author of *One Flew Over the Cuckoo's Nest* (1962), and his Merry Band of Pranksters who drove across the United States in a bus in 1964, celebrating the virtues of LSD and life on the road.

The reality of mobile homes in the United States may not be as colorful and poetic as names like Kerouac and Kesey would imply. Mobile homes make up 6.4 percent of the US housing sector and there were 8.5 million of them in 2013, down slightly on 2011, again according to the US Census Bureau. The number of occupants is not recorded but it is estimated to total about 20 million people. The Census Bureau also noted a strong correlation between the states with the most mobile homes and the lowest incomes. It was at the time of America's Great Depression in the 1930s that people started living in trailers designed for travelling or vacationing but used progressively as real homes. Parked on the outskirts of cities, something like Roma groupings in Europe, these mobile homes came to be associated in many instances with the American poor. Conversely, there was always a glamorous side to mobile homes, with companies like Airstream, created in Los Angeles in the 1920s, widely known for their luxury silver aluminum trailers.

CHRISTOPHER SMITH, "TINY, A STORY ABOUT LIVING SMALL" (P. 6) → P. 72 | MOORMAN'S NEW STANDARD CLASS → P. 60

Bible Wagons Become Leisure Trailers

The distinctions between different types of "mobile" homes are not readily made. In America, a mobile home is usually defined as a pre-fabricated structure that is permanently attached to a chassis. Often, such mobile homes are placed in a semi-permanent fashion on a piece of land, as opposed to travel trailers (also called camper trailers or caravans), like the Airstream, which are towed behind road vehicles. The Bristol Wagon & Carriage Works in England are often credited with the creation of the first "leisure trailer," whose design was based on the Bible Wagons used to preach the gospel in the American West. The ancestor of the Camping and Caravanning Club was created in England in 1901 by Thomas Hiram Holding, who is known as the founder of modern camping. Travel trailers took hold in the United States in the 1920s when it became practical to use a car to move these vehicles. In a related development, motor homes are considered as "self-propelled recreational vehicles."

The distinction between the various types of nomadic residences might well be brought down to classifying just how they can move. In an interesting definition, the US Census Bureau refers to "Manufactured Housing" or mobile homes as being prefabricated housing that is assembled in factories and then transported to its site of use. This book seeks not, of course, to thoroughly catalogue all the different types of mobile homes that exist, but rather to give an idea of the breadth and variety that what might best be called "Nomadic Homes" includes.

Hippy Heaven

Given the origins of modern nomadic homes, it might be a good idea to start with the broad variety of residences on wheels, campers, mobile homes, motor homes, caravans, and, yes, even buses that are converted or built specially to be ready to roll. It has been pointed out that the title *Nomadic Homes* could recall for some that giddy time of the Merry Band of Pranksters, of hippies, long hair, and hallucinogenic substances. Well, if being a hippy is in tune with the times, then one need look no further than the carefully restored and updated Airstream trailers produced by Wally Hofmann (HofArc) in Santa Barbara, California.

For a completely renovated 1979 Airstream Sovereign 31', baptized Elizabeth (2015; see page 38), Hofmann sought and obtained an "authentic Euro style" with a vintage SMEG refrigerator, a 1930s Wedgwood gas stove, and Moroccan mosaic tiles on the bathroom floor. Another client received his 1973 Airstream Sovereign 31', called Michelle, with "state-of-the-art HVAC heating and cooling," high-end electronics functioning with solar panels, and just a touch of reclaimed wood, perhaps to recall the 1967 Beatles song "Michelle" for which this luxurious land cruising home was named.

The hippy feeling is not far from Will Winkelman's 1958 Chevy Viking Short-Bus Retro (2009; see page 32), based on an abandoned vehicle that can either carry 12 or sleep two. His client specifically requested a "hippy Moroccan" vintage atmosphere for this conversion that offers 8.5 square meters of living space. Buses are also very much at the cutting edge of nomadic home design.

Despite assorted efforts to classify movable homes by name, modern aesthetics and design tend to blur the distinctions, whence the chapter divisions of this book. Axel Enthoven's Opera (2009; see page 64) is a bit of a camper, a sort of tent, and was inspired by no less than the Sydney Opera. In fact, the Belgian designer maintains that Opera is "neither a tent, nor a trailer, nor a camping car." This winner of the 2010 German Caravanning Design Award in reality unfolds, providing 21 square meters of living space with a king-size bed, an external shower, and numerous other modern amenities.

Homes on wheels have successfully adapted to the trend toward more and more luxurious camping, or glamping. An example of this is the Animated Forest (South Snowdonia, Wales, 2017; see page 46), which is part of an effort to encourage tourists to discover the country's natural wonders. Designed by the young London team Francis & Arnett, the Animated Forest makes reference to medieval Welsh literature and above all allows guests to fully experience nature while lying in comfort in a "padded luxury bedding area."

At what might be called the opposite end of the spectrum, where luxury is surely not the object, the Chinese firm People's Industrial Design Office has invented what they simply call the Tricycle House (Beijing, China, 2012; see page 76). Using sophisticated CNC techniques on polypropylene, they managed to squeeze a sink and stove, a bathtub, a

BRIAN & JONI BUZARDE, WOODY, LAND ARK PROTOTYPE → P. 82

water tank, and furniture that can transform from a bed to a dining table and bench, to a bench and counter top into this ultimate nomadic home.

Bobbing Up and Down

Though movable homes might most often be imagined on land, the broad seas have been a place where men and women have slept and lived almost as long as they have on terra firma. Just as mobile homes can be of the prefabricated sort that is placed in a more or less permanent way on a site, so, too, boats can be towed and moored in a given location (houseboats) or be conceived to roam the waters.

The Netherlands is of course a place where floating homes or houseboats are frequent. A number of architects in the Netherlands and elsewhere have taken into account the prospect of rising seas due to global warming and pointed out that a floating house may be the best way to avoid the coming flood(s). Koen Olthuis, born in 1971, is one of these. He has designed relatively conventional floating homes, such as the ones published here (IJburg Floating Villas, Amsterdam, 2008; see pages 108, 112), but has also struck out into more ambitious projects like The Westland, a planned floating city to be located near The Hague, and including social housing, floating islands and floating apartment buildings. These structures might well be produced elsewhere and towed into place, but their ultimate vocation is to be as static as the water itself, which is to say, in a certain sense, in constant movement.

The Los Angeles firm Morphosis designed the Float House (New Orleans, 2008–09; see page 96) subsequent to the extensive destruction caused by Hurricane Katrina in 2005. This 88-square-meter residence was imagined precisely to be able to survive floods. Attached to guideposts, it rises more than three and a half meters. Like many other new-generation waterborne houses, this one is conceived with the highest ecological standards in mind, combining solar panels and a ground source heat pump for electricity, heating, and cooling.

The rather unexpected Swedish artist Mikael Genberg has created another type of floating home, one that bobs in the waters of the Indian Ocean near Zanzibar in Tanzania. His Manta Underwater Room (2013; see page 124) is a three-level luxurious hotel facility that features an underwater bedroom with 360° views of the aqua water and sealife.

Where some nomadic homes allow their owners or users to relax in surprisingly wild natural environments, the Manta Underwater Room goes a step further, taking guests below the surface of the ocean.

Being on water, especially near an urban environment, can have another substantial advantage, aside from the capacity to float above the tide. In a city such as Copenhagen in Denmark, the center is far too expensive and densely built to permit students to have a place of residence. This is why the talented young Danish architect Bjarke Ingels (BIG), working with the entrepreneur Kim Loudrup, imagined Urban Rigger, a floating block of 12 apartments made with standard shipping containers and anchored in the harbor of Copenhagen (2016; see page 142). Inexpensive, efficient, and quite literally buoyant, Urban Rigger promises to be a model for future housing development in many port cities.

Tents in the Forest

Though the history of tents goes back nearly as far as that of humanity itself, and would seem to be circumscribed in typologies that must have already existed in the past, tents are, in fact, an area of great variety and innovation. When the idea of climbing mountains for sport arose in the 19th century, the temporary "housing" required could only come in the form of lightweight, portable structures that could be attached to the rock and survive strong winds or storms. This type of survival tent has evolved rapidly with the emergence of new materials. So, too, logically, has a related type of structure meant for campers in general. Thus the London-based firm Tentsile offers a series of different tents that can be suspended from trees, some weighing only seven kilos and capable of carrying loads of 400 kilos once suspended. Though Tentsile's models (see page 180) cost about 300 dollars, other firms and architects offer much more luxurious or glamorous solutions for would-be campers. According to a web site called glamping.com: "Recently, a global trend has caught fire that offers outdoor enthusiasts an upgrade on rest and recreation. It's called glamping, a new word for a new kind of travel, defined as glamorous camping. When you're glamping, there's no tent to pitch, no sleeping bag to unroll, no fire to build. Whether in a tent, yurt, Airstream, pod, igloo, hut, villa, cabin, cube, teepee, or treehouse, glamping is a way to experience the great outdoors without sacrificing luxury."

FRANCIS & ARNETT, ANIMATED FOREST → P. 46

Another suspended tent called the Cocoon Tree (see page 168) was invented by a former advertising agency creative director, Berni du Payrat. It is a spherical, aluminum, waterproof, tree-house pod that can be assembled in less than two hours and weighs 200 kilos (empty). This comfortable nomadic residence comes in different versions best suited to beach or jungle environments.

A Denver firm called Autonomous Tent (see page 164) has set out to create nothing less than a "new form of architecture, which has been engineered as a permanent structure, yet can be raised in just a few days and 'leave without a trace.'" It has a king-size bed, a gas fireplace, and a bathroom with a shower and flushable composting toilet, and all that for just 100 000 dollars. Across the world, in South Korea, Archi-Workshop has pioneered "glamping" structures such as their Stacking Doughnut and Modular Flow (Yang-Pyung, South Korea, 2013; see page 176), modular units that come complete with works of contemporary art specifically created for these modular tentlike homes away from home for the fortunate few.

Protestors, Freaks, Geeks, and Refugees

Movable homes of various types have a very personal aspect. They are often part of a willful attempt to break with standard societal patterns—to strike out into the wilderness as it were. But tents and other forms of temporary dwelling are sometimes grouped for entirely different reasons, as some examples in this book show. Protests are a reason for sit-ins or the occupation of city locations. This type of temporary agglomeration of tents and huts has occurred frequently in recent years, with such examples as the campsite erected by supporters of the Ukrainian opposition leader Viktor Yushchenko on the Central Boulevard of Kiev (December 2004); the Indignados or 15-M movement in Spain at the Puerta del Sol square in Madrid (2011); the various Occupy protests in the United States (2011); or the pro-democracy Umbrella Movement that occupied Hong Kong streets in 2014.

While summer festivals are the occasion for the creation of temporary cities in various parts of the world, the most famous of these is Burning Man, which takes place at the end of the summer in Black Rock City, Nevada. This festival focuses on a number of community values and forms

of artistic expression, but even the tents and campers that are united in a vast semicircular plan in the desert are worthy of note. Photographers NK Guy and Philippe Glade have documented these structures for many years and published books about the architecture of Burning Man, where 65 000 people are briefly grouped together. Although their motivations and artistic expression are very different, other events bring together large numbers of people who live for a time in a small tent. This is the case of Campus Party, a seven-day 24-hour festival that brings together gamers, bloggers, programmers, and others fascinated with technology. Campus Party has occurred on several occasions in Brazil. In 2011, the event was held from January 17 to 23 at the Centro Imigrantes exhibition hall in São Paulo, where nearly 7000 young people grouped together to take advantage of a 10Gb connection provided by the government and local telephone operators. Their hundreds of identical tents were provided with the admission charge and aligned in a rigorous grid.

Those who view aerial images of the vast temporary city created for Burning Man may be troubled by the similarity of this site with the many refugee camps that have sprung up all over the world, particularly subsequent to the Syrian crisis. The Zaatari refugee camp, located near Mafraq, Jordan, created in 2012, currently houses about 85 000 people lodged in various shelters that surely constitute one of the most visible and disturbing types of "nomadic home" in the world. Even in such difficult environments, it is to the honor of groups that work in the West, such as Architects for Society, based in Minneapolis, that designs are being developed to assist those in need in such camps. The Hex House developed by Architects for Society is a 47-square-meter emergency residence made with insulated metal panels for a "passive, low-tech design" (see page 314).

Even Western countries like France have had to deal with an influx of refugees, such as those attempting to reach the UK who were temporarily living in the "Jungle" in Calais. It is curious to note that nomadic housing for the wealthy tends to be seen as a way to escape society and attain isolation, whereas a reverse phenomena occurs for the poorest populations, herded together against their will, hoping only to find a stable life again. UNHCR estimates that there were 65.3 million forcibly displaced people worldwide in 2015. This fact, together with the ebb and flow of people made homeless by disasters other than war, such

GÜTE, COLLINGWOOD SHEPHERD HUT → P. 52

as earthquakes, tsunamis, and storm-driven floods, has encouraged a number of talented architects, such as the Japanese Pritzker Prize winner Shigeru Ban, to try to design better temporary housing, but these individual realizations are a somewhat different subject than the vast camps seen recently in the Middle East for example.

So, too, what the US Census Bureau calls "Manufactured Housing," a category still often associated with poverty or low income in the United States, becomes a more noble exercise in the hands of architects like the Latin American group MAPA who conceived the elegant MINIMOD Cauçaba (Fazenda Catuçaba, SP, Brazil, 2009–15; see page 248) created in modular form in a factory before being trucked to its site.

The noted American architects LOT-EK have experimented with shipping containers to create what they call the M.D.U. or Mobile Dwelling Unit (see page 232), which has push-out extensions in its metal walls offering space for living, working, and storage. When returned to its closed form, the M.D.U. can again take to the roads and the seas with the tens of thousands of shipping containers that move every day across the planet. Exhibited at the Whitney Museum of American Art in New York and at the Walker Art Center in Milwaukee, the Mobile Dwelling Unit is a serious effort to integrate the fundamental nomadism of many people across the world into an industrial system that is in constant movement for other reasons.

Another modular system, called the Wikkelhouse (2016; see page 292), was created by the Dutch group Fiction Factory. This surprising house is made in large part of cardboard and can be readily assembled, enlarged, or removed in 1.2-meter-long interlocking sections. The modules are treated in such a way as to be able to withstand just about any weather conditions and are estimated to have a life of up to 50 years. Thus the nomadic and the temporary can readily adapt to conditions of a more stable existence.

Six Legs to Move Slowly Forward

Quite a few architects and artists have taken the subject of the movable home a few steps further than day-to-day life might suggest, testing the ideas of mobility and of privacy in surprising ways. The Danish group N55 created their WALKING HOUSE in Copenhagen in 2009 (see page 286). This modular dwelling system for up to four people actually walks on six legs propelled by linear actuators. Environmentally friendly, this very unexpected structure was actually inspired in part by nomadic cultures and in particular by traditional Romani horse carriages from the 18th century, combined in this instance with technology and modern materials. Alex Schweder and Ward Shelley imagined their own movable home called *ReActor* in a very different way, preferring to anchor it on a five-meter-high concrete column erected at the Art Omi Center (Ghent, New York, 2016; see page 266). The 15-meter-long glass house actually pivots and moves, depending on winds and the movement of its two inhabitants. The artist and the architect actually lived in *ReActor* during a "five-day inhabitation performance."

Another artist who has questioned the nature of housing and mobility is the American Andrea Zittel. She refers to the "social construction of needs" in presenting works like her *Indy Island*, a floating pod placed in a lake and commissioned by the Indianapolis Museum of Art meant to be occupied each summer. Her Wagon Stations (A-Z West, Joshua Tree, California; Milwaukee, Minnesota, USA, 2003–) are even more surprising. These sleeping pods that can be rented in the grounds of the artist's California domain are relatively tiny movable structures made of metal and wood. Though they do offer residents an opportunity to look out through an opening in the "roof" they are clearly minimal to the point of bringing to mind Japanese "capsule" hotels. Inspired both by the covered wagons that housed possessions and provided shelter from the elements for American settlers moving West, and the station wagon, from which the scale of each of the units is derived, the Wagon Stations, might be considered the *nec plus ultra* of nomadic homes. They could not be much smaller and they are artist-designed, even if they do bring to mind that most minimal (and permanent) of lodgings.

The Challenge of Technology

Nomadic homes are increasingly being designed with an eye to making use of high technology to the end of creating the smallest possible ecological footprint while also making mobile residences for extreme environments or places where no connection to any municipal services is available. Two such unexpected projects are published in this volume.

URBAN RIGGER / BIG, URBAN RIGGER → P. 142

The first of these is the Ecocapusule (see page 212), invented by the young Slovakian architects Tomáš Žáček and Soňa Pohlová, formerly of Nice Architects (Bratislava). This 6.2-square-meter pod is described as a "self-sustainable intelligent micro-home that uses solar and wind energy." Its spherical shape and fiberglass design allow it to collect rainwater and dew while minimizing energy loss. The 1200-kilo structure can fit into a standard shipping container or make use of a specially designed trailer that can be towed by a passenger car, turning it into a fully functional caravan. An even more sophisticated mobile home is the AMIE project (see page 42), carried forward by the architects Skidmore, Owings & Merrill together with the US Department of Energy's Oak Ridge National Laboratory. The 19.5-square-meter shelter is a 3D-printed vehicle intended to demonstrate the highest levels of energy efficiency and waste control. Both the Ecocapsule and the AMIE project demonstrate a high degree of design sophistication as well as pointing the way to the homes of the future.

Space: the Final Frontier

As though to prove that we are all nomads, reference should be made to the ultimate mobile home, the one that goes into space and beyond. For those who grew up with the Star Trek series or perhaps the Star Wars movies, the words will be familiar: "Space: the final frontier. These are the voyages of the starship *Enterprise*. Its five-year mission: to explore strange new worlds, to seek out new life and new civilizations, to boldly go where no man has gone before." Those who explore "the final frontier" are in some sense already floating in space above us, aboard the 419 000-kilo International Space Station. Travelling at about 27 000 kilometers an hour, the astronauts of the ISS are the ultimate nomads, orbiting the earth 15.7 times a day, living in a fatally technological environment, but theirs, too, is a mobile home.

If government authorities and an odd collection of billionaires and visionaries have their way, orbiting the earth will not be the "final frontier" of Star Trek lore. Rather, men will strike out for Mars and then perhaps beyond. The Mars One initiative (see page 228), which aims to put at least four "permanent" settlers on Mars by 2032, represents the most distant imagined outpost of the men to date and thus the furthest ad-

venture of the nomadic home. Be it the brave men who joined Columbus and other explorers, or even those who took their covered wagons to the promised West, the prospect of returning to their former lives must always have been distant. In the case of Mars One the prospects are even more bleak: "There is no way to go back; going to Mars is a decision that you make for the rest of your life. The technology for a return mission does not yet exist."

Returning to Earth

For some, the prospect of going to Mars would seem to be a joke, whereas the life of refugees or people left homeless by natural disaster is in the hands of international organizations—NGOs that can only do so much with limited means. This is why the efforts of architects such as Shigeru Ban are so positive, and give new life to contemporary architecture. Imagine actually helping those in need, and doing so with a cogent analysis of means and ends. Inexpensive temporary housing that can be readily transported near to the site of disasters, or, even more pressing, to the frontiers of lands at war.

Shigeru Ban has made numerous efforts to assist people left without homes after natural disasters. His Container Temporary Housing (Onagawa, Japan, 2011; see page 300) was conceived after the March 11, 2011 earthquake and tsunami that struck the Tohoku region of eastern Japan. It is estimated that four years after the event, 230 000 people were still living in temporary housing. As he had for a number of previous designs, Shigeru Ban employed 6.1-meter shipping containers to build the housing at Onagawa. Due to the lack of appropriate flat sites, he decided to stack the containers three stories high in a checkerboard pattern that created "bright, open living spaces between the containers." He also managed to design three different configurations of living space depending on the size of families to be housed.

Another of Shigeru Ban's emergency relief initiatives, the New Temporary House (Manila, Philippines, 2013; see page 320), is low-cost prefabricated housing, which was tested in the Philippines. Made with fiber-reinforced plastic (FRP) and foam-board sandwich panels, this project allows for better quality temporary housing, and also generates local employment. Just as he does for an even more recent Carbon

DANIEL STRAUB, SEALANDER → P. 138

Fiber Tent that he designed (2017), the architect imagines a number of uses for the New Temporary House, including the possibility of helping in providing housing in low-income regions in countries such as India and Nepal.

Another interesting project, initially conceived for use by refugees but also available for less stressful use, is the SURI (or Shelter Units for Rapid Installation; see page 324) developed by Suricatta Systems in Alicante, Spain. Measuring a bit more than 12 square meters, the SURI units put an accent on readily available local materials including sand bags, although they also use different forms of polyethylene. These shelters are intended to be 100% recyclable and sustainable. All materials are reusable or biodegradable. Solar panels and a rainwater collection system can be integrated where appropriate. The SURI shelter comes as a 580-kilo flat-pack that can be assembled on site by two people without particular skills.

In Search of the Minimum

What a great distance between private jets and super yachts and minimal refugee housing. From the richest to the poorest inhabitants of the planet, and on to those who one day hope to colonize other planets, nomadic housing of one form or another is more the rule than the exception. With housing in general being hard to come by, what is called "Manufactured Housing" offers the possibility of ownership and residence to people who cannot afford to build their own home on site. Others can afford to spend 1.5 million euros on a bus that can be their very own motor home. A number of the architects and artists whose work is reproduced here have been interested in the concept of what constitutes a minimal home. For Renzo Piano, Diogene, a 7.5-square-meter refuge (Weil am Rhein, Germany, 2011–13; see page 202) is a response to the very least that a man or woman can hope for in their life. And yet, with such features as photovoltaic panels, a geothermal heat pump, and low-energy lighting, Diogene is also a product of advances in modern construction technology. The project is named after the Greek philosopher Diogenes, who said: "I am a citizen of the world."

Andrea Zittel's musings on "the social construction of needs" might suggest that people really need far less than society leads them to believe. But do her Wagon Stations elicit anything so much as what the French call "l'ultime demeure"? Making do in a world with finite resources of course implies downsizing, as the urban Japanese long ago sensed. A Japanese house, while not necessarily mobile, often explores the lower limits of appropriate size, this due to very high land costs and scarce availability of space in their urban centers. The very talented Japanese architect Kengo Kuma sought less to explore the frontiers of technology than to look back into the literary history of his country when he designed his Hojo-an (Kyoto, 2012; see page 216). At nine square meters, this movable house made of ETFE sheets, cedar strips, and magnets is a voluntary reminiscence of the work of Kamono Chomei (1155–1216), the author of *Hojo-ki* (*An Account of My Hut*) who lived in a movable house that is often described as the prototype of Japan's compact housing. Kuma's project aimed to reconstruct this house with modern ideas and methods, on the same site in the precinct of the Shimogamo Jinja Shrine. A *hojo* is a cottage measuring about three by three meters. Perhaps just the right size for a nomadic home, built at the frontier between the past and the future?

As it should be readily apparent from this summary collection of movable residences from all over the world and in all types of different contexts, the nomadic spirit of our ancestors the hunter-gatherers is very much alive in the modern world. Where architecture has often sought stability and thus the lack of movement, modernity has brought a sense of the finite, and a good deal of modesty about posterity and longevity. What more contemporary thought could there be than to seek nothing so much as to move, to grow perhaps, but always to move. "A good traveller," said the ancient Chinese philosopher Lao Tzu "has no fixed plans and is not intent on arriving." It is the journey that counts, the point of arrival for all is exactly the same.

Wir sind alle Nomaden

Ada gebar Jabal; er wurde der
Stammvater derer, die in Zelten und beim Vieh wohnen.
1. Mose 4, Vers 20

Es ist nicht verwunderlich, dass das Wort „Nomade" auf die Antike zurückgeht. Es stammt vom lateinischen *nomad* über das griechische Wort *nomás*, das sich auf das Hüten von Viehherden bezieht, oder *némein*, was weiden oder grasen bedeutet. Das Jagen und Sammeln der Nomaden, die den saisonal verfügbaren Wildpflanzen und dem Wild folgten, ist die weitaus älteste Methode des Menschen zum Überleben. Tatsächlich waren bis vor 10 000 Jahren alle modernen Menschen Jäger und Sammler. Vereinfacht ausgedrückt, waren die Menschen ganze 99 Prozent ihres bekannten Daseins auf der Erde Nomaden. Obgleich diese Lebensform in der traditionellen Bedeutung des Wortes allmählich verschwindet, wird sie von vielen Gruppen immer noch praktiziert: zum Beispiel von den Rentierhirten in den Tundragebieten des Nordens, die ihren Tieren im Ablauf der Jahreszeit folgen. Die meisten Nomadenstämme verfolgen ein festgelegtes jährliches oder saisonales System der Bewegung und der Sesshaftigkeit. Nomaden bewegten sich gewöhnlich mithilfe der Kraft von Tieren, auf Kanus oder zu Fuß, aber selbst in die entlegensten Regionen der Welt haben die Technologie und der motorisierte Transport inzwischen Einzug gehalten. Formen der Transhumanz, der saisonalen Wanderung von Menschen mit ihren Viehherden, bedeuten natürlich eine Existenz in konstanter Bewegung, wenn auch üblicherweise zwischen zwei Fixpunkten im Frühjahr und im Herbst.

Aus einleuchtenden Gründen waren Zelte, deren Existenz schon aus der frühen Eisenzeit (in Mitteleuropa aus dem 8. Jahrhundert v. Chr.) bekannt ist, für die Nomadenvölker stets die bevorzugte Form einer „Wohnung". Vorläufer waren das Tipi der nordamerikanischen Prärieindianer, dessen Geschichte wohl bis auf 4000 Jahre zurückgeht, oder die von den Nomaden in den Steppen Zentralasiens seit mindestens 3000 Jahren genutzte Jurte. Die militärische Nutzung von Zelten, etwa der Lederkonstruktionen der römischen Armee, geht auch auf die Antike zurück.

Fahrendes Volk und Voortrekkers

Und doch wäre es ein Fehler, die Vorstellung von nomadischen Lebensformen auf unsere fernen Vorfahren zu beschränken. Volksstämme wie die Roma ziehen seit dem Mittelalter, wenn nicht schon früher, durch Europa. Jedenfalls ist ihre Anwesenheit auf Kreta im Jahr 1322 bezeugt.

Von irischen Nomaden, völlig anderer Herkunft, wurden mehr als 22 000 im Zensus der Republik Irland von 2006 gezählt. Die zuerst in Planwagen oder Wohnwagen reisenden Roma erinnern an „modernere" Bewegungsformen von Volksgruppen, etwa die Eroberung des nordamerikanischen Westens, die zuerst mit „Trecks" oder Gruppen von Planwagen erfolgte, die die Habseligkeiten der Siedler enthielten und ihnen zugleich als Unterkunft dienten. Die burischen Trekboers und Voortrekkers in Südafrika waren nomadische Viehhalter, die im 17. und 18. Jahrhundert von Kapstadt aus nach Norden und Osten zogen. Auch sie nutzten eine Art Planwagen für ihre Reisen.

Unterwegs

Mit Sicherheit hat diese Geschichte der Eroberung des Westens bis heute bei den Amerikanern zu einem häufigeren Wechsel des Wohnorts geführt als bei den meisten anderen Völkern der Welt. Allerdings ist laut dem US Census Bureau im Jahr 2016 der Prozentsatz der Amerikaner, die im Lauf eines Jahres in den Vereinigten Staaten umzogen, auf den tiefsten Stand aller Zeiten, auf 11,2 Prozent, gefallen. Und dennoch, wenn man sich vorstellt, dass von einer Nation von 325 Millionen Einwohnern in nur einem Jahr ganze 35 Millionen umgezogen sind, muss man von einem ernst zu nehmenden Aspekt der amerikanischen Kultur sprechen. Man könnte das die Kultur der Straße nennen, die von Autoren wie Jack Kerouac (*On the Road*, 1957, dt. *Unterwegs*) gepriesen wurde, oder, in anderer Form, von Ken Kesey, dem Autor von *Einer flog über das Kuckucksnest* (1962), und seiner Band Merry Pranksters, die 1964 in einem Bus durch die USA fuhren und die Vorzüge von LSD und dem Leben auf der Straße propagierten.

Die Realität der Mobilheime in den Vereinigten Staaten wird nicht so farbig und poetisch aussehen, wie Kerouac und Kesey uns glauben machen. Mobile Wohnungen nehmen 6,4 Prozent des US-Wohnungssektors ein, und 2013 gab es davon 8,5 Millionen, etwas weniger als 2011, wiederum laut dem US Census Bureau. Die Zahl der Bewohner wird nicht genannt, aber auf insgesamt etwa 20 Millionen geschätzt. Die Statistikbehörde erwähnt auch eine starke Korrelation zwischen den Staaten mit den meisten mobilen Wohnungen und den mit den niedrigsten Einkommen. Zur Zeit von Amerikas großer Wirtschaftskrise in den

CARL TURNER, FLOATING HOUSE (P. 14) → P. 102 | FRIDAY / FERNANDO SEABRA SANTOS, FLOATWING® → P. 116

1930er-Jahren begannen die Leute, in Wohnwagen zu leben, die eigentlich zum Reisen oder für die Ferien bestimmt waren, aber zunehmend dauerhaft genutzt wurden. Diese an den Rändern der Städte, ähnlich wie bei den Roma-Gruppen in Europa, geparkten mobilen Wohnungen wurden oft mit den Bedürftigen in Amerika gleichgesetzt. Umgekehrt gab es aber auch immer glamouröse Mobilheime, zum Beispiel von der in den 1920ern in Los Angeles gegründeten Firma Airstream, die durch ihre luxuriösen, silberfarbigen Aluminiumanhänger weithin bekannt wurde.

Bible Wagons werden zu Freizeit-Wohnwagen

Die Unterschiede zwischen den verschiedenen Arten „mobiler" Wohnungen sind nicht so einfach zu definieren. In den USA wird üblicherweise eine vorfabrizierte, auf einem Chassis angebrachte Konstruktion als Mobile Home bezeichnet. Häufig werden solche quasi permanent auf ein Grundstück gestellt – ganz im Gegensatz zu den Reiseanhängern (auch als Camper oder Wohnwagen bezeichnet) wie die von Airstream, die an Geländefahrzeuge angehängt werden. Den Bristol Wagon & Carriage Works in England wird häufig die Produktion des ersten „Freizeitanhängers" zugeschrieben, dessen Gestaltung auf den Bible Wagons beruhte, die im amerikanischen Westen zur Verkündigung des Evangeliums dienten. Der Vorläufer des Camping and Caravanning Club wurde 1901 von Thomas Hiram Holding in England gegründet, der als Begründer des modernen Camping bekannt wurde. Wohnwagen verbreiteten sich in den Vereinigten Staaten in den 1920er-Jahren, als es üblich wurde, sie zur Beförderung an ein Fahrzeug anzuhängen. Im Gegensatz dazu gelten die motorisierten Wohnmobile als „selbstfahrende Freizeitfahrzeuge".

Der Unterschied zwischen den verschiedenen Formen nomadischer Wohnungen lässt sich auch daran festmachen, wie sie bewegt werden können. In einer interessanten Definition bezeichnet das US Census Bureau „fabrikmäßig hergestellte" oder mobile Wohnungen als vorfabrizierten Wohnungsbau, der in Fabriken zusammengesetzt und dann zum Ort seiner Nutzung transportiert wird. Dieses Buch ist natürlich kein Versuch, alle unterschiedlichen Formen mobilen Wohnens aufzulisten, vielmehr soll es eine Vorstellung vom Umfang und von der Vielfalt

dessen vermitteln, was man vielleicht am besten als „Nomadenwohnungen" bezeichnen könnte.

Der Himmel der Hippies

Angesichts der Ursprünge der modernen Nomadenwohnungen ist es vielleicht sinnvoll, mit der großen Vielfalt der Wohnformen auf Rädern zu beginnen: die Camper, die mobilen und motorisierten Wohnungen, die Caravans und – ja – sogar die Busse, die zu diesem Zweck umgebaut oder speziell dafür produziert wurden. Es wurde bereits erwähnt, dass der Titel *Nomadic Homes* einige an die wilden Zeiten der Band Merry Pranksters erinnern würde – an die Hippies mit langen Haaren und an halluzinogene Substanzen. Wer heute mit den Hippies sympathisiert, braucht nur die von der Firma Wally Hofmann (HofArc) in Santa Barbara, Kalifornien, sorgfältig restaurierten und modernisierten Airstream-Trailer zu betrachten. Für einen komplett renovierten Airstream Sovereign 31' von 1979 namens Elizabeth (2015, siehe Seite 38) suchte und fand Hofmann einen „authentischen Euro Style" mit einem zeitgleichen Kühlschrank von SMEG, einem Wedgwood-Gasofen von 1930 und marokkanischen Fliesen für den Boden des Badezimmers. Ein anderer Kunde erhielt seinen Airstream Sovereign 31' von 1973 namens Michelle mit „modernster Heizung und Klimaanlage", hochwertiger elektronischer Ausstattung mit Solarpaneelen und nur einem Hauch recycelten Holzes, wohl als Erinnerung an den Beatles-Song „Michelle" von 1967, nach dem dieser luxuriöse Straßenkreuzer benannt wurde.

Dem Hippie-Ideal entspricht auch Will Winkelmans Chevy Viking Short-Bus Retro aus dem Jahr 1958 (2009, siehe Seite 32) auf der Basis eines längst aufgegebenen Fahrzeugs, in dem entweder zwölf Personen reisen oder zwei übernachten können. Sein Kunde forderte für diesen Umbau ausdrücklich eine authentische „marokkanische Hippie-Atmosphäre" mit 8,5 m² Wohnfläche. Busse sind auch aktuell sehr gefragt für das moderne Nomadenleben.

Trotz verschiedentlicher Bemühungen, die mobilen Heime namentlich zu klassifizieren, scheinen die moderne Ästhetik und das Design die Unterschiede zu verwischen, daher auch die Kapitelaufteilung in diesem Buch. Axel Enthovens Opera (2009, siehe Seite 64) hat etwas von einem Camper, ist eine Art Zelt und wurde von nichts Geringerem als dem

+31 ARCHITECTS, WATERVILLA WEESPERZIJDE → P. 154

Opernhaus in Sydney inspiriert. In der Tat behauptet der belgische Designer, dass Opera „weder ein Zelt noch ein Trailer noch ein Campingwagen" sei. Dieser Gewinner des German Caravanning Design Award von 2010 bietet realiter 21 m² Wohnraum mit einem großen Doppelbett, einer Außendusche und zahlreichen weiteren modernen Annehmlichkeiten. Die Wohnungen auf Rädern haben sich erfolgreich dem Trend zum immer luxuriöseren Camping oder Glamping angepasst. Ein Beispiel dafür ist der Animated Forest (South Snowdonia, Wales, 2017, siehe Seite 46), der zu einem Programm gehört, das Touristen zur Entdeckung der Naturwunder des Landes anregen soll. Der von dem jungen Londoner Team Francis & Arnett gestaltete Animated Forest nimmt Bezug auf die mittelalterliche walisische Literatur und bietet den Gästen das echte Erlebnis der Natur bei komfortabler Unterbringung „in gepolsterten Luxusbetten".

Sozusagen am anderen Ende des Spektrums, wo Luxus sicher keine Rolle spielt, hat die chinesische Firma People's Industrial Design Office das schlicht Tricycle House genannte Projekt entworfen (Peking, 2012, siehe Seite 76). Mittels hochentwickelter CNC-Technik und Polypropylen ist es der Firma gelungen, in diesem ultimativen Nomadenhaus eine Spüle, einen Ofen, eine Badewanne, einen Wassertank und Möbel unterzubringen, die sich von einem Bett in einen Esstisch und eine Bank oder eine Bank und eine Arbeitsfläche umfunktionieren lassen.

Auf- und Abbewegung

Obgleich man mobile Heime meist an Land vermutet, leben und schlafen die Menschen auch auf den Meeren schon fast so lange wie auf dem Festland. Ebenso wie man vorfabrizierte mobile Wohnungen mehr oder weniger permanent auf ein Grundstück stellen kann, können auch Boote an einem bestimmten Ort (als Hausboote) vertäut und verankert werden oder sind dafür vorgesehen, über das Wasser zu treiben. Die Niederlande sind natürlich ein Land, in dem es viele schwimmende Häuser oder Hausboote gibt. Einige Architekten aus den Niederlanden und von anderswo haben wegen des Ansteigens des Meeresspiegels aufgrund der globalen Erwärmung darauf hingewiesen, dass ein schwimmendes Haus der beste Weg sein könnte, sich gegen künftige Überflutungen zu wappnen. Koen Olthuis (geb. 1971) ist einer von ihnen. Er hat

relativ konventionelle schwimmende Häuser entworfen, zum Beispiel die hier vorgestellten (IJburg Floating Villas, Amsterdam, 2008, siehe Seiten 108, 112), ist aber auch mit ehrgeizigeren Projekten bekannt geworden, etwa mit The Westland, einer schwimmenden Stadt bei Den Haag, einschließlich Sozialwohnungen, schwimmender Inseln und schwimmender Mehrfamilienhäuser. Diese Bauten könnten anderswo hergestellt und an ihren Standort geschleppt werden, sind aber letztlich dafür bestimmt, ebenso statisch wie das Wasser zu sein, das heißt, gewissermaßen in ständiger Bewegung.

Das Büro Morphosis Architects aus Los Angeles plante das Float House (New Orleans, 2008–09, siehe Seite 96) nach der großen Zerstörung 2005 durch den Hurrikan Katrina. Dieses 88 m² große Wohnhaus ist extra dafür vorgesehen, Überschwemmungen zu überstehen. An Leitpfosten befestigt, kann es über 3,5 m ansteigen. Wie viele andere für das Wasser bestimmte Häuser der neuen Generation soll es mit dem höchsten ökologischen Standard ausgestattet werden, mit Solarpaneelen und einer Erdwärmepumpe für Strom, Heizung und Kühlung. Der auf diesem Gebiet eher unbekannte schwedische Künstler Mikael Genberg hat einen anderen Typ eines schwimmenden Hauses geschaffen, das auf dem Wasser des Indischen Ozeans bei Sansibar in Tansania treibt. Sein Manta Underwater Room (2013, siehe Seite 124) ist ein dreigeschossiges Luxushotel mit einem Unterwasser-Schlafraum, der 360-Grad-Ausblicke auf das Wasser und das Leben im Meer gewährt. Während auch einige andere Nomadenhäuser ihren Besitzern oder Nutzern Entspannung in erstaunlich unberührter Natur bieten, geht der Manta Underwater Room noch einen Schritt weiter, indem er die Gäste unter die Meeresoberfläche bringt.

Der Standort auf dem Wasser, besonders in einem städtischen Umfeld, kann, außer der Möglichkeit des Schwimmens bei Überflutung, noch einen weiteren entscheidenden Vorteil haben: In einer Stadt wie Kopenhagen in Dänemark ist das Zentrum viel zu teuer und zu dicht bebaut, um Studenten noch eine Wohnung bieten zu können. Deshalb hat der begabte, junge dänische Architekt Bjarke Ingels (vom Büro BIG) in Zusammenarbeit mit dem Unternehmer Kim Loudrup Urban Rigger entworfen, einen schwimmenden Block mit zwölf Wohnungen aus genormten Transportcontainern, der im Kopenhagener Hafen verankert ist (2016, siehe Seite 142). Der preiswerte, effiziente und im wahren Sinn

TENTSILE, TENTSILE TREE TENTS → P. 180

des Wortes beschwingte Urban Rigger verspricht, ein Modell für künftige Wohnbebauung in vielen Hafenstädten zu werden.

Zelte im Wald

Obwohl die Geschichte des Zeltes fast bis zur Entstehung der Menschheit zurückgeht und sich scheinbar in Typologien umschreiben lässt, die bereits in der Vergangenheit existierten, zeichnen sich Zelte tatsächlich durch große Vielfalt und Innovation aus. Als im 19. Jahrhundert der Sport des Bergsteigens aufkam, waren die benötigten temporären „Wohnungen" nur als leichte, tragbare Konstruktionen denkbar, die sich am Fels befestigen ließen und starken Winden standhalten konnten. Diese Form des Zeltes zum Überleben hat sich mit der Entstehung neuer Materialien sehr schnell weiterentwickelt, logischerweise ebenso die damit verwandte Ausführung für normale Camper. So bietet die Londoner Firma Tensile eine Reihe verschiedener Zelte an, von denen einige nur 7 kg wiegen und die an Bäumen aufgehängt werden können, wobei sie dann Gewichte von bis zu 400 kg tragen können.

Während die Modelle von Tensile (siehe Seite 180) etwa 300 Dollar kosten, bieten andere Firmen und Architekten weitaus luxuriösere und elegantere Lösungen für Möchtegerncamper an. Eine Website namens glamping.com berichtet: „Kürzlich hat ein globaler Trend um sich gegriffen, der Outdoorfans ein Upgrade für Ruhe und Erholung bietet. Man nennt das Glamping, ein neues Wort für eine neue Art zu reisen, das glamouröses Camping bedeutet. Wenn man Glamping macht, braucht man kein Zelt aufzustellen, keinen Schlafsack aufzurollen, kein Feuer zu machen. Ob im Zelt, in der Jurte, im Airstream, im Iglu, in der Hütte, in der Villa, in der Kabine, im Kubus, im Tipi oder im Baumhaus – Glamping ist eine Art, großartige Freiräume zu erleben, ohne auf Luxus zu verzichten."

Ein anderes aufgehängtes Zelt namens Cocoon Tree (siehe Seite 168) wird tatsächlich von einer Firma hergestellt und vertrieben, die sich vielversprechend Glamping Technology nennt. Das vom früheren Chef einer Werbeagentur, Berni du Payrat, erfundene Cocoon Tree ist ein kugelförmiges, wasserdichtes Baumhaus aus Aluminium. Es kann in weniger als zwei Stunden aufgebaut werden und wiegt (leer) 200 kg. Diese behagliche Nomadenwohnung gibt es in verschiedenen Ausführungen und eignet sich besonders für Standorte am Strand oder im Dschungel. Eine Firma aus Denver namens Autonomous Tent (siehe Seite 164) hat begonnen, nichts weniger zu produzieren als eine „neue Form der Architektur, die als permanente Konstruktion errichtet, aber in nur wenigen Tagen abgebaut werden kann, ohne irgendwelche Spuren zu hinterlassen". Sie enthält ein großes Doppelbett, einen Gaskamin und ein Bad mit Dusche und Komposttoilette, und all das für nur 100 000 Dollar. Am anderen Ende der Welt, in Südkorea, hat ArchiWorkshop „Glamping"-Bauten entworfen, zum Beispiel Stacking Doughnut und Modular Flow (Yang-Pyung, Südkorea, 2013, siehe Seite 176) – modulare Einheiten, komplett ausgestattet mit modernen Kunstwerken, die speziell für diese standardisierten, zeltähnlichen Häuser geschaffen wurden, weit weg von daheim für die wenigen Auserwählten.

Protestierer, Freaks, Geeks und Flüchtlinge

Mobile Wohnungen unterschiedlicher Art haben einen sehr persönlichen Aspekt. Häufig sind sie Teil eines bewussten Versuchs, sich den herrschenden sozialen Verhaltensmustern zu entziehen – sich sozusagen in die Wildnis zu schlagen. Aber Zelte und sonstige temporäre Unterkünfte werden manchmal auch für völlig andere Zwecke aufgestellt, wie einige Beispiele in diesem Buch zeigen. Proteste sind ein Grund für Sit-ins oder für die Besetzung von urbanen Orten. Diese Form der temporären Ansammlung von Zelten und Hütten hat es in den vergangenen Jahren häufig gegeben; Beispiele dafür sind das vom Führer der ukrainischen Opposition Viktor Juschtschenko errichtete Campinggelände auf dem zentralen Boulevard von Kiew (Dezember 2004), die Indignados oder Movimiento 15-M in Spanien an der Puerta del Sol in Madrid (2011), die verschiedenen Occupy-Proteste in den Vereinigten Staaten (2011) oder die prodemokratische Regenschirm-Revolution, die 2014 die Straßen von Hongkong besetzte.

Mehrere Sommerfeste in verschiedenen Teilen der Welt bieten die Gelegenheit zur Errichtung temporärer Städte. Das berühmteste von ihnen ist Burning Man, das am Ende des Sommers in Black Rock City, Nevada, stattfindet. Dieses Festival konzentriert sich auf bestimmte gemeinschaftliche Wertvorstellungen und äußert sich in künstlerischen Ausdrucksformen. Aber sogar die Zelte und die Camper, die in einem

ARCHIWORKSHOP, STACKING DOUGHNUT AND MODULAR FLOW → P. 176

großen Halbkreis in der Wüste aufgestellt werden, sind bemerkenswert. Die Fotografen NK Guy und Philippe Glade haben diese Strukturen über viele Jahre dokumentiert und Bücher über Burning Man veröffentlicht, wo 65 000 Menschen sich für kurze Zeit zusammenfinden. Wenngleich mit sehr unterschiedlichen Motivationen und künstlerischen Ausdrucksformen führen auch andere Events große Menschengruppen zusammen, die eine Zeitlang in kleinen Zelten leben. Dies ist der Fall bei der Campus Party, einem siebentägigen, jeweils 24 Stunden dauernden Festival, zu dem Spieler, Blogger, Programmierer und andere Technik-freaks zusammenkommen. Die Campus Party ist mehrere Male in Brasilien abgehalten worden, 2011 vom 17. bis zum 23. Januar in der Ausstellungshalle Centro Imigrantes in São Paulo, wo sich fast 7000 junge Menschen trafen, um von einer von der Regierung und von örtlichen Telefonanbietern eingerichteten 10-GB-Verbindung zu profitieren. Dafür wurden Hunderte identische Zelte gegen eine Gebühr zur Verfügung gestellt und in einem strengen Raster aufgestellt.

Wer Luftaufnahmen von der riesigen temporären, für Burning Man errichteten Stadt sieht, mag bestürzt sein über deren Ähnlichkeit mit den vielen, in der ganzen Welt entstandenen Flüchtlingslagern, vor allem als Folge der Syrienkrise. Das 2012 errichtete Flüchtlingslager Zaatari bei Mafraq in Jordanien beherbergt etwa 85 000 Menschen in verschiedenen Unterkünften, die sicher zu den auffälligsten und verstörendsten „nomadischen Wohnungen" der Welt zählen. Einigen im Westen tätigen Teams, zum Beispiel Architects for Society aus Minneapolis, ist es zu verdanken, dass sie selbst in einem problematischen Umfeld Pläne zur Unterstützung der notleidenden Menschen in solchen Lagern entwickeln. Das von Architects for Society geplante Hex House ist eine 47 m² große Notunterkunft aus isolierten Metallplatten in „passivem Low-Tech-Design" (siehe Seite 314).

Auch westliche Länder wie Frankreich haben sich mit dem Zustrom von Flüchtlingen auseinandersetzen müssen, zum Beispiel denen, die nach England wollten und vorübergehend im „Dschungel" von Calais lebten. Es ist merkwürdig zu beobachten, dass Nomadenhäuser für die Wohlhabenden allgemein als Mittel zur Flucht vor der Gesellschaft und zur Sicherung einer Privatsphäre betrachtet werden, wogegen das umgekehrte Phänomen für die ärmste, gegen ihren Willen zusammengepferchte Bevölkerung gilt, die nur darauf hofft, wieder ein sicheres Leben zu finden. Nach Schätzungen des Flüchtlingshilfswerks der Vereinten Nationen UNHCR gab es im Jahr 2015 weltweit 65,3 Millionen zwangsweise Vertriebene. Diese Tatsache sowie die schwankende Zahl von Menschen, die durch andere Katastrophen als Kriege, etwa durch Erdbeben, Tsunamis und Sturmfluten, heimatlos wurden, haben eine Anzahl von fähigen Architekten dazu veranlasst, bessere Notunterkünfte zu planen, zum Beispiel den japanischen Pritzker-Preisträger Shigeru Ban. Aber diese individuellen Realisierungen sind wohl ein etwas anderes Thema als die riesigen Lager, die man etwa kürzlich im Nahen Osten gesehen hat.

Ebenso wird auch das, was das US Census Bureau „manufactured housing" nennt – eine Kategorie, die in den USA oft mit Armut oder niedrigem Einkommen assoziiert wird –, zu einer noblen Aufgabe in den Händen von Architekten wie der südamerikanischen Gruppe MAPA, die das elegante MINIMOD Catuçaba (Fazenda Catuçaba, São Paulo, 2009–15, siehe Seite 248) plante, das aus modularen Elementen in einer Fabrik produziert und dann an seinen Standort transportiert wurde.

Die bekannten amerikanischen Architekten LOT-EK experimentierten mit Containern bei der von ihnen so bezeichneten M. D. U. oder Mobile Dwelling Unit (siehe Seite 232), von der Erweiterungen aus den Metallwänden ausgefahren werden können, die Raum zum Wohnen, Arbeiten und Lagern bieten. In geschlossenem Zustand kann die M. D. U. wieder auf die Straße oder auf das Wasser gehen – mit den Zehntausenden von Containern, die täglich um den Planeten reisen. Die im Whitney Museum of American Art in New York und dem Walker Art Center in Milwaukee ausgestellte M. D. U. ist ein ernsthafter Versuch, die elementare Wanderlust vieler Menschen in ein industrielles System zu integrieren, das sich aus anderen Gründen in ständiger Bewegung befindet.

Ein weiteres modulares System namens Wikkelhouse (2016, siehe Seite 292) stammt von der niederländischen Gruppe Fiction Factory. Dieses erstaunliche Haus besteht zum großen Teil aus 1,2 m langen, zusammensteckbaren Teilen aus Pappe und kann leicht aufgebaut, erweitert oder abgebaut werden. Die Elemente sind so behandelt, dass sie fast allen Wetterbedingungen standhalten und eine Lebensdauer von voraussichtlich 50 Jahren haben. So lassen sich nomadische und temporäre Konstruktionen durchaus auch an stabilere Lebensbedingungen anpassen.

Sechs Beine zur langsamen Fortbewegung

Einige Architekten und Künstler haben das Thema des mobilen Heims über das alltägliche Leben hinaus weiterentwickelt und die Vorstellungen von Mobilität und Privatsphäre auf ungewöhnliche Weise getestet. Das dänische Team N55 entwarf 2009 das WALKING HOUSE in Kopenhagen (siehe Seite 286). Dieses modulare Wohnsystem für maximal vier Personen läuft in der Tat auf sechs Beinen und wird von linearen Aktoren angetrieben. Dieses umweltfreundliche, sehr ausgefallene Bauwerk wurde von der nomadischen Kultur inspiriert, vor allem von den Pferdewagen der Roma aus dem 18. Jahrhundert, vereint mit Technologie und modernen Materialien. Alex Schweder und Ward Shelley stellten sich ihr eigenes mobiles Heim namens ReActor ganz anders vor; sie zogen vor, es auf einer 5 m hohen Betonstütze des Omi International Arts Center (Ghent, New York, 2016, siehe Seite 266) zu verankern. Das 15 m lange Glashaus dreht und bewegt sich tatsächlich, je nach Windrichtung und den Bewegungen seiner beiden Bewohner. Der Künstler und der Architekt lebten während einer „fünftägigen Wohnvorführung" wirklich im ReActor.

Eine weitere Künstlerin, die sich mit dem Thema Wohnen und Mobilität befasst, ist die Amerikanerin Andrea Zittel. Sie bezieht sich auf die „sozialen Bedürfnisse", wenn sie Werke wie ihre Indy Island vorstellt: eine auf einem See schwimmende Hülle, die jeden Sommer bewohnt werden soll, beauftragt vom Indianapolis Museum of Art. Ihre Wagon Stations (A-Z West, Joshua Tree, Kalifornien; Milwaukee, Minnesota, seit 2003) sind noch erstaunlicher. Diese relativ kleinen, mobilen Konstruktionen aus Metall und Holz können auf dem Wohngelände der Künstlerin in Kalifornien gemietet werden. Obgleich sie den Bewohnern die Möglichkeit bieten, durch eine Öffnung im „Dach" nach außen zu blicken, sind sie so klein, dass sie an japanische „Kapselhotels" erinnern. Die Anregung dazu gaben die Planwagen, welche die Besitztümer der Siedler im amerikanischen Westen enthielten und ihnen Schutz vor den Elementen boten, sowie Kombiwagen, die den Maßstab der einzelnen Einheiten bestimmten. Die Wagon Stations können als das Nonplusultra der nomadischen Wohnung betrachtet werden. Sie könnten nicht viel kleiner sein und sind von einer Künstlerin entworfen, auch wenn sie an diese kleinste (und beständigste) aller Unterkünfte erinnern.

Die Herausforderung der Technik

Nomadenwohnungen werden immer öfter mit hochtechnologischer Ausstattung geplant, um damit höchste Umweltfreundlichkeit, aber zugleich auch ihre Eignung für extreme Standorte zu erreichen, an denen keinerlei Verbindung zu kommunalen Dienstleistungen vorhanden ist. Zwei solcher ungewöhnlichen Projekte werden in diesem Buch vorgestellt. Eines davon ist die von den jungen slowakischen Architekten Tomáš Žáček und Soňa Pohlová (früher Nice Architects) entworfene Ecocapsule (siehe Seite 212). Dieser 6,2 m² große Behälter wird beschrieben als „nachhaltiges, intelligentes Mikrohaus, das Solar- und Windenergie nutzt". Seine Kugelform und das Material Glasfaser ermöglichen das Sammeln von Regen- und Tauwasser bei gleichzeitiger Minimierung des Energieverbrauchs. Die 1200 kg schwere Konstruktion passt in einen üblichen Container oder kann auf einem speziell dafür vorgesehenen Trailer an einen Personenwagen gehängt werden und wird dadurch zu einem voll funktionsfähigen Camper. Ein noch ausgeklügelteres Mobilheim ist das Projekt AMIE (siehe Seite 42), das die Architekten Skidmore, Owings & Merrill zusammen mit dem US Department Energy's Oak Ridge National Laboratory vorgestellt haben. Diese 19,5 m² große Behausung ist ein 3D-gedrucktes Fahrzeug und soll das höchste Niveau an Energieeffizienz und Schadstoffkontrolle demonstrieren. Sowohl die Ecocapsule als auch das AMIE-Projekt zeigen ein hohes Maß an Designqualität und Möglichkeiten für das Wohnhaus der Zukunft auf.

Der Weltraum: die unendlichen Weiten

Gewissermaßen um zu beweisen, dass wir alle Nomaden sind, soll auch das ultimative mobile Heim erwähnt werden, das in den Weltraum und noch weiter fährt. Denen, die mit der Serie Star Trek oder auch den Star-Trek-Filmen aufgewachsen sind, werden diese Worte bekannt sein: „Der Weltraum – unendliche Weiten. Dies sind die Abenteuer des Raumschiffs Enterprise. Seine fünfjährige Mission ist die Entdeckung fremder neuer Welten, unbekannter Lebensformen und neuer Zivilisationen und mutig dorthin vorzustoßen, wo noch niemand zuvor gewesen ist." Jene, die die „unendlichen Weiten" erforschen, schweben schon über uns an Bord der 419 000 kg schweren Internationalen Raumstation. Die Astronauten der ISS sind die ultimativen Nomaden, welche die Erde 15,7 Mal täglich umkreisen, und sie leben in einer schicksalhaft technologischen Umgebung, aber auch ihr Heim ist ein mobiles.

Sollten sich die Regierungsbehörden und eine seltsame Gruppe von Milliardären und Visionären durchsetzen, so wird es sich beim Umkreisen der Erde nicht um die „unendlichen Weiten" des Star-Trek-Märchens handeln. Vielmehr werden die Menschen zum Mars und vielleicht auch noch darüber hinaus reisen. Die Initiative Mars One (siehe Seite 228) will bis 2032 mindestens vier „permanente" Siedler auf dem Mars etablieren, sie tritt für den bis dato entferntesten Außenposten der Menschheit und damit das größte Abenteuer der Nomadenwohnung ein. Bei den kühnen Männern, die Kolumbus und andere Entdecker begleiteten, oder auch jenen, die mit ihren Planwagen in das gelobte Land des Westens aufbrachen, war die Aussicht auf Rückkehr in ihr früheres Leben sehr vage. Bei Mars One sind die Aussichten noch düsterer: „Es gibt keinen Weg zurück. Die Reise zum Mars ist eine Entscheidung für den Rest des Lebens. Es existiert keine Technologie für eine Rückkehr."

Die Rückkehr zur Erde

Für einige wirkt die Aussicht auf eine Reise zum Mars wie ein Scherz; dagegen liegt das Leben von durch Naturkatastrophen heimatlos gewordenen Flüchtlingen in der Hand von internationalen Institutionen – von Nichtregierungsorganisationen, deren Mittel begrenzt sind. Deshalb sind die Bemühungen von Architekten wie Shigeru Ban so wichtig und befruchtend für die zeitgenössische Architektur. Sie sind eine wirkliche Hilfe für die Notleidenden und liefern eine überzeugende Analyse der Möglichkeiten von preiswertem temporärem Wohnungsbau, der schnell in Katastrophengebiete oder, noch dringender, an die Grenzen von kriegführenden Ländern transportiert werden kann.

Shigeru Ban hat zahlreiche Versuche unternommen, um heimatlos gewordenen Menschen nach Naturkatastrophen Hilfe zu leisten. Sein Projekt Container Temporary Housing (Onagawa, Japan, 2011, siehe Seite 300) entstand nach dem Erdbeben und Tsunami vom 11. März 2011 in der Region Tohoku in Ostjapan. Man schätzt, dass vier Jahre nach dem Unglück immer noch 230 000 Menschen in Übergangswohnungen lebten. Wie schon bei einigen früheren Entwürfen verwendete Shigeru Ban 6,1 m große Container für den Bau der Häuser in Onagawa. Da es keine geeigneten ebenen Grundstücke gab, beschloss er, die Container drei Geschosse hoch im Schachbrettmuster übereinanderzustapeln, wodurch „helle, offene Wohnbereiche zwischen den Containern" entstanden. Er plante drei unterschiedliche Anordnungen von Wohnräumen, je nach Größe der Familien, die unterzubringen waren. Eine weitere von Bans Initiativen ist das New Temporary House (Manila, Philippinen, 2013, siehe Seite 320), ein preiswertes, vorfabriziertes Wohnhaus, das auf den Philippinen getestet wurde. Dieses Projekt aus glasfaserverstärktem Kunststoff und Schaumstoff-Sandwichplatten bietet eine bessere Qualität für den temporären Wohnungsbau und schafft auch lokale Arbeitsplätze. Das Gleiche gilt für das kürzlich von ihm entworfene Zelt aus Karbonfaser (Carbon Fiber Tent). Der Architekt hat viele Nutzungen für das New Temporary House vorgesehen, darunter auch die Möglichkeit, in ärmeren Regionen, etwa in Indien und Nepal, Wohnraum zu schaffen.

Ein weiteres interessantes, ursprünglich für Flüchtlinge bestimmtes, aber auch für weniger belastende Nutzungen brauchbares Projekt ist das von Suricatta Systems in Alicante entwickelte SURI (Shelter Units for Rapid Installation, siehe Seite 324). Die etwas über 12 m² großen Einheiten nutzen vor allem schnell vor Ort verfügbare Materialien, zum Beispiel Sandsäcke, aber auch verschiedene Arten von Polyethylen. Diese

BERNI DU PAYRAT, COCOON TREE → P. 168

Unterkünfte sollen zu 100 Prozent recycelbar und nachhaltig sein. Alle Materialien sind wiederverwendbar oder biologisch abbaubar. Solarpaneele und ein System zum Auffangen des Regenwassers können an geeigneter Stelle integriert werden. Die SURI-Elemente werden in 580 kg schweren Flachpackungen geliefert und können vor Ort von zwei Personen ohne Vorkenntnisse montiert werden.

Auf der Suche nach dem Minimum

Welch gewaltiger Unterschied zwischen Privatjets und Superjachten und den Minimalunterkünften für Flüchtlinge! Für die reichsten wie die ärmsten Bewohner unseres Planeten und für jene, die hoffen, eines Tages andere Planeten zu besiedeln, ist nomadisches Wohnen in der einen oder anderen Form eher die Regel als die Ausnahme. Da Wohnraum im Allgemeinen schwer zu bekommen ist, bieten die vorfabrizierten Häuser Leuten, die sich den Bau eines frei stehenden Hauses nicht leisten können, die Möglichkeit, eigenen Wohnraum zu erwerben. Wiederum andere können 1,5 Millionen Euro für einen Bus als ihr eigenes motorisiertes Heim ausgeben. Einige der Architekten und Künstler, deren Werke hier abgebildet sind, haben sich mit dem Konzept einer Minimalwohnung auseinandergesetzt. Für Renzo Piano ist das 7,5 m² große Minihaus (Weil am Rhein, Deutschland, 2013, siehe Seite 202) eine Antwort auf das Minimum, worauf ein Mensch in seinem Leben hoffen kann. Und dennoch ist das mit Solarpaneelen, einer Erdwärmepumpe und Niedrigenergie-Beleuchtung ausgestattete Diogene auch ein Produkt moderner Bautechnik. Das Projekt ist nach dem griechischen Philosophen Diogenes benannt, der gesagt hat: „Ich bin ein Weltbürger."

Andrea Zittels Überlegungen zu den „sozialen Bedürfnissen" könnten andeuten, dass Menschen wirklich viel weniger benötigen, als die Gesellschaft sie glauben lässt. Aber zeigen ihre Wagon Stations wirklich so etwas, was die Franzosen „l'ultime demeure" nennen? Sich zu beschränken in einer Welt der begrenzten Ressourcen bedeutet natürlich auch Verkleinerung, was den japanischen Stadtbewohnern schon längst bekannt ist. Ein japanisches, wenn auch nicht notwendigerweise mobiles Haus liegt aufgrund der sehr hohen Grundstückspreise und des Platzmangels in den Stadtzentren oft an der unteren Grenze der Normalgröße. Der sehr begabte japanische Architekt Kenzo Kuma such-

te weniger die Grenzen der Technologie auszuloten, sondern blickte vielmehr zurück in die Literaturgeschichte seines Landes, als er sein Hojo-an plante (Kioto, 2012, siehe Seite 216). Dieses nur 9 m² große, transportable Haus aus Fluorpolymerplatten (ETFE), Zedernholzlatten und Magneten ist ein bewusster Hinweis auf das Werk von Kamono Chomei (1155–1215), den Autor von Hojo-ki (dt. Aufzeichnungen aus meiner Hütte, Frankfurt am Main 1997), der in einem mobilen Haus wohnte, das oft als Prototyp des japanischen Kompaktwohnhauses geschildert wird. Kumas Projekt zielte auf die Rekonstruktion dieses Hauses nach modernen Vorstellungen und Methoden auf dem selben Gelände des Shimogamo-Schreins in Kioto. Ein hojo ist eine Hütte, die etwa 3 × 3 m misst. Vielleicht ist das genau die richtige Größe für ein an der Schwelle zwischen Vergangenheit und Zukunft errichtetes Nomadenhaus.

Wie aus dieser summarischen Übersicht von mobilen Wohnhäusern aus aller Welt und von allen Typen aus unterschiedlichen Kontexten leicht zu erkennen, ist der nomadische Geist unserer Jäger-und-Sammler-Vorfahren auch in der modernen Welt durchaus noch präsent. Während die Architektur immer nach Stabilität und daher nicht nach Mobilität strebte, hat die Moderne zu einem Gefühl von Begrenztheit und zu einer gewissen Bescheidenheit gegenüber der Nachwelt und der Langlebigkeit geführt. Was könnte es Aktuelleres geben, als vor allem beweglich zu sein, vielleicht auch zu wachsen, aber sich stets zu bewegen. „Ein guter Reisender", sagte der antike chinesische Philosoph Laozi, „hat keine festen Pläne und nicht die Absicht, irgendwo anzukommen." Es ist die Reise, die zählt, der Ort der Ankunft ist für alle immer der gleiche.

Nous sommes tous nomades

*Ada enfanta Yabal ; ce fut lui le père de
ceux qui habitent des tentes avec des troupeaux.*
Genèse, 4-20

Nul ne sera surpris d'apprendre que le mot « nomade » a des origines antiques. Il vient du latin *nomad*, via le grec *nomás* qui évoque des troupeaux, le verbe *némein* signifiant « paître », ou « brouter ». En effet, la chasse et la cueillette nomades, à la recherche des plantes sauvages et du gibier disponibles selon les saisons, sont de loin le plus ancien moyen de subsistance humain. Il y a encore 10 000 ans, les hommes modernes étaient tous chasseurs et cueilleurs. Pour dire les choses plus simplement, les hommes ont été nomades pendant 99 % de la durée connue de leur présence sur Terre. Et si le nomadisme au sens traditionnel du terme disparaît aujourd'hui peu à peu, il est encore pratiqué par certains groupes comme les gardiens de rennes dans la toundra du Nord de l'Europe qui suivent leurs troupeaux au fil des saisons. La plupart adoptent un rythme fixe de déplacements, annuel ou saisonnier. Et si les nomades ont longtemps voyagé à dos d'animaux, en canoë ou à pied, les technologies et les transports motorisés se sont désormais imposés jusque dans les régions les plus éloignées du monde. Les différentes formes de transhumance — le déplacement saisonnier des bergers et de leurs troupeaux — représentent elles aussi une existence en mouvement permanent, mais entre deux points généralement fixes, atteints respectivement au printemps et à l'automne.

Pour des raisons évidentes, les tentes, dont l'existence est connue depuis le début de l'âge de fer (VIIIe siècle av. J.-C. en Europe centrale), ont souvent représenté le type d'« habitat » préféré des nomades, à l'instar des *tipis* utilisés par les Indiens des plaines d'Amérique du Nord, dont l'histoire pourrait remonter à 4 000 ans, ou des *yourtes* dont font usage les nomades des steppes d'Asie centrale depuis au moins 3 000 ans. Les tentes militaires, notamment les structures de toile de l'armée romaine, sont également très anciennes.

Gitans et Voortrekkers

Pourtant, ce serait une erreur de réduire les modes de vie nomades à nos lointains ancêtres. Des populations telles que les Roms (ou gitans) parcourent l'Europe depuis le Moyen Âge, peut-être plus — leur présence est attestée en 1322 en Crète. De même, les Travellers irlandais d'origines diverses sont une population nomade dont le nombre a été évalué à plus de 22 000 par le recensement de 2006 en République d'Irlande. Les Roms, qui ont d'abord voyagé dans des chariots couverts ou des caravanes, renvoient quant à eux des mouvements de population plus « modernes » comme la conquête de l'Ouest américain, dont la progression a d'abord été le fait de convois de chariots ou de groupes de chariots couverts transportant les biens de leurs propriétaires tout en leur servant d'abri. Les paysans voyageurs appelés Trekboers et les Voortrekkers d'Afrique du Sud, enfin, étaient des pasteurs nomades qui ont essaimé au nord et à l'est du Cap aux XVIIe et XVIIIe siècles et utilisaient aussi une forme de chariots couverts pour leurs déplacements.

On the road

Cela s'explique sans doute par l'histoire de la conquête du Far West ; les Américains continuent encore aujourd'hui de changer plus souvent de lieu d'habitation que la plupart des autres populations mondiales. En 2016 cependant, le pourcentage d'Américains à avoir déménagé en un an n'a jamais été aussi bas avec 11,2 % selon le Bureau du recensement des États-Unis. Malgré tout, c'est prendre conscience d'un aspect fondamental de la culture américaine que d'imaginer que, dans une nation de 325 millions d'habitants, pas moins de 35 millions ont déménagé en seulement un an. On pourrait parler à ce sujet de culture de la route, célébrée par des personnalités telles que Jack Kerouac (*Sur la route*, 1951) ou, dans un autre genre, Ken Kesey, l'auteur de *Vol au-dessus d'un nid de coucou* (1962), et sa bande de joyeux drilles qui traversèrent les États-Unis en bus en 1964, célébrant les vertus du LSD et la vie sur la route.

La réalité des mobile homes aux USA n'est peut-être pas aussi colorée et poétique que ce que de grands noms comme Kerouac et Kesey l'ont laissé entendre. Ce type d'habitat représente 6,4 % de l'habitat américain et on en comptait 8,5 millions en 2013, soit légèrement moins qu'en 2011, toujours selon le Bureau du recensement américain. Le nombre de leurs occupants n'a pas été enregistré, mais il est estimé à près de 20 millions. Par ailleurs, le Bureau du recensement a noté une forte corrélation entre les États comptant le plus de mobile homes et ceux dont les revenus sont les plus bas. C'est pendant la Grande

VIPP, VIPP SHELTER (P. 22) → P. 278 | SKIDMORE, OWINGS & MERRILL, ADDITIVE MANUFACTURING INTEGRATED ENERGY (AMIE) → P. 42

Dépression des années 1930 que les caravanes destinées aux voyages ou aux vacances ont progressivement commencé à être utilisées comme des habitations à part entière. Garées en périphérie des villes, un peu comme les camps de Roms en Europe, elles ont fini par être associées dans bien des cas aux Américains pauvres. À l'inverse cependant, les mobile homes ont toujours eu un côté « glamour » grâce à des entreprises comme Airstream, créé à Los Angeles dans les années 1920 et célèbre pour ses caravanes de luxe en aluminium argenté.

Des chariots missionnaires aux remorques de loisirs

Les différents types d'habitat « mobile » ne sont pas faciles à distinguer. En Amérique, un mobile home se définit généralement comme une structure préfabriquée couplée à un châssis. Il est souvent stationné de manière semi-permanente sur un bout de terrain, à la différence des remorques de tourisme (camping-cars ou caravanes) comme l'Airstream, qui sont tractées par des véhicules routiers. Ce sont les usines Bristol Wagon & Carriage Works, en Angleterre, qui passent le plus souvent pour avoir inventé la première « remorque de loisirs », dont le design s'inspirait des chariots missionnaires utilisés par les prédicateurs dans l'Ouest américain. L'ancêtre du club de camping et caravanning a aussi été créé en Angleterre, en 1901, par Thomas Hiram Holding, connu comme le fondateur du camping moderne. Les remorques de tourisme se sont imposées aux États-Unis dans les années 1920 lorsqu'il est devenu pratique d'utiliser une voiture pour les déplacer. Les mobile homes à moteur ont connu un développement voisin et sont considérées comme des « véhicules de loisirs autopropulsés ».

La distinction entre les différents types d'habitats nomades pourrait également reposer sur leur mode de déplacement. Dans sa définition fort intéressante, le Bureau du recensement des États-Unis décrit par exemple les « habitats manufacturés » ou mobile homes comme des logements préfabriqués assemblés en usine avant d'être transportés sur leur lieu d'implantation. Sans chercher à dresser un inventaire précis des différents types de mobile homes, l'ouvrage qui suit vise à donner un aperçu du nombre et de la variété de ce qu'il vaudrait peut-être mieux appeler « habitat nomade ».

Paradis hippie

Étant donné l'origine des habitats nomades modernes, il est peut-être judicieux de commencer par la grande variété de logements sur roues, caravanes, mobile homes, maisons à moteurs, camping-cars, et même bus reconvertis ou spécialement construits. On a vu que le titre *Nomadic Homes* pouvait rappeler à certains l'époque grisante des joyeux drilles, des hippies, des cheveux longs et des substances hallucinogènes. S'il faut être hippie pour vivre avec son temps, il suffit pour s'en convaincre de voir les caravanes Airstream soigneusement restaurées et actualisées produites par Wally Hofmann (HofArc) à Santa Barbara, en Californie. Pour un Airstream Sovereign 31' de 1979 entièrement rénové et baptisé Elizabeth (2015 ; voir page 38), il a cherché et trouvé un « authentique style européen » avec un réfrigérateur SMEG d'époque, un réchaud à gaz Wedgewood des années 1930 et des carreaux de mosaïque marocaines pour le sol de la salle de bains. Un autre client a obtenu son Airstream Sovereign 31' de 1973, appelé Michelle, avec « chauffage et climatisation HVAC dernier cri », électronique haut de gamme fonctionnant grâce à des panneaux solaires et une touche minimale de bois de récupération, peut-être pour rappeler la chanson des Beatles de 1967, « Michelle », d'après laquelle ce luxueux véhicule habitable de croisière a été baptisé.

Le sentiment hippie se retrouve aussi dans le petit Bus Chevrolet Viking de 1958 rénové dans un style rétro par Will Winkelman (2009 ; voir page 32) à partir d'un véhicule à l'abandon, qui peut transporter 12 personnes ou en coucher deux. Le client avait spécialement demandé une ambiance vintage « hippie marocaine » pour ces 8,5 mètres carrés d'espace habitable. Les bus sont aussi très populaires chez les designers d'habitat nomade.

Malgré les multiples efforts entrepris pour classer les logements mobiles par leur nom, l'esthétique et le design modernes ont tendance à gommer les différences, d'où la division du livre en chapitres. L'Opera d'Axel Enthoven (2009 ; voir page 64) est en partie une caravane, mais aussi une sorte de tente, et s'inspire de rien de moins que de l'opéra de Sydney. Le designer belge maintient cependant qu'il ne s'agit « ni d'une tente, ni d'une remorque, ni d'un camping-car ». Salué par le prix allemand du design de caravane en 2010, il se déplie pour offrir

CARWYN LLOYD JONES, DRAGON'S EYE → P. 206

21 mètres carrés d'espace habitable avec un lit king-size, une douche à l'extérieur et bon nombre d'autres équipements modernes.

Les maisons sur roues se sont adaptées avec succès à la tendance vers un camping de plus en plus luxueux, qu'on appelle « glamping ». La Forêt animée (Animated Forest, sud du Snowdonia, Pays de Galles, 2017 ; voir page 46) en est un exemple, qui contribue aux efforts entrepris pour inciter les touristes à découvrir les merveilles naturelles de la région. Conçu par la jeune équipe londonienne de Francis & Arnett, le projet évoque la littérature galloise du Moyen Âge et permet surtout à ses occupants de faire pleinement l'expérience de la nature, allongés confortablement sur une « couche rembourrée de luxe ».

L'extrême inverse pour ainsi dire, qui n'a assurément pas le luxe comme objectif, est incarné par le projet de l'entreprise chinoise People's Industrial Design Office et simplement appelé Maison triporteur (Tricycle House, Pékin, 2012 ; voir page 76). À l'aide de technologies numériques très élaborées, ses inventeurs sont parvenus à caser un évier et une cuisinière, une baignoire, un réservoir d'eau et du mobilier qui peut se transformer d'un lit en une table avec banc ou en un banc avec comptoir, et former ainsi un logement mobile de l'extrême.

Au gré des flots

On imagine sans doute le plus souvent les maisons mobiles à terre. Pourtant les hommes et les femmes ont dormi et vécu presque aussi longtemps sur la haute mer que sur la terre ferme. Et de même que les mobile homes peuvent être des préfabriqués déposés à un endroit de manière plus ou moins permanente, les bateaux peuvent être remorqués et amarrés à un endroit donné (house-boats), ou être conçus pour écumer les mers.

Les Pays-Bas sont, comme il se doit, un pays qui compte beaucoup de maisons flottantes ou house-boats. Mais les architectes sont aussi nombreux, aux Pays-Bas et ailleurs, à avoir pris en compte la montée du niveau de la mer due au réchauffement de la planète et à avoir jugé qu'une maison flottante pourrait bien être le meilleur moyen de remédier aux inondations futures. Koen Olthuis, né en 1971, est l'un d'entre eux. Il a conçu des maisons flottantes assez classiques, comme celles qui sont publiées ici (villas flottantes d'IJburg, Amsterdam, 2008 ;

voir pages 108, 112), mais s'est aussi lancé dans des projets plus ambitieux tels que New Water, une ville flottante prévue pour être amarrée à proximité de La Haye et qui comprend des logements sociaux, des îles flottantes et des immeubles d'appartements flottants. Même si ces structures sont produites ailleurs et remorquées jusqu'à leur lieu d'implantation, leur vocation ultime est d'être aussi immobiles que l'eau, ce qui signifie, en un sens, en perpétuel mouvement.

La société de Los Angeles Morphosis, quant à elle, a conçu la Maison flottante (Float House, New Orleans, 2008–2009 ; voir page 96) après les destructions massives causées par l'ouragan Katrina en 2005. Le logement de 88 mètres carrés a été imaginé précisément pour pouvoir surmonter les inondations. Amarré à des poteaux, il monte avec l'eau à plus de 3,5 mètres et comme beaucoup dans la nouvelle générations de maisons flottantes, il a été conçu dans le respect des normes écologiques les plus strictes, associant des panneaux solaires et une pompe géothermique pour l'électricité, le chauffage et la climatisation.

L'artiste suédois toujours imprévisible Mikael Genberg a, lui, créé un autre genre de maison flottante qui vogue sur les eaux de l'océan Indien, près de Zanzibar, en Tanzanie. Sa chambre sous-marine Manta (2013 ; voir page 124) est un logement hôtelier de luxe à trois niveaux dont la chambre à coucher, située sous l'eau, permet une vue à 360° sur les fonds sous-marins. Si certains habitats nomades offrent à leurs occupants des moments de détente dans des environnements naturels parfois étonnants, la chambre sous-marine Manta fait encore un pas de plus et les transporte sous l'océan.

Vivre sur l'eau, surtout à proximité d'un environnement urbain, peut présenter un autre avantage essentiel, en plus de la possibilité de flotter au-dessus des marées. En effet, dans une ville comme Copenhague, le centre est beaucoup trop cher et densément construit pour permettre aux étudiants d'y trouver domicile. C'est pourquoi le jeune et talentueux architecte danois Bjarke Ingels (BIG), en collaboration avec l'entrepreneur Kim Loudrup, a imaginé Urban Rigger, un ensemble flottant de 12 appartements fait de conteneurs maritimes et ancré dans le port de Copenhague (2016 ; voir page 142). Bon marché, efficace et littéralement à flot, Urban Rigger promet de devenir un modèle pour de futurs développements de l'habitat dans de nombreuses villes portuaires.

BONNIFAIT + GIESEN, PORT-A-BACH → P. 262

Camper dans la forêt

Si l'histoire des tentes est presque aussi ancienne que celle de l'humanité et semble circonscrite aux typologies qui existaient déjà par le passé, elles incarnent en réalité un secteur d'une grande diversité et innovation. Lorsque l'idée de faire de l'ascension des montagnes une discipline sportive est née au XIXe siècle, le « logement » temporaire que cela nécessitait pouvait uniquement prendre la forme de structures légères et portatives capables d'être fixées à la roche et de résister à des vents forts ou des tempêtes. Ce type de tente de survie a cependant rapidement évolué avec l'apparition de nouveaux matériaux. Il en est de même, c'est logique, pour les structures dédiées aux campeurs en général. La société Tentsile, située à Londres, propose ainsi plusieurs tentes à suspendre aux arbres, dont certaines ne pèsent pas plus de sept kilos et peuvent porter des charges de 400 kilos une fois suspendues. Si ces modèles (voir page 180) coûtent autour de 300 dollars, d'autres sociétés et architectes ont imaginé des solutions plus luxueuses ou glamour pour les prétendus campeurs. Le site Web *glamping.com* explique ainsi : « Une tendance s'est récemment répandue comme une traînée de poudre dans le monde entier, elle consiste à offrir aux amoureux de la vie en plein air un niveau supérieur en termes de repos et de loisirs. On appelle cela le "glamping", mot nouveau pour une nouvelle façon de voyager, contraction de "glamorous camping". En glamping, il n'y a plus de tente à dresser, plus de sac de couchage à dérouler, plus de feu à allumer. Sous forme de tente, yourte, Airstream, nacelle, igloo, hutte, pavillon, cabane, cube, tipi ou maison dans les arbres, le glamping est une manière de vivre en pleine nature sans renoncer pour autant au luxe et au confort. »

Une autre de ces tentes suspendues, appelée Cocoon Tree (voir page 168), a été inventée par un ancien directeur créatif d'une agence de publicité, Berni du Payrat. Cette nacelle sphérique imperméable en aluminium à accrocher dans les arbres peut être assemblée en moins de deux heures et pèse à vide 200 kilos. Logis nomade confortable, elle est disponible en différentes versions adaptées à la plage ou à la jungle.

Une société de Denver appelée Autonomous Tent (voir page 164) a entrepris de créer rien de moins qu'« une nouvelle forme d'architecture, élaborée comme une structure permanente mais qui peut être érigée en

seulement quelques jours et "disparaître sans laisser de trace" ». On y trouve un lit king-size, un foyer au gaz et une salle de bains avec douche et toilettes compostables à chasse d'eau, le tout pour 100 000 dollars. Ailleurs dans le monde, en Corée du Sud, ArchiWorkshop est le pionnier des structures « glamping » comme le Beignet empilable (Stacking Doughnut) et le Flux modulaire (Modular Flow) (Yang-Pyung, Corée du Sud, 2013 ; voir page 176), des unités modulaires complètes, comprenant même des œuvres d'art contemporain spécialement créées — des tentes qui n'en sont pas, destinées à quelques privilégiés.

Protestataires, freaks, geeks et réfugiés

Les différents habitats mobiles possèdent un caractère très personnel. Ils s'inscrivent souvent dans une tentative délibérée de rompre avec les modèles standards de société, pour conquérir des étendues sauvages et reculées. Mais les tentes et autres formes de logement temporaire peuvent aussi être regroupées pour des motifs très différents, ainsi qu'en témoignent certains exemples présentés ici. La protestation est notamment l'une des raisons justifiant les « sit-in » ou occupation de sites urbains. Ce type d'agglomération temporaire formée de tentes et de cabanes s'est multiplié depuis quelques années, avec notamment le camping installé par les partisans de Victor Iouchtchenko sur le principal boulevard de Kiev (décembre 2004), les Indignés espagnols ou mouvement 15-M sur la Puerta del Sol à Madrid (2011), les différentes occupations de protestation aux États-Unis (2011) ou le Mouvement des parapluies pro-démocratique qui a envahi les rues de Hong Kong en 2014.

Si de nombreux festivals sont chaque été l'occasion de voir des cités provisoires se créer à plusieurs endroits du monde, le plus célèbre est le Burning Man qui a lieu à la fin de l'été à Black Rock City, dans le Nevada. Centré sur diverses valeurs communautaires et formes d'expression artistique, les tentes et les caravanes regroupées selon un immense plan semi-circulaire dans le désert sont à elles seules dignes de mention. Les photographes NK Guy et Philippe Glade documentent ces structures depuis plusieurs années et ont publié des livres entiers sur l'architecture du Burning Man qui réunit 65 000 personnes pour quelques jours. D'autres évènements aux motivations et expressions artistiques très différentes

MIMA HOUSING, MIMA LIGHT → P. 236

sont eux aussi l'occasion de vastes rassemblements temporaires sous de petites tentes. C'est le cas de Campus Party, un festival de sept jours 24 heures sur 24 qui regroupe gamers, blogueurs, programmeurs et tous ceux que la technologie fascine. Il a eu lieu plusieurs fois au Brésil et a notamment été organisé du 17 au 23 janvier 2011 au palais des expositions Centro Imigrantes de São Paulo où près de 7 000 jeunes gens sont venus profiter d'une connexion 10 Gb fournie par le gouvernement et des opérateurs de téléphonie locaux. Les centaines de tentes identiques qui les abritaient étaient comprises dans le droit d'entrée et parfaitement alignées selon une grille très stricte.

La vue des photos aériennes de l'immense cité provisoire érigée pour le Burning Man peut troubler par sa similitude avec les nombreux camps de réfugiés qui ont surgi dans le monde entier, notamment depuis la crise syrienne. Le camp de Zaatari, ouvert en 2012 près de Mafraq en Jordanie, accueille ainsi aujourd'hui quelque 85 000 personnes dans différents abris qui forment certainement l'un des types d'« habitat nomade » les plus visibles et les plus embarrassants au monde. Mais même dans des situations aussi difficiles, c'est tout à l'honneur de groupes actifs en Occident, tels qu'Architects for Society, basé à Minneapolis, que des concepts soient développés pour venir en aide aux habitants dans le besoin. Ainsi, la Hex House, créée par Architects for Society, est un logement d'urgence de 47 mètres carrés en panneaux de métal isolant pour un « design sommaire passif » (voir page 314).

Même des pays occidentaux comme la France ont été confrontés à un afflux de réfugiés, tels ceux qui tentent d'atteindre le Royaume-Uni et peuplent provisoirement la « jungle » de Calais. On notera avec étonnement que l'habitat nomade destiné aux plus riches tend à être considéré comme un moyen de fuir la société et de s'isoler, tandis que c'est le contraire pour les plus pauvres, rassemblés en troupeaux humains contre leur volonté dans le seul espoir de retrouver une existence stable. Le HCR estime à 65,3 millions le nombre de personnes déplacées de force dans le monde en 2015. Ce chiffre, auquel s'ajoute le flux et le reflux des populations devenues sans-abri à la suite d'autres catastrophes que la guerre, notamment des tremblements de terre, tsunamis et inondations dues aux tempêtes, a poussé bon nombre d'architectes de talent, parmi lesquels le lauréat japonais du prix Pritzker, Shigeru

Ban, à tenter de concevoir des logements temporaires de meilleure qualité — mais ces projets individuels diffèrent quelque peu des immenses camps qu'on a vu récemment sortir de terre au Moyen-Orient et ailleurs.

Il en va de même pour ce que le Bureau du recensement des États-Unis appelle « habitat manufacturé », une catégorie souvent associée à la pauvreté ou aux bas revenus dans le pays qui gagne ses lettres de noblesse entre les mains d'architectes tels que le groupe latino-américain MAPA qui a conçu l'élégant MINIMOD Cauçaba (Fazenda Catuçaba, SP, Brésil, 2009–2015 ; voir page 248), créé en usine sous forme modulaire puis acheminé sur place par camion.

Architectes américains reconnus, LOT-EK ont eux choisi les conteneurs maritimes pour y créer ce qu'ils ont baptisé une M.D.U. pour Mobile Dwelling Unit (Unité d'habitation mobile) (voir page 232) dont les murs de métal forment des extensions vers l'extérieur, offrant des espaces de vie, de travail et de rangement. Une fois refermée, la M.D.U. peut reprendre la route et la mer parmi les dizaines de milliers de conteneurs qui sont transportés chaque jour dans le monde entier. Exposée au Whitney Museum of American Art de New York et au Walker Art Center de Milwaukee, l'Unité d'habitation mobile représente un effort important pour intégrer le nomadisme élémentaire de nombreuses populations du monde à un système industriel en mouvement permanent, mais pour d'autres raisons.

La Wikkelhouse (2016 ; voir page 292) est un autre système modulaire créé par le groupe néerlandais Fiction Factory. Cette étonnante maison pour une grande part en carton se présente sous forme de sections longues de 1,2 mètre enclenchées les unes dans les autres, faciles à assembler, à agrandir ou à démonter. Les modules sont traités pour pouvoir résister à absolument toutes les conditions météorologiques et ont une durée de vie estimée à 50 ans. Le nomade et le temporaire peuvent donc facilement s'adapter aux conditions d'une existence plus stable.

Le lent mouvement de six pattes

Certains architectes et artistes ont fait progresser l'idée de maison mobile de quelques pas de plus que la vie quotidienne ne le laisserait entendre et ont ouvert des voies surprenantes aux concepts de mobilité et d'intimité. Le groupe danois N55 a ainsi créé la MAISON QUI MARCHE (WALKING HOUSE) à Copenhague en 2009 (voir page 286). Cet habitat modulaire qui peut accueillir jusqu'à quatre personnes se déplace sur six pattes actionnées par des vérins linéaires. La structure écologique et totalement inédite s'inspire en partie des cultures nomades, et plus particulièrement des charrettes roms tirées par des chevaux au XVIIIe siècle, associées ici à la technologie et aux matériaux modernes. Alex Schweder et Ward Shelley, quant à eux, ont imaginé leur maison mobile du nom de *ReActor* sur une base très différente, préférant la fixer sur une colonne de béton de cinq mètres de haut érigée à l'Omi International Art Center (Gand, New York, 2016 ; voir page 266). Le bâtiment vitré de 15 mètres de long pivote et bouge au gré des vents et des mouvements de ses deux habitants. L'artiste et l'architecte ont réellement vécu dans *ReActor* pendant une « performance habitationnelle de cinq jours ».

L'artiste américaine Andrea Zittel elle aussi a interrogé la nature de l'habitat et de la mobilité. Elle évoque la « construction sociale des besoins » en présentant des réalisations telles que son Indy Island, une nacelle qui flotte au milieu d'un lac, commandée par l'Indianapolis Museum of Art et destinée à être occupée tous les étés. Ses Wagon Stations (A-Z West, Joshua Tree, Californie ; Milwaukee, Minnesota, 2003) sont plus étonnantes encore. Ces couchettes-capsules, minuscules structures mobiles en bois et métal, peuvent être louées sur le domaine que possède l'artiste en Californie. Si elles permettent à leurs occupants de voir à l'extérieur par une ouverture dans le « toit », elles n'en sont pas moins minimalistes au point de rappeler les hôtels « capsules » japonais. Inspirées à la fois des chariots couverts, qui abritaient les biens des colons américains et les protégeaient des intempéries dans leur avancée vers l'Ouest, et des breaks à l'échelle desquels elles sont conçues, elles peuvent être considérées comme le *nec plus ultra* de l'habitat nomade. Elles ne pourraient guère être plus petites et sont conçues par une artiste, et ce même si elles rappellent le plus minimaliste des logements (permanents).

Le défi technologique

De plus en plus, l'habitat nomade est conçu dans le seul but d'utiliser une technologie de pointe pour une empreinte écologique minimale, tout en créant des logements mobiles adaptés à des environnements extrêmes ou à des emplacements qui ne peuvent être raccordés aux services municipaux. Deux de ces projets insolites sont publiés ici. Le premier est l'Écocapsule (voir page 212) inventée par les jeunes architectes slovaques Tomáš Žáček et Soňa Pohlová, anciens du cabinet Nice Architects (Bratislava). Cette capsule de 6,2 mètres carrés est présentée comme « une micro-maison intelligente et autosuffisante qui exploite l'énergie solaire et éolienne ». Sa forme sphérique et son design en fibre de verre permettent de récupérer l'eau de pluie et la rosée en minimisant les pertes d'énergie. La structure de 1 200 kilos rentre dans un conteneur maritime standard et est utilisable avec une remorque spécialement conçue qui peut être tirée par un véhicule de tourisme, ce qui en fait une caravane parfaitement fonctionnelle. Le projet AMIE (voir page 42) des architectes Skidmore, Owings & Merrill avec le laboratoire national Oak Ridge du ministère américain de l'Énergie est, quant à lui, un mobile home encore plus sophistiqué. Cet abri de 19,5 mètres carrés est un véhicule imprimé en 3D dans l'intention d'atteindre le plus haut niveau d'efficacité énergétique et de gestion des déchets. L'Écocapsule comme le projet AMIE présentent un degré élevé de raffinement dans le design et ouvrent la voie vers l'habitat du futur.

L'espace, l'ultime frontière

Pour prouver, s'il le faut, que nous sommes tous nomades, il suffit de mentionner le mobile home ultime, celui qui va dans l'espace et au-delà. Tous ceux qui ont grandi avec la série *Star Trek* ou peut-être l'univers de *La Guerre des étoiles*, reconnaîtront ces mots : « L'espace, l'ultime frontière. Voici le vaisseau galactique *Enterprise*. Sa mission : explorer des mondes nouveaux et étranges, découvrir de nouvelles formes de

vie et de nouvelles civilisations et s'aventurer dans les recoins les plus éloignés de la galaxie. » Les explorateurs de « l'ultime frontière » flottent déjà dans l'espace, à 419 000 kilomètres au-dessus de nos têtes, à bord de la Station spatiale internationale (ISS). Les astronautes de l'ISS, qui se déplacent à environ 27 000 kilomètres à l'heure, sont les nomades ultimes, décrivant une orbite autour de la Terre 15,7 fois par jour et vivant dans un environnement irrémédiablement technologique, mais disposant eux aussi d'un habitat mobile.

Si le gouvernement et un groupe hétéroclite de milliardaires et de visionnaires parviennent à s'imposer, l'orbite de la Terre ne sera bientôt plus « l'ultime frontière » que connaissent les amateurs de *Star Trek*. Les hommes pourront s'aventurer jusqu'à Mars et peut-être au-delà. L'initiative Mars One (voir page 228), qui prévoit d'installer au moins quatre colons « permanents » sur la Planète rouge d'ici 2032, incarne l'avant-poste le plus lointain jamais encore imaginé par les hommes, et donc l'aventure la plus extrême de l'habitat nomade. En effet, qu'il s'agisse des marins qui ont accompagné Christophe Colomb et d'autres explorateurs, ou de ceux qui sont partis en chariots couverts vers l'Ouest promis, tous gardaient certainement en tête la perspective lointaine de revenir à leur ancienne vie. Mais dans le cas de Mars One, l'avenir est plus que sombre : « Le retour est impossible ; aller sur Mars est une décision que vous prendrez pour le reste de votre vie. Il n'existe aucune technologie pour une mission de retour. »

Retour sur Terre

Certains voient, dans la perspective d'aller sur Mars, une aimable plaisanterie alors que la vie des réfugiés ou des ceux devenus sans-abri à la suite de catastrophes naturelles est entre les mains d'organisations internationales — et les ONG ne peuvent faire plus que ce qu'elles font avec leurs moyens limités. C'est ce qui donne un caractère si positif aux efforts qu'entreprennent des architectes comme Shigeru Ban, qui donne un nouveau souffle à l'architecture contemporaine. L'idée est d'aider réellement les personnes dans le besoin et de le faire dans le cadre d'une analyse pertinente des moyens et des objectifs. Le résultat est un habitat temporaire peu onéreux, facile à transporter à proximité du lieu des catastrophes ou aux frontières de pays en guerre, là où l'urgence est encore plus grande.

Shigeru Ban a beaucoup fait pour aider ceux qui avaient perdu leur toit après des catastrophes naturelles. Ses logements temporaires en conteneurs (Onagawa, Japon, 2011 ; voir page 300) ont été conçus après le tremblement de terre et le tsunami du 11 mars 2011 qui ont frappé la région de Tohoku, dans l'est du Japon. On estime en effet que quatre ans après, 230 000 personnes vivaient encore dans des logements temporaires. Comme il l'a souvent fait dans des projets précédents, Shigeru Ban a construit les logements d'Onagawa avec des conteneurs maritimes de 6,1 mètres. En raison du manque de terrains plats appropriés, il a décidé de les empiler sur trois niveaux en formant un motif à damiers qui a créé « des espaces de vie clairs et ouverts entre les conteneurs », conçus selon trois configurations différentes en fonction de la taille des familles à loger.

La Nouvelle Maison temporaire (New Temporary House, Manille, Philippines, 2013 ; voir page 320), une autre initiative d'aide d'urgence de Shigeru Ban, consiste en logements préfabriqués à bas prix et a été testée aux Philippines. Fait de plastique renforcé par des fibres (PRF) et de panneaux sandwich en carton mousse, le projet permet des logements temporaires de meilleure qualité et crée des emplois sur place. Comme pour sa tente en fibres de carbone, plus récente, l'architecte a imaginé de nombreux usages pour la Nouvelle Maison temporaire, notamment celui de fournir des logements dans des régions pauvres de pays tels que l'Inde ou le Népal.

Parmi les autres projets intéressants, d'abord conçus pour les réfugiés mais également adaptés à des circonstances moins difficiles, citons le projet SURI (Shelter Units for Rapid Installation, Unités refuges pour installation rapide ; voir page 324) développé par Suricatta Systems à Alicante, en Espagne. Les unités SURI mesurent un peu plus de 12 mètres carrés et mettent l'accent sur les matériaux locaux facilement

SURICATTA SYSTEMS, SURI—SHELTER UNITS FOR RAPID INSTALLATION → P. 324

disponibles, dont les sacs de sable, même si elles comprennent aussi différentes formes de polyéthylène. Les abris se veulent recyclables à 100 % et durables, tous leurs composants sont réutilisables ou biodégradables. Des panneaux solaires et un système de récupération des eaux de pluie peuvent être installés selon le climat. Les abris SURI sont distribués sous forme de paquets plats de 580 kilos et peuvent être assemblés sur place par deux personnes sans compétences particulières.

En quête du minimum

Mais que la distance est donc grande entre les jets privés ou les super yachts et les logements minimalistes pour réfugiés ! Des plus riches aux plus pauvres habitants de notre Terre, et jusqu'à ceux qui espèrent coloniser un jour d'autres planètes, l'habitat nomade sous ses différentes formes est plus la règle que l'exception. Devant les difficultés généralisées pour trouver à se loger, l'habitat dit « manufacturé » permet à ceux qui ne peuvent pas se permettre de construire leur maison d'accéder à la propriété et au domicile. Alors que d'autres peuvent dépenser 1,5 million d'euros pour un bus susceptible de devenir leur logement à moteur bien à eux. Parmi les architectes et les artistes dont le travail est présenté ici, bon nombre se sont intéressés au concept d'habitat minimal. Pour Renzo Piano, Diogene, un abri de 7,5 mètres carrés (Weil am Rhein, Allemagne, 2013 ; voir page 202), apporte une réponse à la question du minimum qu'un homme ou une femme peut espérer dans la vie. Pourtant, avec ses panneaux photovoltaïques, sa pompe géothermique et son éclairage à faible consommation d'énergie, Diogene est aussi le fruit du progrès accompli par les techniques modernes de construction. Le projet porte le nom du philosophe grec qui affirmait être un citoyen du monde.

Les errances d'Andrea Zittel sur « la construction sociale des besoins » pourraient bien suggérer elles aussi que les hommes ont en réalité besoin de bien moins que ce que la société leur fait croire. Mais ses Wagon Stations incarnent-ils rien de plus que ce que les Français appellent « l'ultime demeure » ? Car se débrouiller dans un monde aux ressources finies implique bien évidemment de rationaliser les tailles Les Japonais des villes l'ont compris depuis longtemps. Les maisons japonaises, sans être forcément mobiles, atteignent souvent les limites

basses de la surface nécessaire — en raison à la fois des prix très élevés du terrain et du peu d'espace disponible dans les centres urbains. L'architecte japonais de grand talent Kengo Kuma a cependant cherché moins à explorer les limites de la technologie qu'à porter un regard rétrospectif sur l'histoire littéraire de son pays avec son Hojo-an (Kyoto, 2012 ; voir page 216). Cette maison mobile de neuf mètres carrés en feuilles d'ETFE, bandes de cèdre et aimants, constitue une réminiscence voulue de l'œuvre de Kamono Chomei (1155–1216), auteur de *Hojo-ki* (*Notes de ma cabane de moine*), qui habitait une maison mobile souvent décrite comme le prototype du logement compact japonais. Kuma a voulu reconstruire cette maison avec des idées et des méthodes modernes sur le même site, dans l'enceinte du sanctuaire de Shimogamo Jinja. Un *hojo* est un « cottage » de trois mètres sur trois environ — peut-être la taille idéale pour un logis nomade construit à la frontière entre le passé et le futur ?

Ce panorama, forcément restreint, d'habitations mobiles développées toutes les régions du monde et dans tous les contextes le met rapidement en évidence : l'esprit nomade de nos ancêtres chasseurs-cueilleurs est resté très vivant dans le monde moderne. En effet, là où l'architecture a souvent recherché la stabilité, et donc l'absence de mouvement, la modernité a apporté un sens du fini et une bonne dose de modestie face à la postérité et à la longévité. Peut-il y avoir une réflexion plus contemporaine que celle de ne rien tant chercher que bouger, s'agrandir éventuellement, mais toujours bouger. « Le bon voyageur, a dit le philosophe chinois de l'Antiquité Lao-Tseu, n'a pas de plans établis et n'a pas l'intention d'arriver. » C'est le voyage qui compte, l'arrivée est la même pour tous.

WILLIAM WINKELMAN
Maine [USA] — 2009

1958 CHEVY VIKING SHORT-BUS RETRO

Area: 8.4 m² — Client: not disclosed — Cost: not disclosed — Collaboration: Tony Jose,
Linekin Bay Woodworkers, Vince Moulton, Vince Moulton Interiors

Recalling the form of iconic American school buses, this remake combines a retro or vintage feeling with a refit that allows for transport or camping use.

Der Bus greift die Form des bekannten amerikanischen Schulbusses auf und verbindet eine nostalgische Wirkung mit neuer Ausstattung. Er ist als Transporter ebenso wie zum Camping geeignet.

Rappelant la forme des emblématiques bus scolaires américains, ce remake associe une ambiance rétro ou vintage à de nouveaux équipements qui permettent de l'utiliser pour le transport ou le camping.

Starting out with a 1958 Chevy Viking Bus spotted in an essentially abandoned state in a field by a client, the architects added surfaces in quarter-sawn white oak, salvaged hard pine, and used salvaged metal fixtures. Designed to carry up to 12 passengers and a driver, the bus can be converted into a mobile home for two with two beds or a queen-size bed, a toilet and sink, and electrical power. The bus had actually been converted into a camper before Winkelman Architecture took on the project, but the client's desire for a "hippy Moroccan," 1960s "vintage" feeling, and to make it usable both for transport and for camping led the architects to work with woodworkers specialized in custom boat-building (Linekin Bay Woodworkers).

Für ihren Umbau eines Chevy Viking Bus von 1958, den ein Kunde in ziemlich verkommenem Zustand auf einem Feld entdeckt hatte, verwendeten die Architekten radial geschnittene Flächen aus weißer Eiche und recyceltem Kiefernholz sowie aufbereitete alte Metallarmaturen. Der für zwölf Passagiere plus Fahrer ausgelegte Bus kann zu einem mit elektrischem Strom ausgerüsteten Wohnmobil für zwei Personen mit zwei einzelnen oder einem Doppelbett, einer Toilette und einem Waschbecken umfunktioniert werden. Das Fahrzeug war schon zu einem Camper umgebaut worden, als die Architekten das Projekt übernahmen. Doch die Auftraggeber wünschten sich einen nostalgischen „1960er-Hippie-Marokko-Look" und wollten den Bus nicht nur zum Campen, sondern auch als Transporter nutzen. Die Architekten suchten daher die Zusammenarbeit mit Schreinern, die maßgeschneiderte Bootsausstattungen herstellen (Linekin Bay Woodworkers).

À ce bus Chevrolet Viking de 1958 presque à l'abandon, repéré dans un champ par le client, les architectes ont ajouté des surfaces de chêne blanc débité sur quartiers et de pin dur récupéré, avec des accessoires métalliques d'occasion. Conçu pour transporter jusqu'à 12 passagers et un conducteur, il peut aussi être converti en mobile home pour deux avec deux lits ou un grand lit, des toilettes, un lavabo et l'électricité. Le bus avait par ailleurs déjà été transformé en camping-car avant que Winkelman Architecture n'entreprenne son projet, mais le client souhaitait une ambiance années 1960 « hippie marocaine » et pouvoir l'utiliser pour le transport et le camping. C'est pour accéder à cette demande que les architectes ont collaboré avec des menuisiers spécialisés dans la construction de bateaux sur mesure (Linekin Bay Woodworkers).

1979 AIRSTREAM SOVEREIGN 31', ELIZABETH

Area: 16.7 m² — Client: not disclosed — Cost: not disclosed

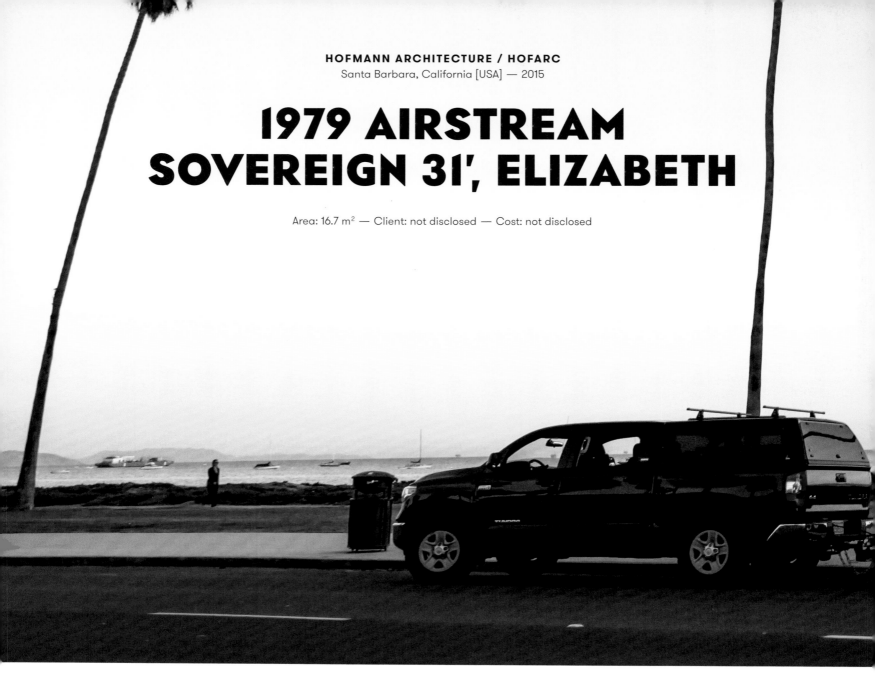

The owner of this Airstream trailer parks it in northern California. Elizabeth features 12 automated skylight windows and two further sets of operable windows, in the front and back. A vintage SMEG refrigerator and a 1930s Wedgewood gas stove are centerpieces of the "authentic Euro-style kitchen." Moroccan mosaic tiles are used on the bathroom floor, walls, and ceiling. A Petite Kensington upholstered sofa marks the living area, where reclaimed barn wood mounted on white Plexiglas is used for the walls. Filament bare Edison bulbs contribute to the "retro" atmosphere, but the light comes from solar energy. Amenities include radiant floor heating, reclaimed wood shelving in the kitchen, and reclaimed oak flooring. As is the case with their other Airstream refits, Hofmann Architecture finishes the job by thoroughly polishing the stainless-steel exterior of the vehicle.

Der Besitzer dieses Airstream-Trailers parkt ihn im Norden Kaliforniens. Elizabeth hat zwölf vollautomatisierte Oberlichter und zwei weitere verstellbare Fenster vorne und hinten. Ein Vintage-SMEG-Kühlschrank und ein Wedgewood-Gasherd aus den 1930er-Jahren sind die zentralen Elemente der „Küche im authentisch europäischen Stil". Boden, Wände und Decke des Badezimmers sind mit marokkanischen Mosaikfliesen ausgelegt. Ein Sofa im Petite-Kensington-Stil steht im Wohnraum, der mit auf weißem Plexiglas angebrachtem Altholz aus Scheunen verkleidet ist. Nackte Glühbirnen tragen zur „Retro"-Atmosphäre bei, das Licht wird aber mit Solarstrom erzeugt. Zu den weiteren Annehmlichkeiten zählen die Fußbodenheizung, Küchenregale aus recyceltem Holz und Fußböden aus wiederverwendeter Eiche. Wie auch bei ihren anderen Airstream-Restaurierungen beendeten Hofmann Architecture ihren Auftrag mit einer gründlichen Politur der Edelstahl-Außenhaut des Wohnwagens.

Cette caravane Airstream est stationnée dans le nord de la Californie. Elizabeth possède 12 lucarnes à ouverture automatique et deux autres séries de fenêtres ouvrantes à l'avant et à l'arrière. La « cuisine en authentique style européen » est articulée autour d'un réfrigérateur SMEG d'époque et d'un réchaud à gaz Wedgewood des années 1930. Des carreaux de mosaïque marocaine recouvrent le sol, les murs et le plafond de la salle de bains. Un canapé rembourré Petite Kensington occupe l'espace salon dont les murs sont garnis de bois de grange récupéré sur du Plexiglas blanc. Des ampoules nues Edison à incandescence contribuent à l'atmosphère « rétro », mais l'éclairage est assuré par l'énergie solaire. Les équipements comprennent un chauffage au sol à rayonnement, des étagères en bois de récupération dans la cuisine et un plancher en chêne récupéré. Comme pour les autres caravanes Airstream restaurées par Hofmann Architecture, l'ensemble est complété par un polissage parfait de l'extérieur en acier inoxydable.

The rounded, polished aluminum bodies of Airstream trailers were first created in the 1930s and remain in production in varying forms. Below, a plan of this 2015 refit of a 1979, 9.5-meter-long model.

Die abgerundeten, polierten Chassis der Airstream-Wohnwagen wurden erstmals in den 1930er-Jahren gebaut und werden in unterschiedlichen Formen weiterhin produziert. Unten: Ein Grundriss dieses 9,5 m langen, 2015 neu ausgestatteten Modells aus dem Jahr 1979.

Les carrosseries arrondies des remorques Airstream, en aluminium poli, ont été inventées dans les années 1930 et sont encore produites aujourd'hui sous diverses formes. Ci-dessous, le plan d'un modèle de 1979 long de 9,5 m, réaménagé en 2015.

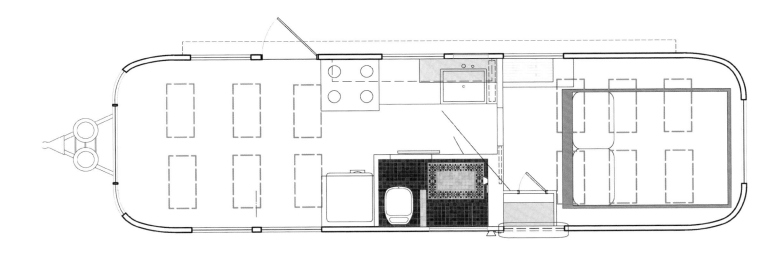

The interiors of the trailer are finished with vintage elements, such as an upholstered sofa, a SMEG (Italian) refrigerator, a 1930s Wedgewood gas stove, and reclaimed wood, giving a "Euro style" to the whole.

Das Innere des Wohnwagens ist mit Vintage-Möbeln ausgestattet: einem Sofa, einem SMEG-Kühlschrank aus Italien, einem Gasherd von Wedgewood aus den 1930er-Jahren und recyceltem Holz, das dem Ganzen eine „euro-päische" Note verleiht.

Les finitions intérieures de la remorque comprennent des éléments d'époque tels qu'un canapé rembourré, un réfrigérateur SMEG (italien), un réchaud à gaz Wedgewood des années 1930 et du bois de récupération qui confère un « style euro-péen » à l'ensemble.

SKIDMORE, OWINGS & MERRILL
Knoxville, Tennessee [USA] — 2015

ADDITIVE MANUFACTURING INTEGRATED ENERGY (AMIE)

Area: 19.5 m² — Client: Oak Ridge National Laboratory, University of Tennessee College of Architecture and Design — Cost: not disclosed

The Additive Manufacturing Integrated Energy (AMIE) demonstration project, a 3D-printed building, is a research and design collaboration between SOM and the US Department of Energy's (DOE) Oak Ridge National Laboratory (ORNL). The building was designed by SOM to produce and store renewable power and to share energy wirelessly with a 3D-printed vehicle, developed by the DOE. SOM states: "The project illustrates the potential of a clean energy future for a rapidly urbanizing world by demonstrating the use of bidirectional wireless energy technology and high-performance materials to achieve independence from the power grid at peak-demand times." Super high-efficiency atmospherically insulated panels are attached to the interior ribs of the building. A natural gas-powered generator and flexible photovoltaic panels provide energy for lighting and a central micro-kitchen produced by GE.

Das Demonstrationsprojekt Additive Manufacturing Integrated Energy (AMIE), ein 3-D-gedrucktes Gebäude, ist das Ergebnis einer Zusammenarbeit in Forschung und Planung von SOM mit dem Oak Ridge National Laboratory (ORNL) des US Department of Energy (DOE). Das Gebäude wurde von SOM entworfen, um erneuerbare Energie zu produzieren und zu speichern und Energie drahtlos auf ein 3-D-gedrucktes, von der DOE entwickeltes Fahrzeug zu übertragen. SOM erklären: „Das Projekt zeigt das Potenzial einer Zukunft mit sauberer Energie für eine sich ständig weiter verstädternde Welt. Es demonstriert die Anwendung bidirektionaler drahtloser Energietechnologie und hoch leistungsfähiger Materialien mit dem Ziel, zu Spitzenzeiten unabhängig vom Stromnetz zu sein." Auf die Rippen im Inneren des Bauwerks wurden hocheffiziente Isolierplatten aufgebracht. Ein gasbetriebener Generator und flexible Fotovoltaikpaneele liefern die Energie zur Beleuchtung und für eine zentrale, von General Electric produzierte Mikro-Küche.

Le projet pilote Additive Manufacturing Integrated Energy (AMIE), construit par impression 3D, est le résultat d'une collaboration de recherche et de design entre SOM et le laboratoire national Oak Ridge (ORNL) du ministère américain de l'Énergie (DOE). Le bâtiment a été conçu par SOM afin de produire et de stocker l'énergie renouvelable qu'il partage sans fil avec un véhicule imprimé en 3D développé par le DOE. « Le projet illustre le potentiel d'un avenir énergétique propre dans un monde à l'urbanisation rapide, explique SOM. Il témoigne de l'emploi des technologies de transfert d'énergie bidirectionnel sans fil et des matériaux haute performance pour assurer l'indépendance du réseau électrique pendant les pics de consommation. » Des panneaux isolés à très haut rendement atmosphériquement sont fixés aux nervures intérieures de l'abri. Un générateur au gaz naturel et des panneaux photovoltaïques souples fournissent l'énergie nécessaire à l'éclairage et à une mini-cuisine centrale fabriquée par GE.

The AMIE project aims for "zero-waste construction, reduced material consumption, and buildings that can be recycled and reprinted for new forms and uses." Flexible photovoltaic panels are integrated into the roof and work in conjunction with a natural gas-powered generator.

Das Projekt AMIE zielt auf „abfallfreie Produktion, reduzierten Materialverbrauch und Bauten, die recycelt sowie in neue Formen und für neue Nutzungen umgestaltet werden können". In das Dach sind flexible Fotovoltaikpaneele eingelassen, die mit einem gasbetriebenen Generator kombiniert sind.

Le projet AMIE vise « une construction zéro déchet, une consommation de matériel réduite et des bâtiments qui peuvent être recyclés et réimprimés pour de nouvelles formes et de nouveaux usages ». Des panneaux photovoltaïques souples sont intégrés au toit et fonctionnent conjointement avec un générateur au gaz naturel.

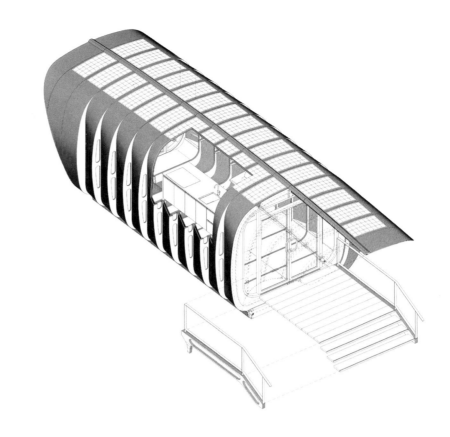

AMIE is part of an effort to "identify and develop innovative strategies of achieving a sustainable balance between the world's rapidly growing cities, their energy demands and the natural environment."

AMIE ist Teil der Bemühungen, „innovative Strategien zu erkennen und zu entwickeln, um einen nachhaltigen Ausgleich zwischen dem schnellen Wachstum der Städte, deren Energieverbrauch und der natürlichen Umwelt zu erzielen".

AMIE s'inscrit dans un effort d'« identification et développement des stratégies innovantes pour parvenir à un équilibre durable entre la croissance rapide des villes dans le monde entier, leurs besoins en énergie et l'environnement naturel ».

FRANCIS & ARNETT
Southern Snowdonia, Wales [UK] — 2016–17

ANIMATED FOREST

Area: 15 m² — Client: Epic Retreats, Welsh Government — Cost: £11 000

This small cabin was originally intended to sit on legs high above the ground. It explores the theme of the "animated forest" that shapes the Welsh landscape. According to the designers, it was inspired by the poem *Cad Goddeu*, meaning "Battle of the trees," from the medieval Welsh manuscript called the "Book of Taliesin." The structure is made of blackened timber and Corten steel, and seeks to "resemble a creature meandering through the landscape." Digital modeling and fabrication techniques were used to create the structure with a limited budget, in which skylights allow residents to view the forest and sky. The large circular door rolls open to reveal the raw spruce cladding of the interior with a padded luxury leather bedding area and tailored sink and plumbing. A dark-stained shower space is lit from above. Quoting from the novel *Moby Dick* (Herman Melville, 1851), the designers present Animated Forest in unexpected terms: "It is some systematized exhibition of the whale in his broad genera, that I would now fain put before you. Yet is it no easy task. The classification of the constituents of a chaos, nothing less is here essayed."

Diese kleine Hütte sollte ursprünglich aufgeständert sein. Sie ist ein Beitrag zum Thema „belebter Wald", der die walisische Landschaft prägt. Laut Auskunft der Planer wurde sie vom Gedicht *Cad Goddeu* (was „Kampf der Bäume" bedeutet) aus dem mittelalterlichen walisischen Manuskript *Book of Taliesin* angeregt. Das Gebäude besteht aus geschwärztem Holz und Corten-Stahl und soll „einem Geschöpf ähneln, das durch das Gelände streift". Digitale Entwurfs- und Produktionstechniken wurden für die Entstehung des Bauwerks mit kleinem Etat genutzt. Oberlichter gewähren den Bewohnern Ausblicke auf den Wald und zum Himmel. Die große, kreisförmige Tür wird zur Seite gerollt und zeigt dann die Innenverkleidung aus unbehandeltem Fichtenholz mit einem luxuriösen, ledergepolsterten Schlafbereich, maßgefertigtem Waschbecken und Sanitärbereich. Die dunkel gefleckte Duschkabine wird von oben beleuchtet. Die Architekten präsentieren den Animated Forest in überraschenden Worten aus dem Roman *Moby Dick* (Herman Melville, 1851): „Was ich hier vorlegen möchte, ist ein einigermaßen geordneter Abriss der hauptsächlichen Walfischarten. Es ist dies freilich keine leichte Aufgabe. Ordnung in ein Chaos zu bringen, nichts Geringeres ist es, was hier angestrebt wird."

Cette petite cabane devait au départ être posée sur des pieds très au-dessus du sol. Elle renvoie au thème de la « forêt animée » qui a donné forme au paysage du Pays de Galles. Selon ses créateurs, elle s'inspire du poème « Cad Goddeu » (« Le Combat des arbres ») qu'on trouve dans le manuscrit médiéval gallois du *Livre de Taliesin*. La structure est en bois d'œuvre noirci et acier Corten afin de « ressembler à une créature qui vagabonde dans la campagne ». Les techniques de modélisation numérique et de fabrication utilisées ont permis de réduire son budget de production. Des lucarnes permettent aux occupants de contempler la forêt et le ciel, tandis que la large porte circulaire roule pour révéler l'intérieur revêtu d'épicéa brut, sa luxueuse zone de couchage rembourrée en cuir, son évier et sa plomberie sur mesure. L'espace douche teinté de sombre est éclairé par le haut. Citant le roman *Moby Dick* (Herman Melville, 1851), les designers présentent leur Animated Forest en ces termes surprenants : « C'est une exposition systématique de la baleine au sein de son espèce, dans un ensemble plus vaste, que je voudrais mettre sous vos yeux. Ce qui n'est certes pas chose facile. C'est l'organisation d'un véritable chaos qu'il nous faut essayer de faire ici ; rien de moins que cela. »

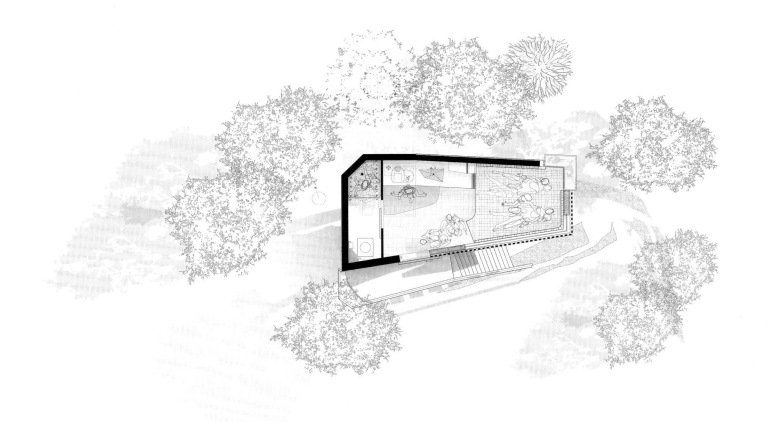

A large, round, sliding entrance door and skylights give residents a clear feeling that they are living in the natural setting. A wood-burning stove and natural wood interiors are visible below and left.

Eine große, runde Tür und Oberlichter geben den Bewohnern das sichere Gefühl, in einer natürlichen Umgebung zu leben. Ein Holzofen sowie Einbauten aus Naturholz sind unten und links zu erkennen.

La large porte ronde coulissante et les lucarnes donnent aux occupants de la cabane le sentiment manifeste de vivre dans le décor naturel. Ci-dessous et à gauche, on aperçoit le poêle à bois et l'intérieur en bois naturel.

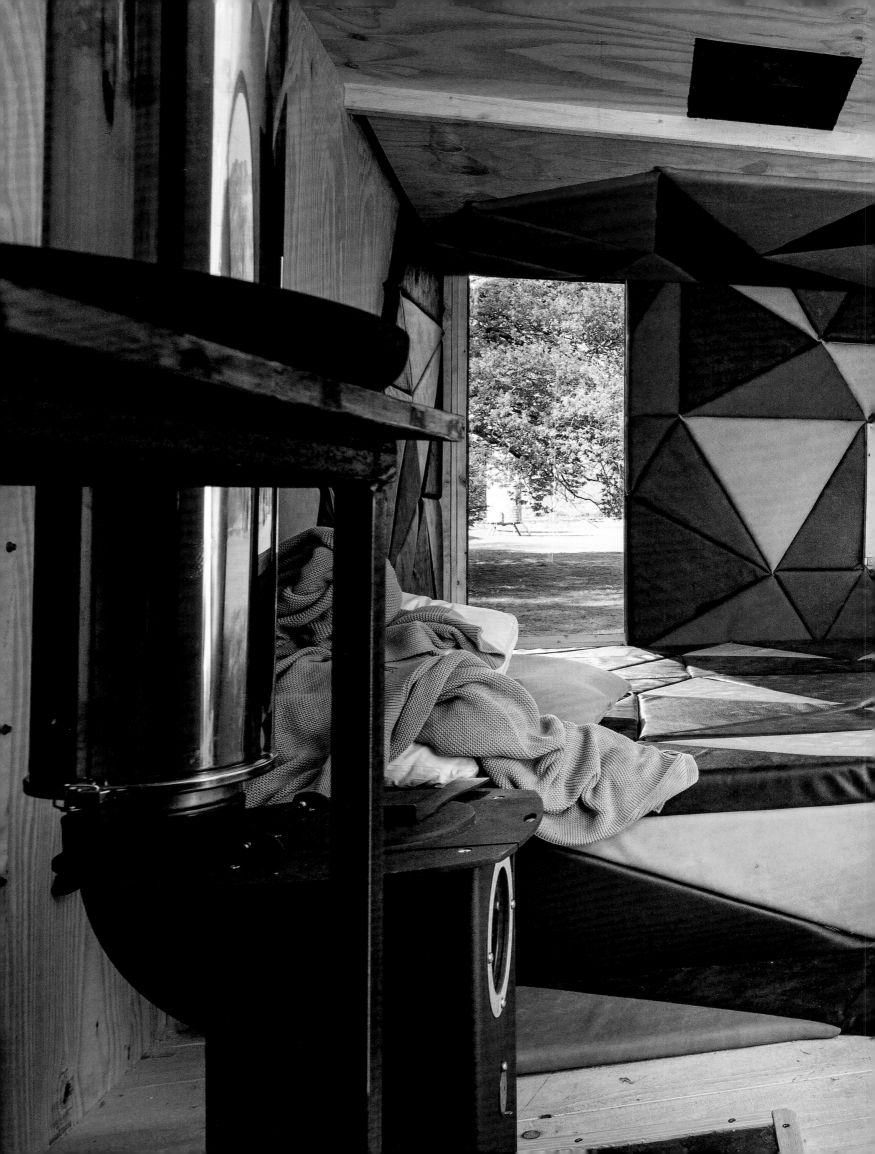

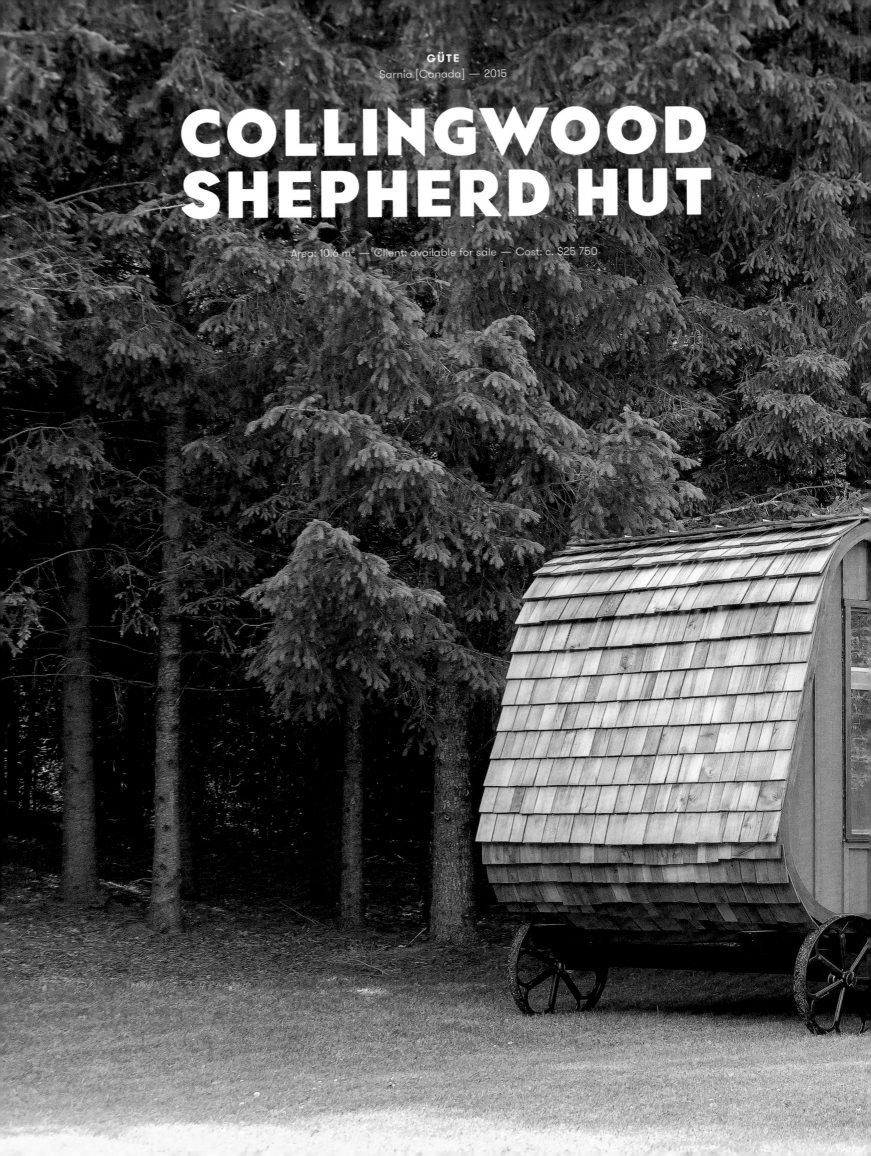

GÜTE
Sarnia [Canada] — 2015

COLLINGWOOD SHEPHERD HUT

Area: 10.6 m² — Client: available for sale — Cost: c. $25 750

In the words of the designers: "We built the Collingwood Shepherd Hut without clear distinctions of where the walls become the floor or roof… We wrapped the roof all the way around in a fluid wooden framed structure that sheds off every kind of bad weather." Natural Western red cedar shingles over an ice and water shield were used for the exterior. The roof is clad in galvanized steel. Interiors are in poplar with a painted pine floor and an insulated floor substructure. The designers offer a variety of different reclaimed woods including chestnut, Douglas fir, beech, ash, maple, and pine. Thermal glass panes are set in solid cedar frames and sashes. The door, frame, and sill are made with solid white oak. Inspired by 19th-century mobile homes, the Collingwood Shepherd Hut is meant as a combination of "German precision and technical mastery with the warmth and coziness of natural materials." Its design allows for the mobile home to be installed even where no traditional building is allowed for environmental reasons.

Die Designer sagen: „Wir bauten die Collingwood Shepherd Hut, ohne klar zu definieren, wo die Wände zum Fußboden oder zum Dach werden … Wir wickelten das Dach als geschwungene, fließende Holzrahmenkonstruktion ganz ums Haus, die jeder Art von schlechtem Wetter trotzt." Schindeln aus naturbelassenem Rotzedernholz über einer Schutzabdeckung gegen Eis und Wasser bilden die Außenhaut. Das Dach ist mit verzinktem Stahl gedeckt. Der Innenraum ist mit Pappelholz verkleidet und hat einen lackierten Kiefernholzboden auf einer isolierten Unterkonstruktion. Die Designer nutzten viele verschiedene Althölzer: Kastanie, Douglasie, Birke, Esche, Ahorn und Kiefer. Die Fenster haben Isolierglasscheiben in Rahmen aus massivem Zedernholz. Die Tür, der Türrahmen und die Türschwelle sind aus massiver Weißeiche. Die von Mobilheimen des 19. Jahrhunderts inspirierte Collingwood Shepherd Hut soll eine Kombination aus „deutscher Präzisionsarbeit und technischer Meisterschaft mit der Wärme und Gemütlichkeit natürlicher Materialien" darstellen. Seine Form macht es möglich, dieses mobile Heim überall dort aufzustellen, wo aus Gründen des Umweltschutzes konventionelle Bauten verboten sind.

Voici ce qu'en disent les designers : « Nous avons construit Collingwood sans distinguer clairement là où les murs deviennent le sol ou le toit… Nous avons entièrement emballé le toit dans une structure de bois fluide qui résiste à tous les mauvais temps. » L'extérieur est en bardeaux de cèdre rouge d'Occident sur un écran étanche à l'eau et à la glace. Le toit est recouvert d'acier galvanisé. L'intérieur est en peuplier avec un plancher de pin peint et isolé. Les designers ont utilisé différents bois de récupération, parmi lesquels du châtaignier, du sapin de Douglas, du hêtre, du frêne, de l'érable et du pin. Les vitres en verre thermique sont fixées dans de robustes cadres de cèdre et des châssis à guillotine. La porte, la charpente et le seuil sont en chêne blanc massif. Inspirée par les roulottes du XIXe siècle, cette « cabane de berger » est censée associer « la précision et la maîtrise technique allemandes à la chaleur et au confort des matériaux naturels ». Son design permet de la stationner même aux endroits interdits aux constructions traditionnelles pour des raisons de protection de l'environnement.

Despite its small size, the structure is bright and apparently spacious inside. Solid pine flooring and solid wood board are used for the interior surfaces.

Trotz seiner bescheidenen Größe wirkt das Haus innen hell und geräumig. Die Böden sind aus massivem Kiefernholz, wie auch die übrigen Flächen aus Massivholz bestehen.

Malgré sa taille réduite, l'ensemble est clair et l'intérieur, avec son sol en pin massif et ses planches en bois massif, semble spacieux.

HRISTINA HRISTOVA
Burgas [Bulgaria] — 2015

KOLELIBA

Area: 9 m² — Client: Georgievi family — Cost: €8500
Collaboration: Amillee Design (Furniture)

This tiny vacation house was made with white, oiled pine, lumber cladding and plywood. The size of the structure was determined by restrictions related to road traffic. With a height of 2.4 meters and full-height glazing, the designer was able to avoid any claustrophobic feeling. A bench spanning across the main façade with a canopy was created to allow friends to come and visit. Exterior lighting was added to permit gatherings to go on after dark. "Koleliba," says the designer, "is our response to the invading consumerism that encourages us to always want our homes to be bigger, better, and unnecessarily luxurious. It's a step back to a simpler life without excesses but full of free time, happy moments, and friends that we often have to sacrifice in our never-ending drive for more."

Dieses kleine Ferienhaus wurde aus weißem, geöltem Kiefernholz, Sperrholz und mit Holzverkleidung errichtet. Die Größe des Gebäudes orientiert sich an dem, was die Straßenverkehrsordnung zulässt. Mit einer Höhe von 2,4 m und ebenso hoher Verglasung konnte die Planerin aber eine klaustrophobische Stimmung vermeiden. Eine überdachte Bank erstreckt sich entlang der Hauptfassade, um Besuch empfangen zu können, was dank der Außenbeleuchtung auch nach Einbruch der Dunkelheit noch möglich ist. „Koleliba", sagt die Architektin, „ist unsere Reaktion auf das Eindringen des Konsumzwangs in unser Leben, der uns nach immer größeren, besseren und unnötig luxuriösen Häusern streben lässt. Es ist ein Schritt zurück zu einem einfacheren Leben ohne Überfluss, aber mit viel Freizeit, glücklichen Momenten und Freunden, die wir oft wegen unseres unaufhörlichen Strebens nach mehr vernachlässigen."

Cette minuscule maison de vacances est en pin blanc huilé, bois de charpente pour le revêtement et contreplaqué. La taille en a été déterminée en fonction des restrictions de la circulation routière, mais la designer est parvenue à éviter toute sensation de claustrophobie grâce à la hauteur de 2,4 mètres entièrement vitrée. Un banc court le long de la façade principale sous un auvent et invite aux visites, tandis que l'éclairage extérieur permet aux réunions de se prolonger à la nuit tombée. « Koleliba, explique la créatrice, est notre réponse à la frénésie de consommation qui nous incite à vouloir des habitations toujours plus grandes, plus belles et inutilement luxueuses. C'est un pas en arrière vers une vie plus simple, sans excès, mais avec du temps libre, des moments de bonheur et des amis en abondance, alors que nous devons souvent les sacrifier dans notre course sans fin vers toujours plus. »

The nine-square-meter size of Koleliba (a made-up name meaning "hut with wheels") was determined by road restrictions. Oiled wood and plywood were used to give a feeling of warmth despite the small dimensions.

Die Größe des Koleliba (ein Kunstwort, das „Hütte auf Rädern" bedeutet) von 9 m² orientiert sich an den Verkehrsvorschriften. Geöltes Holz und Sperrholz sollen den kleinen Raum wohnlich wirken lassen.

Les 9 m² de Koleliba (un nom inventé qui signifie « cabane à roues ») ont été déterminés en fonction des restrictions de circulation routière. Le bois huilé et le contreplaqué donnent néanmoins un sentiment chaleureux.

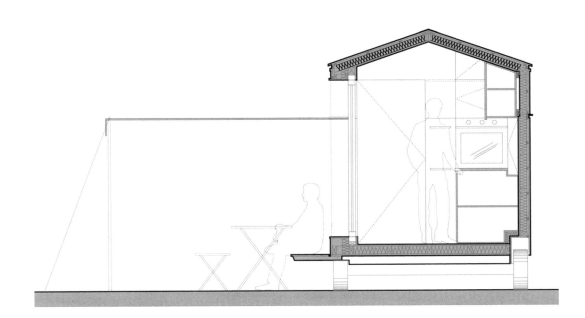

A section drawing (above) shows the folding canopy (also seen in the photos), a built-in oven, and storage, as well as full-height glazing at the entrance.

Der Schnitt (oben) zeigt das (auch auf dem Foto zu sehende) faltbare Vordach, einen eingebauten Ofen und Abstellflächen sowie die geschosshohe Verglasung am Eingang.

Le schéma en coupe (ci-dessus) montre l'auvent pliant (aussi visible sur les photos), un four encastré et des rangements, ainsi que le vitrage sur toute la hauteur de l'entrée.

The plan (left) shows the toilet visible to the left, a built-in boiler (top, center), as well as the extendable canopy seen in the photo above.

Der Grundriss (links) zeigt links die Toilette, einen eingebauten Boiler (Mitte oben) sowie das auf dem Foto oben sichtbare ausfaltbare Vordach.

Le plan (à gauche) montre les toilettes à gauche, une chaudière encastrée (en haut au milieu) et l'auvent à rallonge qu'on voit sur la photo ci-dessus.

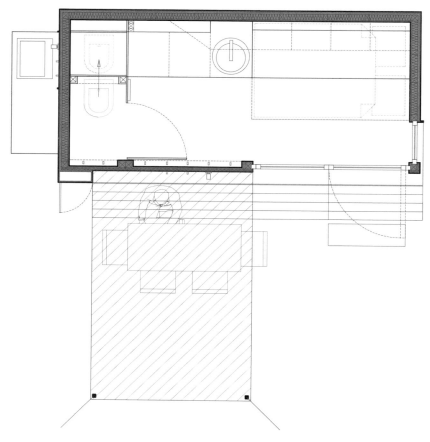

A couch near the kitchen space folds out to become a bed. Storage space is provided for wherever possible.

Die Couch neben der Küchenzeile lässt sich zu einem Bett ausziehen. Für Stauraum wurde gesorgt, wo immer es ging.

À côté de l'espace cuisine, un canapé se déplie pour se transformer en lit. Des rangements sont prévus à tous les endroits possibles.

NILS HOLGER MOORMANN
Aschau im Chiemgau [Germany] — 2016

MOORMANN'S NEW STANDARD CLASS

Area: 4.3 m² — Client: Nils Holger Moormann — Cost: c. €90 000
Collaboration: CB Fahrzeugbau GmbH & Co. KG, www.custom-bus.de

Nils Holger Moormann appears to prefer living in a camper than staying in a hotel, for example. Using a VW Minibus, Moormann and his team sought to eliminate "everything that could possibly be omitted," leaving the exterior appearance of the vehicle essentially untouched. Furniture surfaces in nanotech thermolaminate matt and seat covers made of Merino wool show the kind of surprising contrasts sought by the designer. The bus has four linen compartments, one space for hanging clothes, another for laundry, a cosmetic compartment, two illuminated bookshelves, four compartments for kitchen utensils, where there is a stainless-steel work surface and a 65-liter refrigerator with freezer compartment. A 1.25-meter-wide sofa bed, oak floorboards, and ceiling panelling made with untreated oak, all lit with a sophisticated system including LED atmosphere lights, again demonstrate the combination of "authentic materials" with advanced technology, such as the central LED control panel that shows the status of the 28-gallon fresh water supply or the battery charge level.

Nils Holger Moormann hält sich offenbar lieber in einem Camper als in einem Hotel auf. Er und sein Team versuchten in einem VW-Minibus alles wegzulassen, „auf das man verzichten kann", wobei sie das Äußere des Fahrzeugs weitgehend unverändert ließen. Möbeloberflächen aus mattem Nanotech-Thermolaminat und Polsterbezüge aus Merinowolle zeigen die vom Designer gewollten überraschenden Kontraste. Der Bus hat vier Kleiderschrankfächer, eine Garderobe mit Kleiderstange, ein Schmutzwäschefach, eine Kosmetikschublade, zwei beleuchtete Bücherregale, vier Schränke für Küchengeräte, eine Arbeitsfläche aus Edelstahl und einen 65-Liter-Kühlschrank mit Gefrierfach. Auch ein 1,25 m breites Schlafsofa, Schiffsboden und Deckenverkleidung aus Eiche sowie ein ausgeklügeltes System zur Raumbeleuchtung mit LED-Leuchten demonstrieren die Kombination „authentischer Materialien" mit fortschrittlicher Technologie, so auch das zentrale LED-Kontrollfeld, das den Stand des 105-l-Frischwasserbehälters oder der Batterieladung anzeigt.

Nils Holger Moormann semble préférer vivre dans une caravane plutôt qu'à l'hôtel, par exemple. Avec son équipe et un minibus VW, il a essayé d'éliminer « tout ce qu'il était possible d'oublier » sans toucher pour l'essentiel à l'aspect extérieur du véhicule. Les surfaces du mobilier en thermostratifié mat produit par nanotechnologie et les housses des sièges en laine de mérinos ne sont que l'un des surprenants contrastes recherchés par le designer. Le bus comporte quatre compartiments à linge, un espace où suspendre des vêtements, un autre destiné au linge sale, un compartiment toilette, deux bibliothèques éclairées, quatre compartiments pour les ustensiles de la cuisine à surface de travail en acier inoxydable et un réfrigérateur de 65 L avec un compartiment congélation. Un canapé-lit de 1,25 mètre de large, le sol en lattes de chêne et les panneaux du plafond en chêne non traité, le tout éclairé par un système complexe d'éclairage à LED, affichent là aussi le mélange de matériaux « authentiques » et de technologie de pointe, avec notamment le panneau de commande central des LED qui indique le niveau du réservoir d'eau potable d'une trentaine de litres ou le niveau de charge de la batterie.

The interiors include illuminated bookshelves, while the 125-centimeter-wide bed is designed for two people. Sophisticated LED lighting and dark surfaces contribute to the modern appearance.

Zur Innenausstattung gehören beleuchtete Bücherregale und ein 125 cm breites Bett für zwei Personen. Raffinierte LED-Beleuchtung und schwarze Flächen tragen zur modernen Optik bei.

À l'intérieur, des bibliothèques éclairées et un lit deux places de 125 cm. L'éclairage raffiné à LED et les surfaces sombres contribuent à donner une impression de modernité.

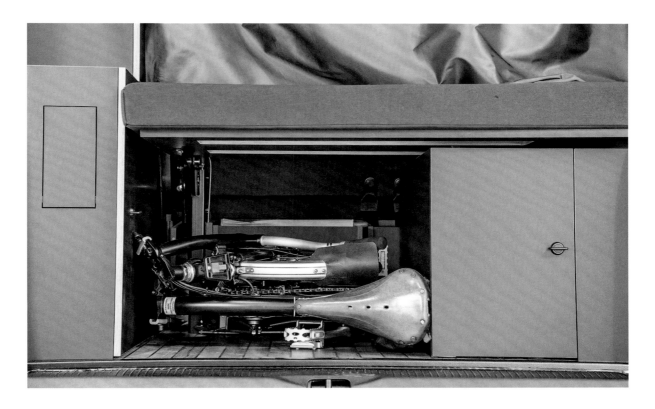

Interiors are designed with an eye to modernity and a minimalist sense of using every available inch of space. Materials used include stainless steel and Nanotech laminate. Above, a compartment for a folding bicycle.

Die Innengestaltung zeigt einen Bezug zur Moderne und zum Minimalismus, indem jeder verfügbare Raum ausgenutzt wird. Die Materialien sind Edelstahl und Nano-tech-Thermolaminat. Oben: Ein Fach für ein Klappfahrrad.

L'intérieur a été conçu avec une volonté de modernité et un minimalisme qui exploite le moindre centimètre carré disponible. Les matériaux comprennent de l'acier inoxydable et du stratifié produit par nanotechnologie. Ci-dessus, un placard pour vélo pliant.

AXEL ENTHOVEN
Valkenswaard [The Netherlands] — 2009

OPERA, YOUR SUITE IN NATURE (YSIN)

Area: 21 m² — Client: not disclosed — Cost: not disclosed — Collaboration: YSIN Rob Vos

YSIN (Your Suite In Nature) is a Dutch start-up created in 2008 by Rob Vos to develop "a new and unprecedented camping experience." Together with Enthoven Associates, they created Opera, which is described as "neither a tent, nor a trailer, nor a camping car." In fact, it is a bit of all of these. Closed, Opera looks like a fairly normal covered car trailer; it is 4.87 meters long and just 1.11 meters high. With the structure in its open position, an area measuring almost seven meters in length and three meters in width is deployed. It has a climate control system, a king-size bed, an external shower, a small kitchen with a stainless-steel sink, ceramic sanitary equipment, a barbecue, and a teak veranda. A boiler supplies hot water and it is equipped with low-energy LED lights. Its exterior forms were inspired by those of the Sydney Opera House, whence the name Opera. Opera was first presented at the Design at Work fair in Kortrijk in 2009, and it won a 2010 German Caravanning Design Award. The jury for that award wrote: "The tent trailer is a good example of innovative symbol design which, creating a new archetype, departs from conventional geometric forms. Borrowing from yacht design, it features inspiring and high-quality solutions that, enhanced by the use of materials such as hard wood, stainless steel, and leather, form a unified whole with a distinct identity of its own."

YSIN (Your Suite in Nature) ist eine 2008 von Rob Vos gegründete holländische Start-up-Firma für die Entwicklung „eines neuen und noch nie dagewesenen Camping-Erlebnisses". Gemeinsam mit Enthoven Associates schufen sie Opera, das „weder Zelt noch Trailer noch Wohnwagen" sein soll. Tatsächlich hat es ein bisschen von allem. In zusammengeklapptem Zustand sieht Opera eigentlich aus wie ein normaler, geschlossener Pkw-Anhänger, der 4,87 m lang und nur 1,11 m hoch ist. In geöffnetem Zustand bietet er eine Fläche von fast 7 m Länge und 3 m Breite. Er hat eine Klimaanlage, ein großes Doppelbett, eine Außendusche, eine kleine Küche mit einem Edelstahlbecken, Badausstattung aus Keramik, einen Grill und eine Teak-Veranda. Opera ist mit einem Boiler für Warmwasser und mit Niedrigenergieleuchten ausgestattet. Seine Außenform wurde vom Opernhaus in Sydney angeregt, daher auch der Name. Opera wurde erstmals 2009 auf der Messe Design at Work in Kortrijk vorgestellt und gewann 2010 den deutschen Caravaning Design Award. Das Preisgericht schrieb dazu: „Der Zeltcaravan ist ein gutes Beispiel für innovatives wegweisendes Design, das einen neuen Archetyp erzeugt und sich von konventionellen geometrischen Formen abwendet. Vom Yacht-Design beeinflusst, bietet er anregende und hochkarätige Lösungen, die, verstärkt durch die Verwendung von Materialien wie Hartholz, Edelstahl und Leder, ein einheitliches Ganzes mit einer ausgesprochen eigenständigen Identität bilden."

YSIN (Your Suite In Nature) est une start-up néerlandaise fondée en 2008 par Rob Vos pour développer « un camping nouveau et sans précédent ». Avec Enthoven Associates, elle a créé Opera, décrit comme n'étant « ni une tente, ni une remorque, ni un camping-car », mais un peu de tout à la fois. Fermé, Opera ressemble à une remorque couverte parfaitement normale, longue de 4,87 mètres et haute de seulement 1,11 mètre. En position ouverte, elle déploie pourtant un espace de presque 7 mètres de long et 3 mètres de large. Elle est équipée d'un système de régulation du climat, d'un grand lit, d'une douche extérieure, d'une petite cuisine avec évier en acier inoxydable, de sanitaires en céramique, d'un grill et d'une véranda en teck. Une chaudière fournit l'eau chaude, les lampes sont éclairées par des LED à faible consommation. La forme extérieure s'inspire de l'opéra de Sydney, d'où son nom. Opera a été présenté au salon Design at Work de Courtrai en 2009 et a reçu le Prix allemand du design de caravane en 2010. Selon le jury, « cette tente-remorque est un bon exemple de design symbolique innovant qui, en créant un nouvel archétype, s'écarte des formes géométriques traditionnelles. Sa forme empruntée à celle des yachts présente des solutions stimulantes de qualité supérieure qui, rehaussées par les matériaux utilisés, du bois dur à l'acier inoxydable et au cuir, forment une unité dotée d'une identité propre ».

Opera has a teak veranda, a boiler, LED lighting, a ceramic toilet, and a Corian sink. Two separate beds can easily be converted into a large single bed.

Opera hat eine Veranda aus Teakholz, einen Boiler, LED-Beleuchtung, eine Keramiktoilette und ein Waschbecken aus Corian. Zwei Einzelbetten können leicht zu einem Doppelbett umgebaut werden.

Opera possède une véranda en teck, une chaudière, un éclairage à LED, des sanitaires en céramique et un évier en corian. Les deux lits séparés peuvent facilement être transformés en un grand lit.

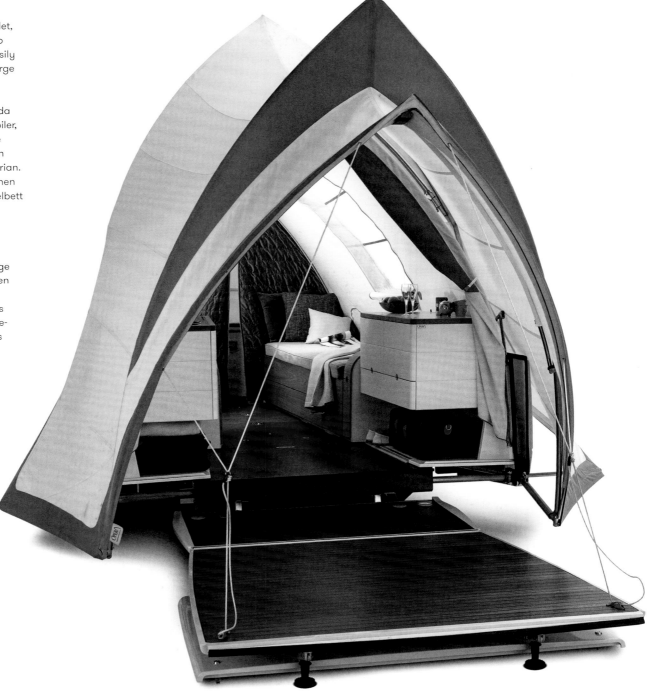

In the folded position, Opera is just 111 centimeters high, while fully opened it is 340 centimeters high, more than three meters. Its total length increases from 487 to 670 centimeters when unfolded.

Opera in geschlossenem Zustand. Es ist nur 111 cm hoch, ganz geöffnet jedoch 340 cm. Ausgeklappt wird aus dem 487 cm langen Anhänger ein 670 cm langer Raum.

Replié, Opera est haut de seulement 111 cm, contre 340 cm entièrement déployé, soit plus de 3 m. Sa longueur totale passe de 487 à 670 cm.

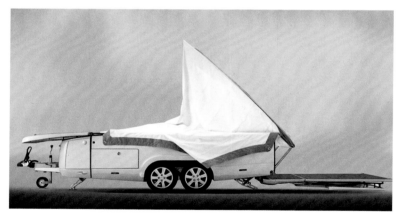

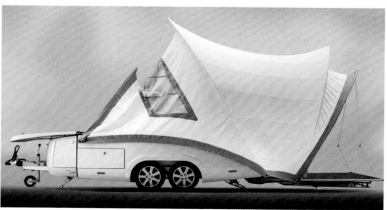

The interior has a coated teak floor, also used for the veranda. Interior finishings are in oak, Corian, and stainless steel. Electronically operated slats admit or exclude light on both sides.

Der Innenraum hat wie auch die Veranda einen beschichteten Teakboden. Die Innenausstattung besteht aus Eichenholz, Corian und Edelstahl. Elektronisch verstellbare Lamellen auf beiden Seiten regulieren den Einfall von Tageslicht.

À l'intérieur, le sol est recouvert de teck, bois également utilisé pour la véranda. Les finitions intérieures sont en chêne, corian et acier inoxydable. Des stores à lamelles à ouverture électronique font entrer ou cachent la lumière de chaque côté.

CHRISTOPHER SMITH
Boulder, Colorado [USA] — 2011–12

"TINY, A STORY ABOUT LIVING SMALL"

Area: 18.6 m² (with loft) — Client: Christopher Smith and Merete Mueller
Cost: $26 000 (not including labor) — Collaboration: Merete Mueller

Christopher Smith's documentary movie (made with Merete Mueller) covers his efforts to build his own tiny house in Boulder, Colorado, beginning in 2011. His intention was to bring the house to Hartsel, Colorado, a small town in the middle of the state where he purchased a small piece of land. Smith admitted to having no building experience, no plans, and not much money. The film includes interviews with proponents of off-grid, self-sufficient housing and describes the difficulties the couple had over a period of one year with construction, weather, and costs. Bluestain pine and reclaimed wood for floors, windows, and doors are the main materials used for the house, which was finished in May 2012 and moved to Hartsel as planned. The couple used the house "for a few days or a week at a time," but also spent a good deal of time in New York and elsewhere working on the film and proceeding to other work that they have undertaken since that time.

Der Dokumentarfilm von Christopher Smith (mit Merete Mueller) schildert die Mühen, die der Bau seines eigenen kleinen Wohnhauses in Boulder, Colorado, ab 2011 ihm bereitete. Er hatte die Absicht, das Haus nach Hartsel zu bringen, eine Kleinstadt in der Mitte des Staates Colorado, wo er ein kleines Grundstück erworben hatte. Smith bekannte, keinerlei Erfahrung mit dem Bauen, keine Pläne und nur wenig Geld zu haben. Der Film enthält Interviews mit Menschen, die autark abseits des Versorgungsnetzes leben, und schildert die ein Jahr andauernden Schwierigkeiten der Besitzer mit dem Bau, dem Wetter und den Kosten. Kiefernholz und Altholz für Böden, Fenster und Türen waren die wichtigsten Baumaterialien für das Haus, das im Mai 2012 fertiggestellt und wie geplant nach Hartsel transportiert wurde. Das Paar nutzt das Haus „immer mal für ein paar Tage oder eine Woche", verbringt aber auch viel Zeit in New York und anderswo beim Filmen oder mit anderen Projekten, die sie seither übernommen haben.

Christopher Smith a réalisé, avec Merete Mueller, un film documentaire qui retrace les efforts entrepris pour construire sa minuscule maison à Boulder, dans le Colorado, à partir de 2011. Son but était d'amener la maison à Hartsel, une petite ville au centre du Colorado où il avait acheté un petit terrain. Smith reconnaît qu'il ne possédait aucune expérience de la construction, aucun plan et peu d'argent. Le film comprend des interviews avec des adeptes de l'habitat autosuffisant non raccordé au réseau électrique, et décrit les difficultés techniques, météorologiques et financières auxquelles le couple a été confronté pendant un an. Les principaux matériaux sont le pin bleui et le bois de récupération pour les sols, les fenêtres et les portes de la maison, qui a été terminée en mai 2012 et a rejoint Hartsel comme prévu. Le couple y a habité « quelques jours ou une semaine de temps en temps », mais a aussi passé beaucoup de temps à New York et ailleurs, à travailler sur le film et d'autres projets développés depuis.

The story of this house is told by Merete Mueller and Christopher Smith, on www.youtube.com/watch?v=e7zXG-pUCTA.

Merete Mueller und Christopher Smith erzählen die Geschichte dieses Hauses auf www.youtube.com/watch?v=e7zXG-pUCTA.

L'histoire de cette maison, racontée par Merete Mueller et Christopher Smith, est visible sur https://www.youtube.com/watch?v=e7zXG-pUCTA.

PEOPLE'S INDUSTRIAL DESIGN OFFICE
Beijing [China] — 2012

TRICYCLE HOUSE

Area: 5 m² — Client: Get It Louder Exhibition, 2012 — Cost: $14 552

In China, private ownership of land still does not exist, therefore, according to the designers, "the Tricycle House suggests a future embrace of the temporary relationship between people and the land they occupy." The Tricycle House was created for the Get It Louder 2012 art exhibition in Beijing. The designers used folded polypropylene plastic for the Tricycle House, cut with a CNC router, scored, folded, and welded into shape. Polypropylene can be folded without losing its strength, and expanded like an accordion. The translucent nature of the plastic provides for some privacy while admitting daylight or the light of street lamps at night. The house includes a sink and stove, a bathtub, a water tank, and furniture that can transform from a bed to a dining table and bench, to a bench and counter top. The sink, stove, and bathtub are designed to collapse into the front wall of the house.

In China gibt es immer noch keinen privaten Grundbesitz, daher erläutern die Planer: „Das Tricycle House empfiehlt eine künftige Intensivierung der temporären Beziehung von den Menschen zu dem Land, das sie bewohnen." Das Tricycle House entstand 2012 für die Kunstausstellung Get It Louder in Beijing. Die Architekten verwendeten dafür mit einem CNC-Router geschnittenen Polypropylen-Kunststoff, der gefaltet und in Form geschweißt wurde. Polypropylen kann gefaltet und ausgezogen werden wie ein

Akkordeon, ohne seine Stärke zu verlieren. Die Lichtdurchlässigeit des Kunststoffs sichert die Privatsphäre, lässt jedoch Tageslicht oder nachts das Licht der Straßenlaternen ein. Das Haus enthält ein Waschbecken und einen Ofen, eine Badewanne, einen Wassertank und Möbel, die von einem Bett in einen Esstisch und eine Bank sowie in eine Bank und eine Arbeitsfläche umgebaut werden können. Das Waschbecken, der Ofen und die Wanne lassen sich in die Außenwand des Hauses einklappen.

La propriété privée de la terre n'existe pas en Chine, c'est pourquoi, selon les designers, « la Tricycle House suggère l'étreinte future de la relation temporaire entre les gens et le terrain qu'ils occupent. » Elle a été créée pour l'exposition artistique Get It Louder 2012 de Pékin. Les designers ont utilisé du polypropylène plié, découpé avec une machine à commande numérique, incisé, plié et soudé en forme. En effet, le polypropylène peut être plié sans perdre de sa solidité et déplié comme un accordéon. Le plastique translucide garantit une certaine intimité tout en laissant pénétrer la lumière du jour ou des lampadaires la nuit. Le logement comporte un évier et une cuisinière, une baignoire, un réservoir d'eau et du mobilier transformable, d'un lit à une table avec banc à un banc et comptoir. L'évier, la cuisinière et la baignoire sont conçus pour être repliés dans la paroi avant.

The structure of the Tricycle House is made of folded polypropylene plastic. The translucent material can be folded or expanded without losing its structural strength.

Das Tragwerk des Tricycle House besteht aus Polypropylen. Das lichtdurchlässige Material kann gefaltet oder ausgezogen werden, ohne an Stabilität zu verlieren.

La structure de la Tricycle House est en polypropylène plié. Ce matériau plastique translucide peut être plié ou étiré sans perdre de sa résistance structurelle.

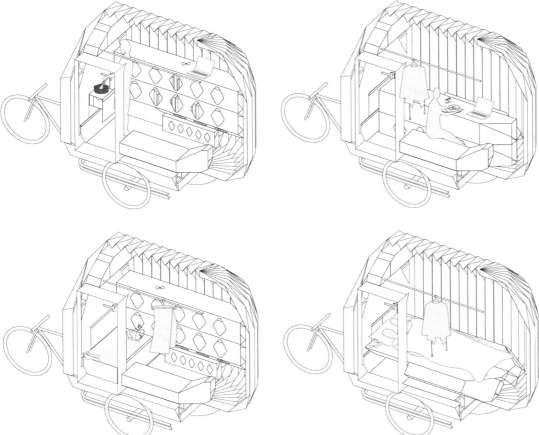

Section drawings show the contents of the design. Left, a sink, stove and, most surprising, a bathtub fold out from the front of the house.

Die Schnitte zeigen das Innere des Projekts. Links: Waschbecken, Herd und – sehr erstaunlich – eine Badewanne lassen sich aus der Vorderfront des Hauses klappen.

Les schémas en coupe montrent l'intérieur du projet. À gauche, un évier, une cuisinière et, plus étonnant, une baignoire se déplient depuis l'avant.

The project also includes what the architects call the "Tricycle garden," which can be planted with grass, vegetables, and even small trees. Several gardens can be combined to create a green space.

Zum entwurf gehört auch der sogenannte Tricycle-Garten, der mit Gras, Gemüse und sogar kleinen Bäumen bepflanzt werden kann. Mehrere Gärten können zu einer Grünfläche zusammengestellt werden.

Le projet comprend aussi ce que les architectes ont baptisé le « Tricycle Garden » qui peut être planté de pelouse, de légumes, ou même de petits arbres. Plusieurs jardins peuvent être regroupés pour créer un espace vert.

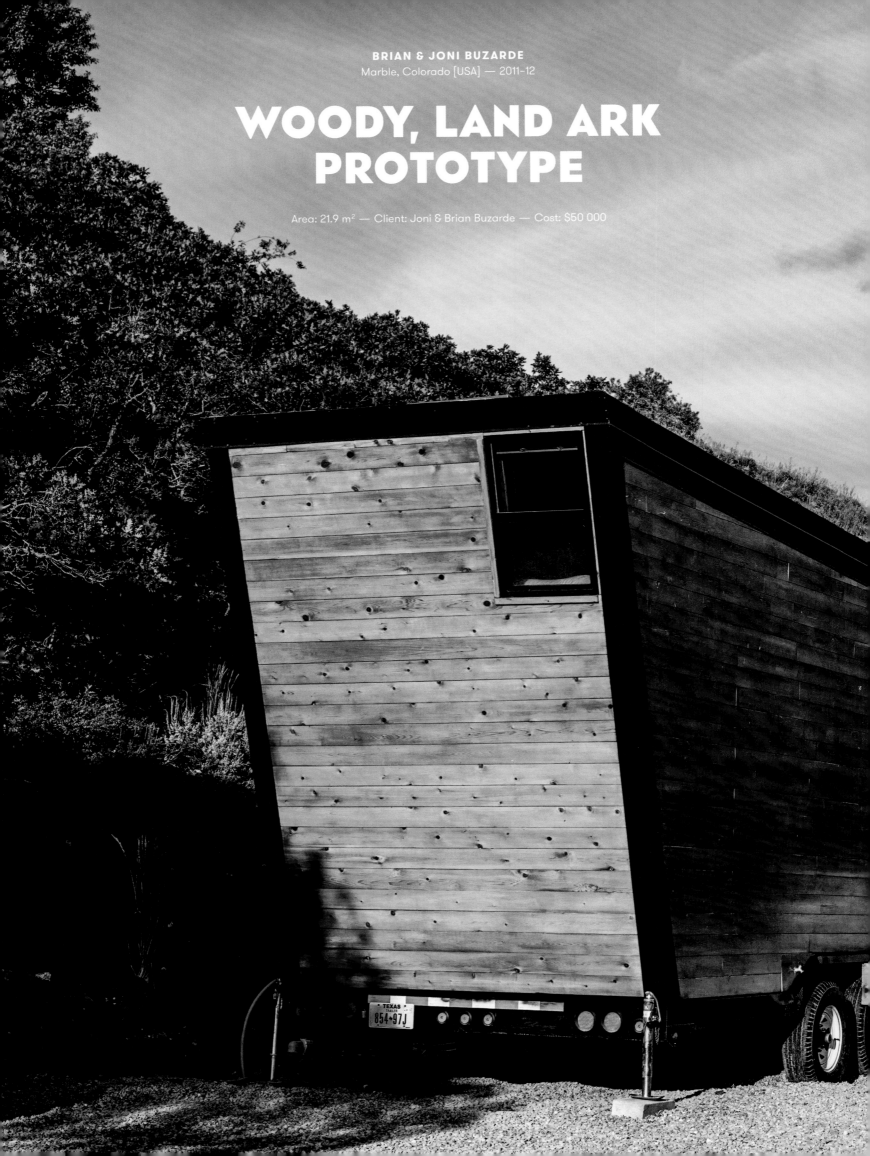

BRIAN & JONI BUZARDE
Marble, Colorado [USA] — 2011–12

WOODY, LAND ARK PROTOTYPE

Area: 21.9 m² — Client: Joni & Brian Buzarde — Cost: $50 000

Brian and Joni Buzarde explain: "Woody was designed and built as a direct response to seemingly opposing goals: we wanted our own home and we wanted location flexibility. We wanted clean lines, ample light, ample storage, and a singular simplicity. We also wanted something original that wasn't trying to look like a tiny version of a house; we wanted an authentic solution to our unorthodox goals and challenges." The trailer home they designed was moved from Austin, Texas, to its current location Marble, Colorado. The couple purchased an eight-meter-long, 2.6-meter-wide flatbed trailer chassis for $7000 and then added SIP (Structural Insulated Panel). Other materials are cedar T&G (tongue and groove) exterior siding, windows manufactured by Milgard, and Velux skylights. Birch plywood interior was used for interior finishing. The house includes a loft bed, a small refrigerator, storage compartments under the floor, and a bathtub made with a galvanized-steel cow trough. The home is 4.1 meters high and thus can be transported on US highways without special authorization.

Brian und Joni Buzarde erklären: „Woody wurde zur Vereinbarung scheinbar widersprüchlicher Ziele geplant und gebaut: Wir wünschten uns ein eigenes Heim, und wir wollten örtlich ungebunden sein. Wir wollten klare Linien, viel Licht, ausreichend Stauraum und etwas ganz Einfaches. Wir wollten auch etwas Originelles, das nicht wie die kleine Version eines Wohnhauses aussah; wir wollten eine authentische Lösung für unsere unorthodoxen Ziele und Ansprüche." Das Zuhause im Trailer, das sie entwarfen, wurde von Austin, Texas, zum gegenwärtigen Standort Marble in Colorado befördert. Das Paar kaufte für 7000 Dollar ein 8 m langes und 2,6 m breites Chassis eines Tiefladeranhängers und brachte darauf verstärkte isolierte Paneele (SIP) an. Weitere Elemente sind eine Nut-und-Feder-Außenverkleidung aus Zedernholz, von der Firma Milgard produzierte Fenster und Velux-Oberlichter. Für die Innenausstattung wurde Birkenfurnierholz verwendet. Das Haus enthält ein Hochbett, einen kleinen Kühlschrank und Stauraum unter dem Fußboden. Eine Viehtränke aus verzinktem Stahl dient als Badewanne. Mit einer Höhe von 4,1 m darf das Haus ohne Sondergenehmigung auf US-Highways transportiert werden.

Comme l'expliquent Brian et Joni Buzarde, « Woody a été conçu et réalisé comme une réponse directe à des buts en apparence contraires : nous voulions une maison à nous et nous voulions pouvoir en choisir l'emplacement. Nous voulions des lignes nettes, de la lumière en abondance, de nombreux rangements et une simplicité particulière. Nous voulions aussi quelque chose d'original qui ne donne pas l'impression d'une maison miniature ; nous voulions une véritable solution à nos désirs et défis peu orthodoxes ». La remorque habitable qu'ils ont créée a été déplacée d'Austin, au Texas, à son emplacement actuel à Marble, dans le Colorado. Le couple a d'abord acheté un châssis de remorque à plateau long de 8 mètres et large de 2,6 mètres pour 7 000 dollars, et y a ajouté des panneaux SIP (panneaux structurels isolants). Les autres matériaux comprennent des bardages latéraux extérieurs en cèdre à rainure et languette, des fenêtres Milgard et des Velux. Les finitions intérieures sont en contreplaqué de bouleau. L'ensemble comprend un lit mezzanine, un petit réfrigérateur, des compartiments de rangement sous le sol et une baignoire faite d'un abreuvoir à vaches en acier galvanisé. La maison est haute de 4,1 mètres et peut donc être transportée sur les grandes routes américaines sans autorisation spéciale.

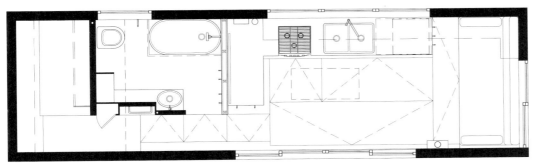

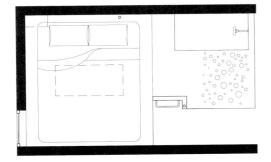

Self-built by the owners, who call it Woody, this trailer was made with structural insulated panels and cedar cladding, with birch-veneer plywood inside.

Dieser von den Besitzern selbst gebaute Trailer, den sie Woody nennen, besteht aus tragenden, isolierten Platten mit Zedernholzverkleidung und ist innen mit Birkenfurnier ausgestattet.

Construite par ses propriétaires, qui l'ont appelée Woody, cette remorque est faite de panneaux structurels isolants et de bardage en cèdre, avec un placage en contreplaqué de bouleau à l'intérieur.

HOMES
on water

DUBLDOM HOUSEBOAT

Area: 26 m² — Client: Dmitriy Sobinyakov
Cost: €20 700 (house), €5 000 (pontoons)

This DublDom Houseboat is moored near the Volga River, three hours north of Moscow. It is used as a floating suite for the Hotel Paluba in Kalyazin.

Dieses DublDom-Hausboot liegt auf der Wolga und dient dem Hotel Paluba in Kalyazin, das drei Stunden Fahrzeit von Moskau entfernt ist, als schwimmende Suite.

Cette maison DublDom est amarrée près du fleuve Volga, à 3 h au nord de Moscou. L'hôtel Paluba de Kalyazin l'utilise comme suite flottante.

The DublDom is a "serial modular home" that is prefabricated and designed to be installed in a single day, making it ideal for temporary or vacation installation, transported by truck. The basic structures are either 40 square meters or 26 square meters like the one published here, which was erected on pontoons. Standard features include the necessary sanitary equipment, furniture, and household appliances. It is insulated, and plumbing and wiring are preinstalled. The DublDom Houseboat has a timber frame. The exterior is finished in corrugated metal sheeting, and the interior in wood. The DublDom Houseboat has the same design and floor plan as its land-based equivalents. An open living area in front with a fully glazed wall facing a covered porch. The bedroom area and bathroom are in the back corners.

DublDom ist ein „serienmäßiges, modulares Haus", das vorgefertigt wird und sich in nur einem Tag aufstellen lässt. Es kann per Lastwagen transportiert werden und ist ideal für eine temporäre Nutzung oder als Ferienhaus. Die Grundkonstruktion hat eine Größe von entweder 40 oder – wie das hier abgebildete, auf Pontons errichtete Haus – 26 m². Zur Grundausstattung gehören die erforderlichen Sanitäranlagen, die Möblierung sowie die Kücheneinrichtung. Das Haus ist isoliert, Hausinstallation und elektrische Leitungen sind eingebaut. Das Hausboot DublDom hat eine Holzkonstruktion, die außen mit Wellblech und innen mit Holz verkleidet ist. Es hat das gleiche Design und den gleichen Grundriss wie die entsprechenden Modelle an Land. Vorne befindet sich ein offener Wohnraum mit einer verglasten Wand zur überdachten Terrasse. Schlafbereich und Bad liegen im hinteren Hausbereich.

DublDom est une « maison modulaire standardisée » préfabriquée, conçue pour être installée en un jour et transportée par camion, ce qui en fait une solution idéale pour des séjours temporaires ou pour les vacances. Les modèles de base ont une superficie de 40 ou 26 mètres carrés, comme celui qui présenté ici, construit sur des pontons. La version standard comprend les installations sanitaires, le mobilier et les appareils électroménagers nécessaires. Elle est isolée, la plomberie et l'électricité étant préinstallées. La charpente est en bois d'œuvre. Les finitions extérieures sont en feuilles de métal ondulé, l'intérieur en bois. Le design et le plan au sol sont identiques à ceux des modèles terrestres : un espace séjour ouvert à l'avant avec une façade entièrement vitrée face à un porche couvert, la chambre et la salle de bains à l'arrière, dans les angles.

A plan of the houseboat shows its simple
rectilinear design, with the covered terrace
seen on the left page visible to the right
of the drawing.

Der Grundriss des Hausboots (rechts)
zeigt seine schlichte, rechtwinklige Form
mit der überdachten Terrasse, die auf
der linken Seite abgebildet ist.

Le plan de la maison révèle une conception
rectiligne simple, avec terrasse couverte
visible sur la page de gauche et à droite sur
le schéma.

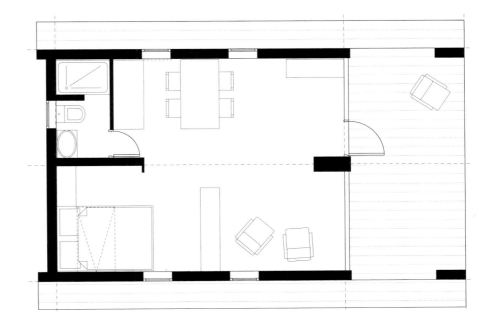

The house has a double bed, a double folding sofa, a folding children's bed, a kitchen, a sunbed, a bathroom with a shower cabin, heating, and hot water.

Das Haus enthält ein Doppelbett, eine ausklappbare Doppelcouch, ein Kinderklappbett, einen Liegestuhl sowie ein Bad mit Duschkabine, Heizung und Warmwasser.

La maison comprend un lit double, un canapé-lit double, un lit d'enfant pliant, une cuisine, un lit pliant, une salle de bains avec cabine de douche, chauffage et eau chaude.

MORPHOSIS
New Orleans, Louisiana [USA] — 2008–09

FLOAT HOUSE

Area: 88 m² — Client: Make It Right Foundation — Cost: not disclosed
Collaboration: UCLA Architecture and Urban Design (AUD)

The architects state: "The Float House is a new kind of house: a house that can sustain its own water and power needs; a house that can survive the floodwaters generated by a storm the size of Hurricane Katrina; and, perhaps most importantly, a house that can be manufactured cheaply enough to function as low-income housing." Based on the typology of the local "shotgun" house, this residence is perched on a raised base containing the mechanical, electrical, and plumbing system. Assembled on site from prefabricated elements, the house can rise up to 3.65 meters on guideposts in case of flooding. Although the house is thus capable of moving upward, it remains anchored to its site with six 13.7-meter-deep concrete piles. Designed to obtain a LEED Platinum rating, the house uses solar panels, rainwater collection, efficient plumbing and insulation systems, and a ground-source heat pump for heating and cooling.

Die Architekten erklären: „Das Float House ist ein neuer Haustyp: ein Haus, das seinen Bedarf an Wasser und Energie selbst erzeugen kann; ein Haus, das den Überschwemmungen, die von Stürmen wie dem Hurrikan Katrina verursacht werden, Widerstand leistet, und, was vielleicht noch wichtiger ist, ein Haus, das so preiswert produziert werden kann, dass es sich auch Menschen mit geringem Einkommen leisten können." Das Wohnhaus ist an der in der Region Shotgun-Haus genannten, lang gestreckten Hausform orientiert. Es steht auf einem erhöhten Fundament, das die Mechanik, Elektrik und Sanitärtechnik enthält. Der Bau wird aus Fertigteilen vor Ort

montiert und kann bei Überflutungen auf Pfosten bis zu einer Höhe von 3,65 m angehoben werden. Auch wenn es angehoben wird, bleibt es auf sechs 13,7 m tief eingelassenen Betonpfeilern an seinem Standort verankert. Das Haus ist mit Solarpaneelen, einem Regenwasser-Auffangsystem, effizienter Sanitärtechnik und Isolierung sowie einer Wärmepumpe für Heizung und Kühlung ausgestattet und erfüllt die Anforderungen des höchsten Umweltstandards der USA, LEED Platinum.

Selon les architectes, « c'est un nouveau type de maison : une maison qui peut satisfaire elle-même ses besoins en eau et en électricité, qui peut survivre aux inondations après un ouragan de l'ampleur de Katrina et, ce qui est peut-être le plus important, une maison suffisamment bon marché à fabriquer pour servir de logement social ». Empruntant au type local de maison dite « shotgun » (fusil), elle repose sur une base surélevée qui contient les éléments mécaniques, le système électrique et la tuyauterie. Assemblée sur place à partir d'éléments préfabriqués, elle peut monter jusqu'à 3,65 mètres sur ses poteaux en cas d'inondation mais n'en reste pas moins ancrée au terrain par six piliers de béton enfoncés à 13,7 mètres de profondeur. Conçue pour obtenir la certification LEED platine, la maison possède des panneaux solaires, un système de récupération des eaux de pluie, des systèmes de plomberie et d'isolation efficaces, ainsi qu'une pompe à chaleur géothermique pour le chauffage et la climatisation.

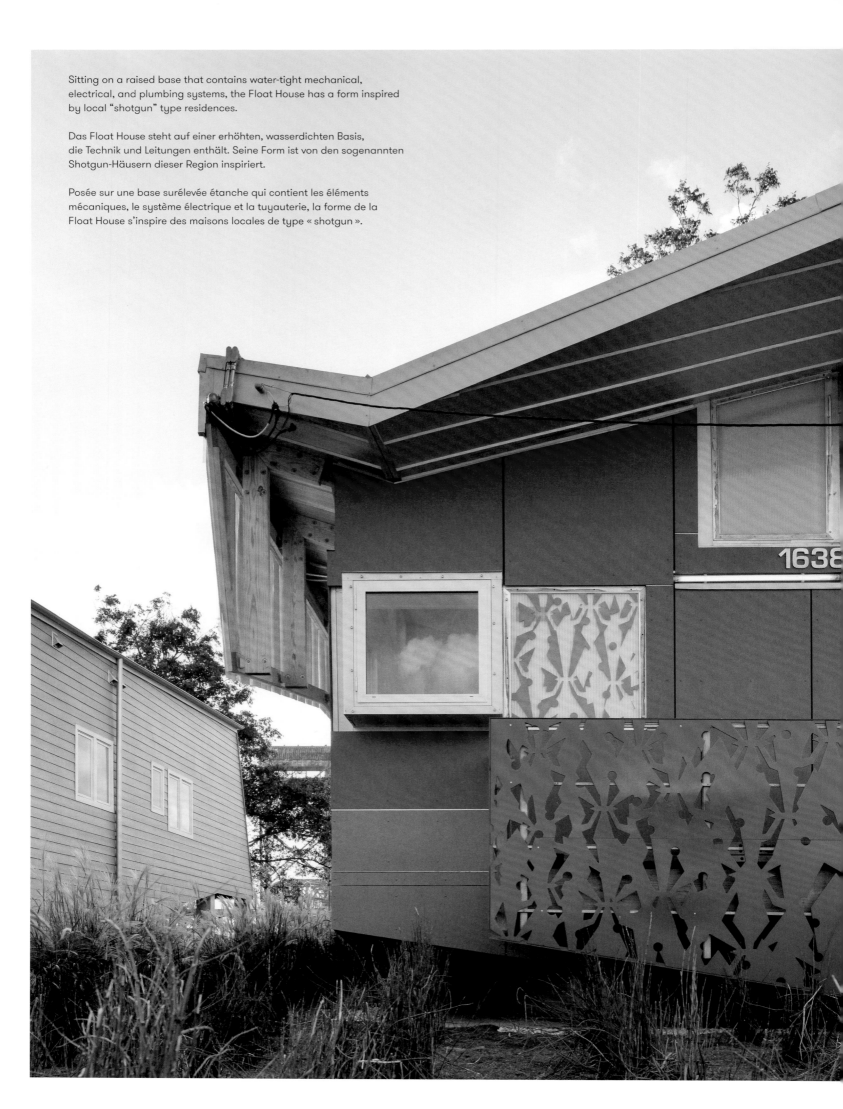

Sitting on a raised base that contains water-tight mechanical, electrical, and plumbing systems, the Float House has a form inspired by local "shotgun" type residences.

Das Float House steht auf einer erhöhten, wasserdichten Basis, die Technik und Leitungen enthält. Seine Form ist von den sogenannten Shotgun-Häusern dieser Region inspiriert.

Posée sur une base surélevée étanche qui contient les éléments mécaniques, le système électrique et la tuyauterie, la forme de la Float House s'inspire des maisons locales de type « shotgun ».

1638

Made from prefabricated elements, the Float House is intended to be assembled on site. In case of flooding, the house can rise up to 3.65 meters, held by anchored guide posts.

Die Montage des aus Fertigteilen bestehenden Float House soll vor Ort erfolgen. Im Falle einer Überschwemmung kann das an Leitpfosten verankerte Haus bis in 3,65 m Höhe angehoben werden.

Faite d'éléments préfabriqués, la Float House est conçue pour être assemblée sur place. En cas d'inondation, elle peut monter jusqu'à 3,65 m grâce à ses piliers profondément ancrés dans le sol.

CARL TURNER
[UK] — 2016

FLOATING HOUSE

Area: 190 m² — Client: not disclosed — Cost: c. €200 000

The architects proposed this Floating House as a result of the increasing likelihood of flooding. They have aimed to make the residence carbon neutral and self-sufficient. The structure could be on piles or on a floating pontoon. The "hull" of the residence would be made by a contractor and shuttering could be manufactured with CNC milling. They state: "The solid timber structure (Cross Laminated Timber) can be ordered from a CLT manufacturer, who can then build it on site in just one to two weeks. Windows can be supplied and fitted by the manufacturer and people can choose to what extent they wish to Do It Themselves and customize the design of their new home." To be built with concrete, steel, cross-laminated timber, polycarbonate, and plywood for the furniture, the plans of the house are available on the open-source site paperhouses.co/architect/carl-turner-architects.

Die Architekten entwarfen dieses schwimmende Haus, weil die Gefahr von Überflutungen zunimmt. Ihr Ziel war ein klimaneutrales und autarkes Wohnhaus. Der Bau könnte auf Pfeilern oder auf einem Ponton stehen. Der „Rumpf" des Wohnhauses sollte von einem Bauunternehmen ausgeführt und die Verschalung mittels CNC-Fräsen hergestellt werden. Die Planer erklären: „Die massive Brettsperrholzkonstruktion kann beim Hersteller bestellt werden, der sie am Standort in nur ein bis zwei Wochen aufstellen kann. Auch die Fenster können von der Fabrik geliefert und eingebaut werden, und der Käufer kann entscheiden, in welchem Ausmaß er Eigenleistung einbringen und die Gestaltung seines neuen Heims selbst bestimmen will." Die Pläne des aus Beton, Stahl, Brettschichtholz, Polykarbonat und Sperrholzmobiliar bestehenden Hauses sind als Open-Source-Software bei paperhouses.co/architect/carl-turner-architects verfügbar.

Par cette maison flottante, les architectes entendent répondre au problème des inondations de plus en plus fréquentes. Ils l'ont voulue autosuffisante et affichant un bilan carbone neutre. La structure peut reposer sur des piliers ou un ponton flottant. La « coque » est réalisée par un entrepreneur extérieur et le coffrage par fraisage à commande numérique. Comme l'expliquent les architectes, « la structure robuste en bois d'œuvre (stratifié croisé) peut être commandée à un fabricant qui peut ensuite la monter sur place en seulement une à deux semaines. Les fenêtres peuvent être fournies et montées par le même fabricant et chacun peut choisir dans quelle mesure il souhaite mettre la main à la pâte pour personnaliser sa nouvelle maison ». Les plans de la maison à construire en béton, acier, bois d'œuvre stratifié croisé, polycarbonate et contreplaqué pour le mobilier sont disponibles sur le site open source paperhouses.co/architect/carl-turner-architects.

Sitting on a concrete hull, the Floating House has polycarbonate walls with 84 square meters of integrated photovoltaic panels and a rooftop rainwater-harvesting tank.

Das auf einer Betonplatte stehende Floating House hat Wände aus Polycarbonat mit 84 m² Fotovoltaikpaneelen und auf dem Dach einen Behälter zum Sammeln von Regenwasser.

Posée sur une coque en béton, la Floating House a des murs en polycarbonate intégrant 84 m² de panneaux photovoltaïques et un réservoir pour récupérer l'eau de pluie sur le toit.

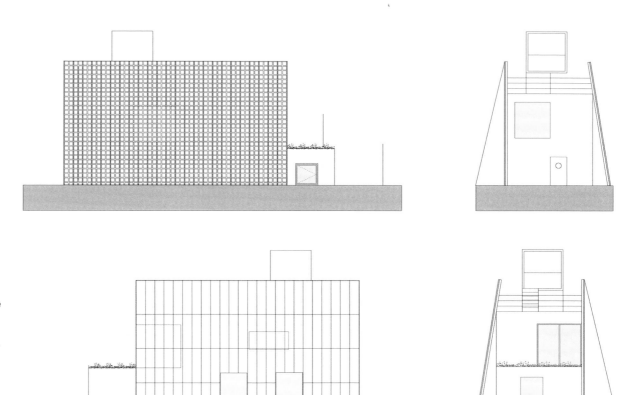

The house has a cross-laminated timber frame and a 50-square-meter roof terrace. It also includes a floating garden.

Das Haus hat eine Brettsperrholzkonstruktion und eine 50 m² große Dachterrasse. Auch ein schwimmender Garten gehört dazu.

La structure de la maison est en bois d'œuvre lamellé croisé avec une terrasse de 50 m² sur le toit. Elle possède aussi un jardin flottant.

WATERSTUDIO.NL

Amsterdam [The Netherlands] — 2008

FLOATING VILLA IJBURG, PLOT 3

Area: 175 m² — Client: not disclosed — Cost: not disclosed

Like the related design on Plot 13, this house had to deal with a strict building envelope limited to 2.5 stories and a limited budget. The architects state: "The location at the end of the pier, where the view should be focused on the water while shielding off the dwelling from adjacent houses, provided the initial starting point." The main volume is formed by a stucco slab on the back wall and roof of the first story, where an open view is created for the living area. A second volume in wood is outlined by a terrace floor that curves up to create a banister. The ceiling of the living room is made with the same wood. There are three bedrooms and a bathroom on the lower level. Here again, the ground floor is essentially open but has an integrated cupboard containing a television. The top floor includes a wide terrace where the wooden decking continues both inside and out. With the large sliding doors open, this makes exterior and interior "blend together."

Ebenso wie der ähnliche Entwurf auf Parzelle 13 musste auch dieses Haus sich an die strengen Vorschriften, die zweieinhalb Geschosse forderten, und einen beschränkten Etat halten. Die Architekten erklären: „Der Standort am Ende des Piers, wo der Blick auf das Wasser gerichtet, aber das Haus von den Nachbargebäuden abgeschirmt sein sollte, bildete den Ausgangspunkt." Das Hauptvolumen wird von einer Gipsplatte als Rückwand und Dach über dem Obergeschoss gebildet, wodurch ein freier Ausblick aus dem Wohnraum entsteht. Ein weiteres Volumen aus Holz wird von einer Terrassenfläche begrenzt, die aufwärts gekrümmt ist und ein Geländer bildet. Die Decke im Wohnraum besteht aus dem gleichen Holz. Auf der unteren Ebene liegen drei Schlafräum und das Bad. Das Erdgeschoss ist auch hier weitgehend offen, hat aber einen eingebauten Schrank mit Fernseher. Das Obergeschoss enthält eine breite Terrasse, deren Holzboden sich von innen nach außen erstreckt. Sind die großen Glasschiebetüren geöffnet, gehen Innen- und Außenbereich ineinander über.

Comme le projet apparenté du lopin 13, cette maison devait respecter un cahier des charges strict qui limitait son enveloppe à 2,5 étages avec un budget réduit. Comme l'expliquent les architectes, « l'emplacement à l'extrémité de la jetée, où la vue porte essentiellement sur l'eau et où le logement est protégé des maisons mitoyennes, a constitué le point de départ ». Le volume principal est formé d'une plaque de stuc sur le mur du fond et le toit du premier étage qui permet d'y ouvrir une vue dégagée pour le salon. Un second volume en bois est délimité par le sol de la terrasse qui décrit une courbe ascendante et forme une rampe. Le plafond du salon est fait du même bois. Trois chambres et une salle de bains occupent le niveau inférieur. Le rez-de-chaussée est lui aussi en grande partie ouvert, à l'exception d'un placard qui contient la télévision. L'étage supérieur comporte une vaste terrasse au plancher en bois continu entre intérieur et extérieur pour les faire « fusionner » lorsque les grandes portes coulissantes sont ouvertes.

Because of its pier-end location, the house has an open view to the water and a closed white stucco façade facing other houses.

Aufgrund seiner Lage am Ende des Piers hat man vom Haus einen freien Blick auf das Wasser, aber eine geschlossene, weiß verputzte Wand zu den anderen Häusern.

En raison de son emplacement à l'extrémité de la jetée, la maison dispose d'une vue dégagée sur l'eau et présente une façade de stuc blanche du côté des autres maisons.

Full-height glazing and outdoor wooden terraces make interior and exterior blend together almost seamlessly in the warmer months.

Geschosshohe Verglasung und Holzterrassen lassen in den wärmeren Monaten den Innen- und Außenraum fast nahtlos ineinander übergehen.

Le vitrage sur toute la hauteur et les terrasses en bois font fusionner intérieur et extérieur en faisant disparaître toute transition pendant les mois les plus chauds de l'année.

WATERSTUDIO.NL
Amsterdam [The Netherlands] — 2008

FLOATING VILLA IJBURG, PLOT 13

Area: 175 m² — Client: not disclosed — Cost: not disclosed

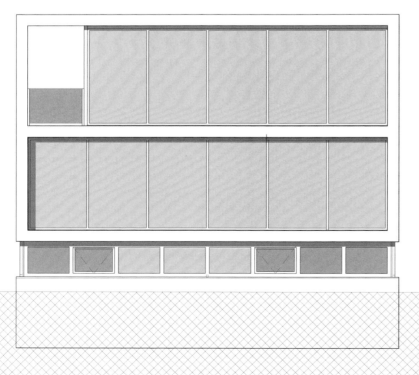

The architects made use of the permitted building envelope entirely and then filled the skin of the resulting metal frame with glazing.

Die Architekten nutzten den genehmigten Gebäudeumfang voll aus und füllten dann die Metallkonstruktion mit Glasflächen aus.

Les architectes ont utilisé la totalité de l'enveloppe autorisée et ont rempli de vitres les vides de la charpente métallique obtenue.

This design and that for Plot 3 were for an Amsterdam urban expansion site with a specific area designated to have only floating houses. Urban rules imposed strict formal guidelines on the designs but Olthuis pushed these regulations to their logical limits. Where the top level was only to be 50% occupied, the architect extended the white frame to enclose the other half, made up of an outdoor terrace. The lower floor, which is partly beneath the water level, contains a bedroom, bathroom with sauna, storage space, and study rooms. The entrance is located at the "ground" level, where two blocks form an entrance hallway and close off the stairwell, leaving the rest of the space almost completely open. The blocks contain a toilet, storage space, and kitchen equipment. The entire level is a living space and kitchen. The upper-floor volume with further living space has a curved outline that alleviates the otherwise austere form of this Floating Villa.

Dieser und der Entwurf für Parzelle 3 waren für ein Amsterdamer Stadterweiterungsgebiet bestimmt, in dem ein Bereich nur für schwimmende Häuser vorgesehen war. Die städtischen Vorschriften geben strenge formale Gestaltungsrichtlinien vor, aber der Architekt Koen Olthuis reizte diese bis an die Grenzen aus. Wo die obere Ebene nur zur Hälfte bebaut sein durfte, erweiterte der Architekt den weißen Rahmen, um auch die andere Hälfte, die aus einer Terrasse besteht, einzufassen. Das untere Geschoss, das zum Teil unter der Wasseroberfläche liegt, enthält einen Schlafraum, ein Bad mit Sauna, Stauraum und Arbeitszimmer. Der Eingang liegt im „Erdgeschoss", wo zwei Blöcke eine Eingangshalle bilden und das Treppenhaus abschotten, den übrigen Raum aber fast ganz offen lassen. Die Blöcke enthalten eine Toilette, einen Abstellraum und die Küchengeräte. Die gesamte übrige Ebene wird vom Wohnraum und der Küche eingenommen. Das Obergeschoss mit weiterer Wohnfläche hat eine gekrümmte Außenform, die die ansonsten strenge Gestaltung dieser schwimmenden Villa mildert.

Ce projet et celui du lopin 3 ont été conçus pour un site d'expansion urbaine à Amsterdam dont une partie était exclusivement réservée à des maisons flottantes. Les règlements d'urbanisme imposaient des contraintes formelles strictes qu'Olthuis a pourtant poussées jusqu'à leurs limites logiques. Ainsi, lorsque le niveau supérieur ne devait être occupé qu'à 50 %, il a prolongé le cadre blanc afin d'englober l'autre moitié composée d'une terrasse. L'étage du bas, en partie sous le niveau de l'eau, abrite une chambre, une salle de bains avec sauna, un espace de rangement et des salles de travail. L'entrée est située au niveau du « sol » où deux blocs forment un vestibule et ferment la cage d'escalier, laissant l'espace restant presque totalement ouvert. Ils contiennent des toilettes, des rangements et le matériel de cuisine. L'étage est tout entier occupé par le salon et la cuisine. Le volume de l'étage supérieur, qui accueille d'autres espaces à vivre, présente une silhouette courbe qui allège la forme sinon austère de la villa flottante.

On the ground floor, where the entrance is situated, most of the space is used as an open kitchen and living area.

Das Erdgeschoss, in dem sich auch der Eingang befindet, wird fast ganz von der offenen Küche und dem Wohnraum eingenommen.

Au rez-de-chaussée où est située l'entrée, la plus grande partie de l'espace est occupée par une cuisine ouverte et un espace séjour.

FLOATWING®

Area: 22 to 64 m² — Client: not disclosed — Cost: €74 000 to €270 000 — Collaboration: Pedro Brigida

The width of this houseboat is fixed at six meters, but its length ranges from 10 to 18 meters. It is equipped with two small outboard motors and can be moved at a speed of up to five knots. As the design is modular, the house and all of its equipment and furniture can easily be stored and moved in two or three standard shipping containers. The house produces up to 80% of its own energy needs with thermal and photovoltaic solar panels, and is self-sufficient for at least seven days when fully charged. When moored it can be readily connected to municipal networks. The floating house includes a wastewater treatment plant (WWTP) that is capable of full treatment, allowing treated wastewater to be freely disposed of while respecting the relative EEC Directive. Drawing only 0.7 meters of draught, the boat can be used in very shallow water and can be configured to have up to three bedrooms.

Die Breite dieses Hausboots ist auf 6 m festgelegt, aber es kann 10 bis 18 m lang sein. Es ist mit zwei Außenbordmotoren ausgestattet und kann in einer Geschwindigkeit von bis zu 5 Knoten bewegt werden. Da es sich um einen modularen Entwurf handelt, können das Haus und seine gesamte Ausstattung einschließlich des Mobiliars ganz einfach in zwei üblichen Containern gelagert und transportiert werden. Das Hausboot erzeugt bis zu 80 Prozent seines Energiebedarfs selbst mit Fotovoltaikpaneelen und ist, mit voll aufgeladener Batterie, mindestens sieben Tage autark. Angedockt kann es leicht an das städtische Versorgungsnetz angeschlossen werden. Das schwimmende Haus hat eine voll leistungsfähige Kläranlage, die das Abwasser in EU-Vorschriften entsprechendes Wasser umwandelt. Mit nur 0,6 m Tiefgang ist das Boot auch in sehr flachem Wasser nutzbar. Es kann so aufgeteilt werden, dass es bis zu drei Schlafräume hat.

La largeur de ce house-boat est fixée à 6 mètres, mais sa longueur varie de 10 à 18 mètres. Il est équipé de deux petits moteurs hors-bord et peut se déplacer à une vitesse maximale de trois nœuds. Le design est modulaire, de sorte que la maison, ses équipements et son mobilier peuvent facilement être stockés et transportés dans deux conteneurs maritimes standard. La maison produit jusqu'à 80 % de ses besoins énergétiques grâce à des panneaux solaires thermiques et photovoltaïques et est autosuffisante pendant au moins sept jours à pleine charge. Elle peut aussi être raccordée aux réseaux municipaux lorsqu'elle est amarrée. Elle comprend une installation de recyclage des eaux usées qui permet leur traitement complet pour une élimination en toute liberté conformément à la directive CEE applicable. Avec un tirant d'eau de seulement 0,6 mètre, le bateau peut flotter dans des eaux très peu profondes et être configuré pour disposer de trois chambres à coucher.

The Floatwing produces 30 to 80% of the energy it requires, depending on location and the number of solar panels installed, and can be moved at a speed of 5 knots.

Das Floatwing erzeugt, je nach Standort und Anzahl der installierten Solarpaneele, 30 bis 80 Prozent seiner benötigten Energie selbst und kann mit einer Geschwindigkeit von 5 Knoten bewegt werden.

Floatwing produit entre 30 et 80 % de ses besoins en énergie selon l'emplacement et le nombre de panneaux solaires installés ; l'ensemble peut se déplacer à une vitesse de 5 nœuds.

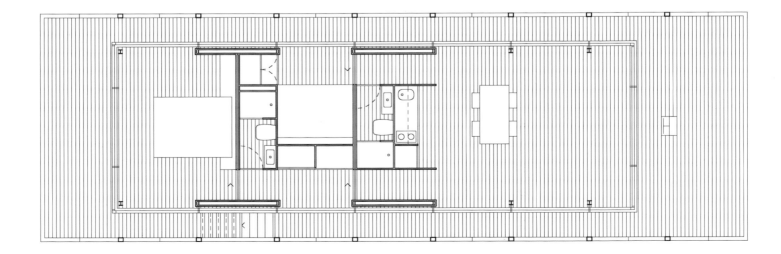

The basic design—seen in the plan to the left—can give rise to up to 300 different house layouts, with varying combinations of platform dimensions, balcony size, or the number and size of bedrooms.

Aus dem Basisplan, wie er im Grundriss links zu sehen ist, können bis zu 300 verschiedene Hausvariationen mit diversen Plattform- und Balkongrößen sowie Zimmern in unterschiedlicher Größe und Anzahl entworfen werden.

Le concept de base – sur le plan à gauche – peut donner naissance à plus de 300 configurations de maisons différentes en variant les combinaisons des dimensions de la plateforme, de la taille du balcon ou du nombre et de la taille des chambres.

The Floatwing, available in five different sizes ranging from 10 to 18 meters in length, is intended to contrast with existing houseboat typologies.

Das Floatwing ist in fünf verschiedenen Größen, von 10 bis 18 m Länge, lieferbar und soll einen Kontrast zur bestehenden Hausboottypologie darstellen.

Floatwing est disponible en cinq tailles différentes, de 10 à 18 m de long, et cherche à se différencier des types de house-boats existants.

MIKAEL GENBERG
Pemba Island, Zanzibar [Tanzania] — 2013

MANTA UNDERWATER ROOM

Area: not disclosed — Client: Manta Resort — Cost: not disclosed

The Manta Underwater Room has a lounge area and bathroom facility on the landing deck, while a ladder leads up to another lounge area on the roof. A double bed is located below the level of the sea offering a nearly 360° underwater view with numerous reef fish hovering nearby. Underwater spotlights attract normally shy creatures such as squid or octopus. Manta, which describes itself as a "sustainable luxury resort," received a tourism innovation award in 2016. The Manta Resort sponsors a community based project called Kwanini Africa (meaning "Why Africa?") that combines sustainable tourism with high-end luxury accommodation. Since its inception in 2007, Kwanini Africa has supported the creation of a school for villagers' children and a football club, advanced the conservation of the unique marine fauna along the coast of Africa, and provided additional income for the people of Pemba Island. Although the waters of Zanzibar clearly offer different attractions from those of Sweden, Mikael Genberg's concept seems clearly to be quite adaptable.

Der Manta Underwater Room hat einen Wohnraum und ein Bad auf dem Landedeck; eine Leiter führt zu einem weiteren Aufenthaltsbereich auf dem Dach. Unter der Meeresoberfläche befindet sich ein Doppelbett mit Unterwasser-Rundumblick auf die vielen dort lebenden Riff-Fische. Scheinwerfer locken normalerweise scheue Kreaturen wie Tintenfische und Oktopusse an. Manta, das sich selbst als „nachhaltiger Luxus-Ferienort" beschreibt, erhielt 2016 eine Auszeichnung für innovativen Tourismus. Das Manta Resort sponsert ein gemeinschaftlich betriebenes Projekt namens Kwanini Africa (Warum Afrika?), das nachhaltigen Tourismus mit luxuriöser Unterbringung verbindet. Seit seiner Gründung 2007 hat Kwanini Africa die Einrichtung einer Dorfschule und eines Fußballklubs unterstützt, den Schutz der einmaligen Meeresfauna an den Küsten Afrikas gefördert und zusätzliche Verdienstmöglichkeiten für die Bevölkerung der Insel Pemba generiert. Obgleich das Meer von Sansibar natürlich andere Attraktionen bietet als das Schwedens, scheint Mikael Genbergs Konzept sich für beide zu eignen.

La chambre sous-marine Manta possède un espace salon et une salle de bains sur le pont, ainsi qu'un autre espace détente sur le toit, accessible par une échelle. Le lit double est situé sous le niveau de la mer et offre une vue à 360° sur les nombreux poissons coralliens qui peuplent ses abords. Des projecteurs sous-marins attirent naturellement les animaux plus farouches comme les calmars ou les pieuvres. Le complexe Manta, qui se présente lui-même comme un « hôtel de luxe durable », a reçu un prix de l'innovation touristique en 2016. Il sponsorise un projet communautaire appelé Kwanini Africa (« Pourquoi l'Afrique ? »), qui associe tourisme durable et hébergement de luxe très haut de gamme. Depuis ses débuts en 2007, Kwanini Africa a contribué à la fondation d'une école pour les enfants des villages et d'un club de football, fait progresser la préservation de la faune marine unique le long des côtes africaines et fourni un revenu supplémentaire aux habitants de Pemba. Et même si les eaux de Zanzibar possèdent indéniablement d'autres charmes que les eaux suédoises, le concept de Mikael Genberg semble parfaitement transposable.

The landing deck, at sea level, has a lounge area and a bathroom facility. A ladder leads up to the roof which is intended as a lounging area.

Das Landedeck auf Meeresniveau hat einen Wohnraum und ein Bad. Eine Leiter führt auf das Dach, das auch als Aufenthaltsbereich gedacht ist.

Le pont, au niveau de la mer, abrite un espace salon et une salle de bains. Une échelle mène au toit, conçu lui aussi comme un espace salon.

The bedroom is entirely below sea level with windows offering a view of almost 360°. Spotlights offer guests a chance to see the underwater domain even after dark.

Der Schlafraum liegt ganz unter dem Wasserspiegel; seine Fenster bieten einen fast vollständigen Rundumblick. Dank der Scheinwerfer können die Gäste die Unterwasserwelt auch bei Nacht betrachten.

La chambre est entièrement située sous le niveau de la mer et ses fenêtres dévoilent une vue à 360° sur l'océan. Des projecteurs permettent aux clients de contempler le monde sous-marin après la tombée de la nuit.

PORTAGE BAY
FLOATING HOME

Area: 167 m² (including decks) — Client: Denise Draper — Cost: $500 000
Collaboration: Kim Mankoski (Interior Designer)

Space in the house was planned to maximize views of the bay and mountains beyond; capturing southern light and northern breezes were also objectives of the architect.

Die Räume des Hauses wurden so geplant, dass sie den bestmöglichen Ausblick auf die Bucht und die Berge dahinter bieten. Ziel des Architekten war es, das Licht aus dem Süden und die Brise des Nordens einzufangen.

L'espace intérieur de la maison a été conçu pour optimiser les vues de la baie et au-delà des montagnes, mais l'architecte voulait aussi profiter de la lumière du sud et des brises du nord.

The early inhabitants of the floating homes on Portage Bay were loggers and sailors who built residences on fallen logs. Ryan Mankoski states: "Our primary design intent with the Portage Bay Floating Home was to create a modern dwelling that paid homage to the historical character of the Lake Washington Ship Canal." This new home was built on a 100-year-old log float. "We chose materials such as raw steel and reclaimed cedar siding for the exterior of the home so that, with weather, they would age in a natural way reminiscent of the surrounding industrial context," state the architects. Materials used also include reclaimed timber and bamboo. Radiant floor heating is used in the house. Use of reclaimed wood and radiant heating are indicative of the designer's affirmation of green design principles.

Die ersten Bewohner der schwimmenden Häuser von Portage Bay waren Holzfäller und Seeleute, die Wohnhäuser auf gefällten Baumstämmen errichteten. Ryan Mankoski erklärt: „Unser wichtigstes Planungsziel war es, ein modernes Wohnhaus zu schaffen, das dem historischen Charakter des Lake Washington Ship Canal gerecht wird." Dieses neue Heim wurde auf einem 100 Jahre alten Holzfloß errichtet. „Als Materialien wählten wir Rohstahl und eine Außenverkleidung aus Zedern-Altholz, damit das Haus natürlich altern kann und zugleich an die industrielle Umgebung anknüpft", sagen die Architekten. Weitere verwendete Materialien sind recyceltes Holz und Bambus. Das Haus hat eine Fußbodenheizung. Diese Heizung und der Gebrauch von Altholz sind Indizen für das Bekenntnis des Architekten zu umweltschonenden Entwurfsprinzipien.

Les premiers habitants des maisons flottantes de Portage Bay étaient des bûcherons et des marins qui ont bâti des maisons sur des rondins abattus. Ryan Mankoski raconte : « Notre première intention était de créer un habitat moderne qui rende hommage au caractère historique du canal maritime entre le lac Washington et l'océan. » La nouvelle maison a été construite sur un ponton de rondins vieux de 100 ans. « Pour l'extérieur, nous avons choisi des matériaux tels qu'acier brut et bardage en bois de cèdre récupéré afin qu'ils vieillissent naturellement sous l'effet des intempéries et rappellent le contexte industriel tout autour », précisent les architectes. Le bois d'œuvre récupéré et le bambou sont aussi utilisés. La maison possède un chauffage au sol à rayonnement qui, avec l'emploi du bois de récupération, s'accorde avec les principes écologiques dont se réclame le designer.

Steel and raw wood were chosen as main building materials to emphasize the aging process, while old timber was recovered from an existing house on the same site.

Stahl und unbehandeltes Holz wurden als Hauptmaterialien gewählt, um den Alterungsprozess zu betonen. Das Altholz wurde von einem Haus auf demselben Grundstück gewonnen.

L'acier et le bois brut ont été choisis comme principaux matériaux de construction afin de mettre en valeur le processus de vieillissement, tandis que du bois d'œuvre ancien a été récupéré sur une maison qui existait sur le site.

Although this is indeed a floating house, its style and design are closely connected to its location in Portage Bay, Seattle.

Obgleich dies wirklich ein schwimmendes Haus ist, entspricht es in Stil und Form seinem Standort in Portage Bay, einem Stadtteil von Seattle.

Bien qu'elle flotte, le style et la conception de la maison sont étroitement liés à l'environnement de Portage Bay, à Seattle.

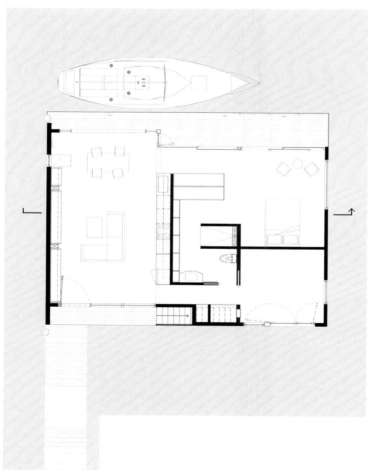

Wood cladding and full-height glazing are significant features of the house. Left, a plan shows Portage Bay to the top and an existing pier linking to the house at the bottom.

Holzverkleidung und geschosshohe Verglasung sind entscheidende Merkmale des Hauses. Links: Der Grundriss zeigt oben die Bucht von Portage und unten einen bestehenden Pier, der zum Hausboot führt.

Ses caractéristiques principales sont le bardage en bois et le vitrage sur toute la hauteur. À gauche, un plan représente Portage Bay en haut et le ponton qui donne accès à la maison en bas.

DANIEL STRAUB
Kiel [Germany] — 2011–14

SEALANDER

Area: 4.5 m² — Client: various — Cost: €15 000

The Sealander weighs approximately 500 kilos, depending on the equipment ordered, and can advance on water with an electric motor at a speed of just under 5 knots. Materials include handmade reinforced fiberglass, which forms the majority of the monocoque shell of the structure, stainless steel and wood. The vehicle can be towed by a car, has an opening roof, and a seating area and a tabletop that can be transformed into a bed. Various options are offered including an added toilet, cooking and washing areas, an audio installation, and fitted curtains and cushions. As the Sealander models are custom-built in a factory in Germany, different colors and finishes are available with an eight-week delivery time. Daniel Straub describes the vehicle as a "camper" but also a "yacht," which may be a little ambitious given the size of the Sealander, but his invention does appear to be the first water-going camper, with a capacity of about four people.

Der Sealander wiegt ungefähr 500 kg, abhängig von seiner Ausstattung, und kann sich auf dem Wasser mittels eines Elektromotors in einer Geschwindigkeit von beinahe 5 Knoten fortbewegen. Zu seinen Materialien zählen handgefertigte, armierte Glasfaser für den überwiegenden Teil der Monocoque-Schale, Edelstahl und Holz. Das Boot kann an ein Auto angehängt werden, hat eeinen Sitzbereich und eine Tischplatte, die zu einem Bett umgebaut werden kann, und ein Dach, das sich öffnen lässt. Verschiedene Ausführungen werden angeboten, darunter eine mit Toilette, Herd und Waschgelegenheit, einer Audioanlage sowie Gardinen und Kissen. Da die Sealander-Modelle serienmäßig in einer Fabrik in Deutschland produziert werden, sind sie mit einer Lieferzeit von acht Wochen in verschiedenen Farben und Ausstattungen verfügbar. Daniel Straub beschreibt das Fahrzeug als „Camper", aber auch als „Yacht", was angesichts der Maße des Sealanders etwas ambitioniert klingt. Aber er ist anscheinend der erste wassertaugliche Camper und kann vier Personen aufnehmen.

Dépendant de son équipement, le Sealander pèse environ 500 kilos et peut avancer sur l'eau à une vitesse maximale de 5 nœuds grâce à son moteur électrique. Les matériaux utilisés comprennent de la fibre de verre moulée à la main et renforcée par du plastique pour la majeure partie de la structure monocoque, ainsi que de l'acier inoxydable et du bois. Le véhicule peut être tracté par une voiture, il dispose d'un toit ouvrant, de places assises et d'une tablette qui se transforme en lit. Diverses options sont possibles, notamment des toilettes, des coins cuisine et toilette, une installation audio et des rideaux et coussins intégrés. Il est fabriqué sur mesure dans une usine allemande, et donc disponible en différentes couleurs et finitions, pour un délai de livraison de huit semaines. Daniel Straub décrit son véhicule comme une « caravane », mais parle aussi d'un « yacht », ce qui peut paraître un peu ambitieux vu la taille du Sealander. Son invention semble pourtant bel et bien être la première caravane à aller sur l'eau, avec sa capacité de quatre personnes environ.

Plans show the vehicle, which is 4.06 meters long and 3.72 meters wide and thus easily transportable as a towed trailer. The amphibious nature of the Sealander is only really clear when it is in the water.

Die Pläne zeigen das 4,06 m lange und 3,72 m breite und dadurch als Anhänger leicht transportierbare Vehikel. Als amphibisches Fahrzeug entpuppt sich der Sealander erst, wenn er im Wasser ist.

Les plans montrent le véhicule long de 4,06 m et large de 3,72 m, facilement tractable par une voiture. La nature amphibie du Sealander n'apparaît véritablement que lorsqu'il est dans l'eau.

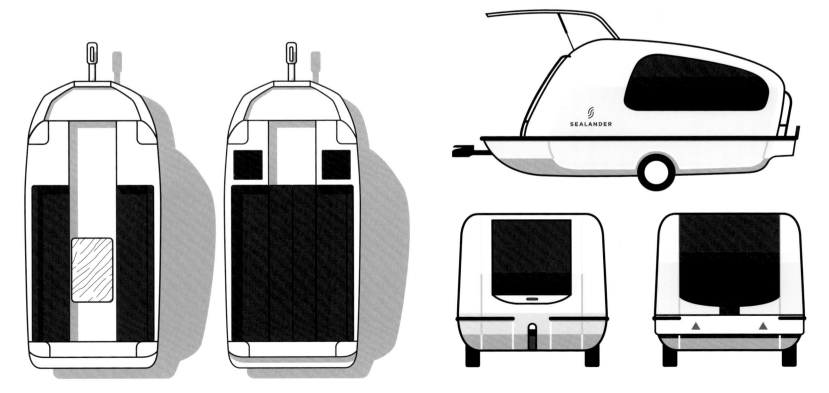

A small outboard motor is installed on the rear of the Sealander, whose wheels can readily be used to push it into the water.

Hinten am Sealander, der sich dank seiner Räder leicht ins Wasser schieben lässt, ist ein kleiner Außenbordmotor angebracht.

Un petit moteur hors-bord est monté à l'arrière du Sealander dont les roues peuvent servir à le pousser dans l'eau.

URBAN RIGGER

Area: total 680 m²; living 300 m² (12 apartments) — Client, Inventor and Patent Holder: Udvikling Danmark A/S – Urban Rigger ApS
Cost: not disclosed — Collaboration: BIG A/S, Danfoss A/S, Grundfos A/S, Miele AG, Hanwha Q CELLS Ltd.

The triangular composition of the Urban Rigger allows for the creation of a common, central space, but also minimizes the footprint of the pontoon and opens views to the water.

Im Zentrum der dreieckigen Form des Urban Rigger, die die Fläche des Pontons minimiert und Ausblicke zum Wasser eröffnet, befindet sich ein Gemeinschaftsbereich.

La disposition en triangle d'Urban Rigger permet de créer un espace central commun, tout en réduisant au minimum l'empreinte et en ouvrant la vue sur l'eau.

The housing shortage for students in Denmark is combined with the lack of available land for construction in Copenhagen. Kim Loudrup and the architects, Bjarke Ingels Group, noted that the harbor near the city center is an "underutilized and underdeveloped area." Using standard Corten shipping containers, they propose a solution that is easy to assemble at a low cost and which will allow students to live very close to the city center. They write: "By stacking nine container units in a circle, we can create 12 studio residences that frame a centralized winter garden; this is used as a common meeting place for students. The Urban Rigger floats due to water displacement principles (like a boat) and weighs in at 650 tonnes, which in turn gives it extreme stability. Thus it can be replicated in other harbor cities where affordable housing is needed, but space is limited." Interest in this project has been considerable and Urban Rigger was working on several new installations in European countries as this book went to press.

Fehlender Wohnraum für Studenten geht in Kopenhagen einher mit einem Mangel an geeigneten Bauplätzen. Kim Loudrup und die Architekten der Bjarke Ingels Group erkannten, dass der nahe am Zentrum gelegene Hafen ein „zu wenig genutztes und unterentwickeltes Gebiet" ist. Mit gewöhnlichen Containern aus Corten-Stahl bieten sie eine einfache und preiswert zu montierende Lösung, die den Studenten Wohnungen nah am Stadtzentrum bietet. Sie schreiben: „Wenn neun Container im Kreis aufgestellt werden, können wir zwölf Atelierwohnungen um einen zentralen Wintergarten errichten, der als gemeinschaftlicher Treffpunkt für die Studenten dient. Die Wohnungen sind auch schwimmfähig wie ein Boot und können daher ebenso in anderen Hafenstädten errichtet werden, in denen preiswerter Wohnraum fehlt, aber der Platz zum Bauen begrenzt ist." Das Interesse an diesem Projekt ist groß, und Urban Rigger waren an mehreren neuen Baustellen in europäischen Ländern tätig, als dieses Buch in Druck ging.

La pénurie de logements étudiants au Danemark va de pair avec le manque de terrains à bâtir à Copenhague. Les architectes ont cependant remarqué que le port, à proximité du centre-ville, constituait un « espace sous-utilisé et sous-développé ». À l'aide de conteneurs maritimes standard en acier Corten, ils ont imaginé une solution facile à assembler à moindres frais qui permettra aux étudiants de vivre tout près du centre-ville. « En empilant neuf conteneurs disposés en cercle, nous pouvons créer 12 studios autour d'un jardin d'hiver central qui sert de pièce commune aux étudiants, expliquent-ils. L'habitat flotte comme un bateau et peut donc être reproduit dans d'autres villes portuaires à l'espace limité, où le besoin de logements abordables est grand. » Le projet a suscité un intérêt considérable ; au moment où ce livre a été mis sous presse, Urban Rigger travaillait à plusieurs nouvelles installations dans différents pays européens.

Above, the central winter garden of the Urban Rigger. Below, a model shows the three levels of the structure and a stairway linking to the rooftop terrace.

Oben: Der zentrale Wintergarten des Urban Rigger. Unten: Das Modell zeigt die drei Ebenen des Bauwerks sowie die Treppe zur Dachterrasse.

Ci-dessus, le jardin d'hiver central. Ci-dessous, une maquette montre les trois niveaux de la structure et l'escalier qui mène à la terrasse sur le toit.

Generous openings in the container
walls make for luminous interior spaces,
here arranged for housing in a harbor-
side setting that would normally be inac-
cessible to students.

Großzügige Öffnungen in den Container-
wänden erzeugen einen hellen Innenraum,
hier zum Wohnen in der Hafengegend,
was für Studenten normalerweise unbezahl-
bar wäre.

De vastes ouvertures dans les parois
des conteneurs créent des espaces intérieurs
lumineux, aménagés ici dans un environnement proche du port, normalement inacces-
sible aux étudiants.

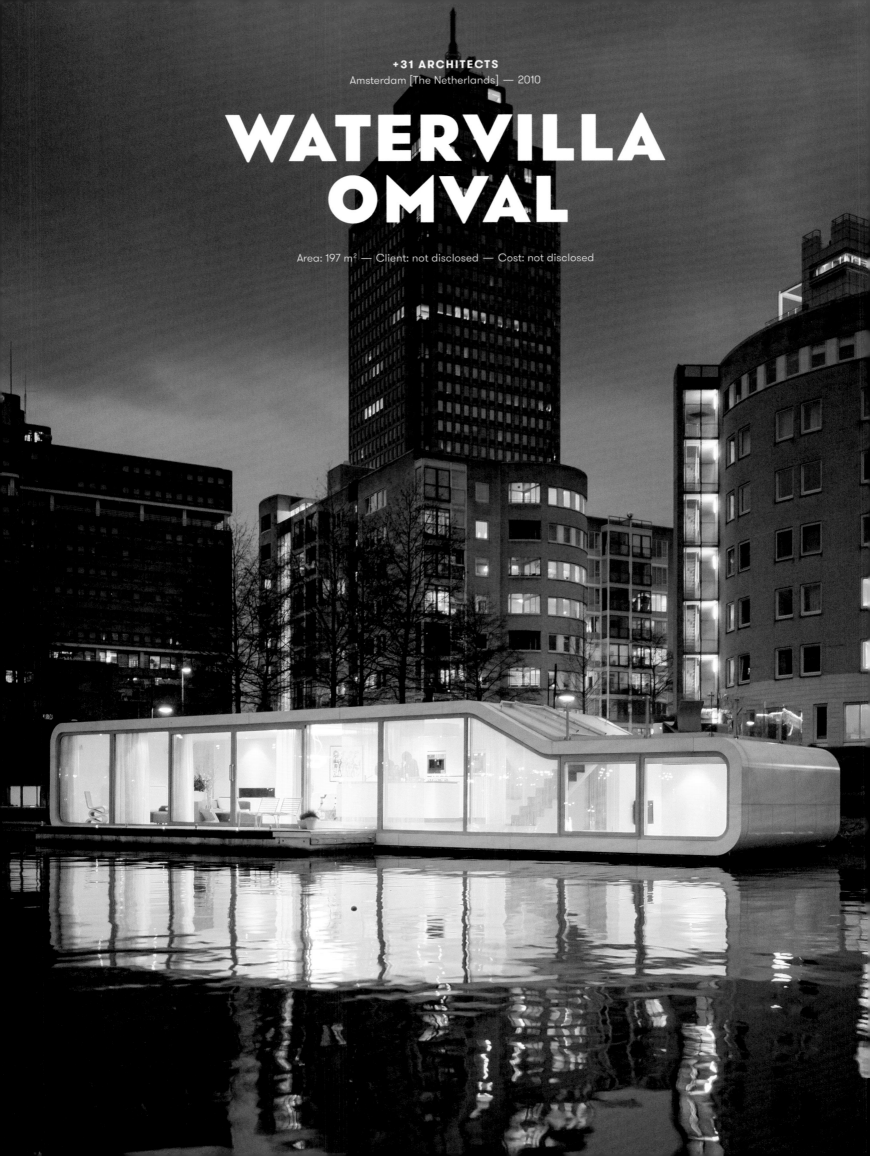

+31 ARCHITECTS
Amsterdam [The Netherlands] — 2010

WATERVILLA OMVAL

Area: 197 m² — Client: not disclosed — Cost: not disclosed

The living area and open kitchen are located on the waterfront (left), and offer residents a panoramic view of the Amstel. Above, the more closed entrance façade.

Der Wohnraum und die offene Küche sind zum Wasser orientiert (links) und bieten den Bewohnern eine Panoramaaussicht auf die Amstel. Oben: Die geschlossenere Eingangsfassade.

L'espace séjour et la cuisine ouverte sont placés du côté de l'eau (à gauche) et offrent aux occupants une vue panoramique sur l'Amstel. Ci-dessus, la façade de l'entrée, plus fermée.

The architects liken living on the Amstel River in Amsterdam to "being on holiday forever." The house has aluminum cladding and windows and was intended to be "very contemporary without losing the characteristic appearance of the typical houseboat." According to the architects: "The clients wanted a boat with an open floor plan where they could enjoy the views to the water and the outdoor space to a maximum. The distinguished curved line of the façade directly derives from this desire and the restriction that the boat couldn't be more than three meters above the water." The bedroom is located on a split level that makes it possible to create a terrace on the south side without exceeding the maximum allowed height. White plastered walls and ceilings follow the curve of the façade creating "a seamless transition from the exterior to the interior." The Watervilla Omval was nominated for the Gouden AAP 2011, Amsterdam Architecture Prize, for the best building realized in 2010–11.

Die Architekten vergleichen das Leben auf der Amstel in Amsterdam mit einem „nie endenden Urlaub". Das Haus hat eine Verkleidung und Fenster aus Aluminium und sollte „sehr zeitgemäß sein, ohne auf die charakteristischen Merkmale eines typischen Hausboots zu verzichten". Sie erklären weiterhin, dass „die Auftraggeber ein Boot mit einem offenen Grundriss wünschten, von dem aus sie den Ausblick auf das Wasser und den Außenbereich am besten genießen könnten. Die auffällig geschwungene Linie geht unmittelbar auf diesen Wunsch und die Vorschrift zurück, dass das Boot nicht mehr als 3 m über der Wasserfläche aufragen durfte." Der Schlafraum liegt in einem Zwischengeschoss, wodurch es möglich wurde, auf der Südseite eine Terrasse anzulegen, ohne die maximal zulässige Höhe zu überschreiten. Die weiß verputzten Wände und Decken folgen der Fassadenkrümmung und bilden „einen nahtlosen Übergang vom Außen- zum Innenbereich". Für die Watervilla Omval wurden die Architekten mit dem Amsterdamer Architekturpreis Gouden AAP 2011 für das beste 2010/11 errichtete Bauwerk ausgezeichnet.

Les architectes comparent la vie sur la rivière Amstel, à Amsterdam, à « des vacances perpétuelles ». Le revêtement et les fenêtres de la maison sont en aluminium, le but étant de la rendre « très contemporaine, mais sans perdre l'aspect caractéristique des house-boats traditionnels ». Les architectes expliquent que « les clients souhaitaient un bateau avec un plan au sol ouvert pour profiter le plus possible des vues sur l'eau et de l'espace extérieur. L'élégante ligne courbe de la façade répond directement à ce désir, de même que la hauteur restreinte à trois mètres au-dessus de l'eau ». La chambre est située à un niveau séparé, ce qui a permis de créer une terrasse côté sud sans dépasser la hauteur maximale autorisée. Les murs et les plafonds crépis de blanc épousent la courbe de la façade, formant « une transition tout en douceur de l'extérieur vers l'intérieur ». En 2001, la Watervilla d'Omval a été nommée au Gouden AAP, le prix d'architecture d'Amsterdam du meilleur bâtiment réalisé entre 2010 et 2011.

The rounded lines of the aluminum façade are carried through to the white plastered walls and ceilings inside.

Die abgerundeten Linien der Aluminiumfassade setzen sich in den weiß verputzten Wänden und Decken im Inneren fort.

Les lignes courbes de la façade en aluminium se prolongent à l'intérieur avec les murs et les plafonds crépis de blanc.

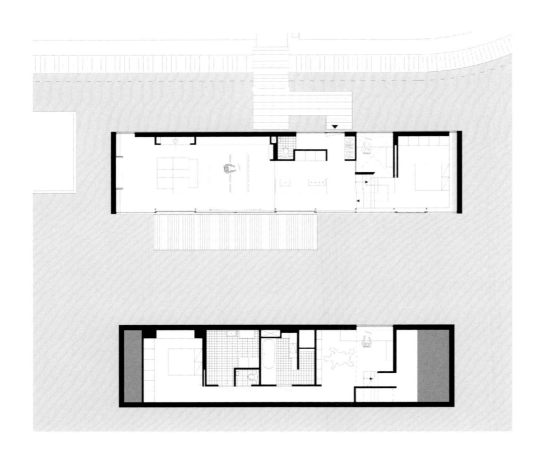

Left, plans show the two levels of the house (Level 0, top; Level -1, below). The master bedroom is on the 0 Level while a guestroom and bathroom are on -1.

Links: Die Pläne zeigen die beiden Ebenen des Hauses (Ebene 0, oben; Ebene -1, unten). Das große Schlafzimmer liegt auf Ebene 0, während ein Gästezimmer und das Bad sich auf Ebene -1 befinden.

À gauche, plan des deux niveaux de la maison (niveau 0 en haut, niveau -1 en bas). La chambre à coucher est située au niveau 0, tandis que la chambre d'amis et la salle de bains sont au -1.

+31 ARCHITECTS
Amsterdam [The Netherlands] — 2014

WATERVILLA WEESPERZIJDE

Area: 240 m² — Client: not disclosed — Cost: not disclosed

The clients for this project were inspired by the modern design of the Watervilla Omval, and they intended to dock their houseboat a bit further downstream on the Amstel. Large sliding glass doors are placed on the waterside to give the broadest possible views from the living area and kitchen of the house. A floating terrace was designed to be moored along the full length of the house. Floor surfaces extend unchanged between interior and exterior giving the impression of a much larger living area. Bedrooms and bathrooms are located in the "basement" and are acceded to via a "floating" stairway that inhabits a void that brings light into the lower level. Three large motor-operated sunscreens are integrated into the waterfront side of the house. Holes in the quayside façade of the house delineate the number of the house (1099), highlighted at night by a large LED strip placed behind the surface of the house. The architects state: "The film frame-like glass façade offers great views on the water but occasionally also gives a glimpse into the life of the residents. For the boats that are passing it looks as if a movie is being played like a small intimate reality show."

Die Auftraggeber dieses Projekts waren vom modernen Design der Watervilla Omval angetan und hatten die Absicht, ihr Hausboot etwas weiter flussabwärts an der Amstel festzumachen. Die zum Wasser gerichtete Seite hat große Glasschiebefenster, um von Wohnraum und Küche aus den bestmöglichen Ausblick zu haben. Eine schwimmende Terrasse wurde an der ganzen Länge des Hauses verankert. Der Fußboden erstreckt sich einheitlich von innen nach außen und lässt den Wohnbereich damit viel größer wirken. Schlafräume und Bäder liegen im „Untergeschoss" und werden über einen „schwimmenden" Treppenaufgang erschlossen, der sich einen Freiraum befindet, durch den Tageslicht in die untere Ebene einfällt. An der Wasserseite sind auch drei große, motorbetriebene Sonnenschutzelemente angebracht. Mit Löchern in der Uferfassade ist die Hausnummer (1099) angezeigt, die nachts von einem großen LED-Streifen von hinten beleuchtet wird. Die Architekten erklären: „Die einem Filmstreifen gleichende Glasfassade bietet großartige Ausblicke auf das Wasser, gelegentlich aber auch Einblicke in das Leben der Bewohner. Vorbeifahrenden Booten erscheint das wie ein Film, wie eine kleine intime Realityshow."

Inspirés par le design moderne de la Watervilla d'Omval, les clients voulaient amarrer leur house-boat un peu en aval sur l'Amstel. De larges portes coulissantes vitrées ont été placées du côté de l'eau afin d'offrir la vue la plus large possible depuis le séjour et la cuisine. Une terrasse flottante a été spécialement conçue pour être ancrée sur toute la longueur de la maison. Les sols sont identiques à l'intérieur et à l'extérieur, ce qui agrandit visuellement l'espace à vivre. Les chambres et les salles de bains sont situées au « sous-sol » et accessibles via un escalier « flottant » qui occupe un puits faisant pénétrer la lumière au niveau inférieur. Trois pare-soleil automatiques de grandes dimensions sont intégrés à la maison du côté de l'eau, tandis que côté quai, des trous dans la façade forment le numéro (1099), éclairés la nuit par un vaste bandeau LED placé par derrière. D'après les architectes, « la façade vitrée encadrée comme une image de film offre des vues fantastiques sur l'eau, mais aussi un aperçu de la vie des habitants. Pour les bateaux qui passent, c'est comme le film d'un petit reality-show intime ».

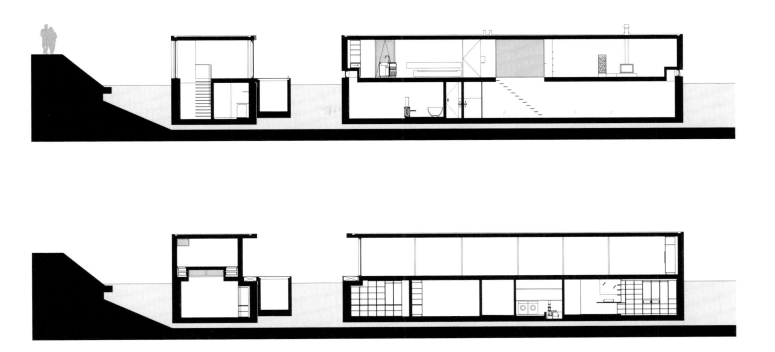

Above, section drawings show the spaces above and below the waterline. Left, the entrance façade and below, a waterside view with the full-length floating terrace visible.

Oben: Die Schnitte zeigen die Räume über und unter dem Wasserspiegel. Links: Die Eingangsfassade und (unten) eine Ansicht der Wasserseite mit der schwimmenden Terrasse, die sich über die ganze Hauslänge erstreckt.

Ci-dessus, schémas en coupe des espaces au-dessus et en-dessous de la surface. À gauche, façade d'entrée et ci-dessous, vue du côté de l'eau avec la terrasse flottante sur toute la longueur de la maison.

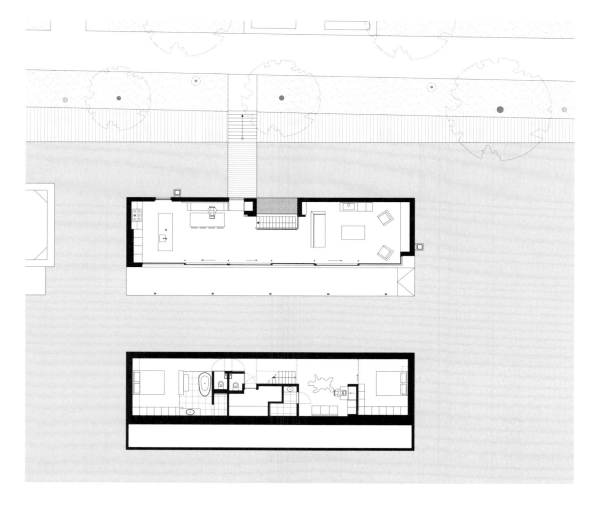

Plans show the two levels of the house and also its floating terrace on the waterside. The upper-level living area is almost entirely open.

Die Grundrisse zeigen die zwei Ebenen des Hauses mit der schwimmenden Terrasse an der Wasserseite. Der Wohnraum auf der oberen Ebene ist fast ganz offen.

Plans des deux niveaux de la maison et de sa terrasse flottante côté eau. Le séjour du niveau supérieur est presque entièrement ouvert.

Left page, the stairway leading down form the main living/dining area. Cabinetry was designed by Forsa Meubels, Utrecht. Furnishings are modern, in keeping with the design of the house itself.

Linke Seite: Die vom Wohn-Ess-Bereich hinunterführende Treppe. Die Möblierung wurde von Forsa Meubels in Utrecht entworfen. Sie ist modern und steht im Einklang mit dem Stil des Hauses.

Page de gauche, l'escalier vers le bas forme l'espace principal qui sert de séjour/salle à manger. Le mobilier moderne a été conçu par Forsa Meubels, Utrecht, en accord avec le design de la maison.

HOME
in a tent

AUTONOMOUS TENT
Treebones Resort, Big Sur, California [USA] — 2015–16

AUTONOMOUS TENT

Area: 46.5 m² (indoor), 28 m² (outdoors) — Client: Treebones Resort — Cost: $100 000 — Collaboration: Harry H. Gesner (Architect), Phil Parr (President, Autonomous Tent Co. LLC)

The Autonomous Tent is described as a "new form of architecture that has been engineered as a permanent structure, yet can be raised in just a few days and 'leave without a trace.'" The tent has an open floor plan and a high ceiling, leading it to be compared to a traditional yurt, but its high-technology nature is evident. This tent is powered by its own solar array. Inside, it has a king-size bed, a gas fireplace, and a bathroom with a shower and flushable composting toilet. The membrane fabric of the tent allows daylight to come in and makes the structure glow in the dark when it is lit inside. The structure was built with aluminum ground screws, a Douglas fir deck frame, steel-tube tent frame, high-performance composite tent membrane, a Beetle kill pine entryway and interior walls, and a bamboo floor and deck.

Das Autonome Zelt wird beschrieben als eine „neue Form der Architektur, die als permanente Konstruktion ausgeführt ist, aber dennoch in wenigen Tagen aufgestellt und ‚spurlos' wieder abgebaut werden kann". Das Zelt hat einen offenen Grundriss und eine hohe Decke und kann mit einer traditionellen Jurte verglichen werden, seine Hightech-Ausstattung ist aber nicht zu übersehen. Es hat eine eigene Solaranlage. Innen befinden sich ein Doppelbett, ein Gasofen und ein Bad mit Dusche und Kompost-Wasserklosett. Durch den Membranstoff kommt Tageslicht in das Zelt, und bei eingeschaltetem Licht leuchtet es in Dunkelheit. Es wurde mit Aluminium-Bodenschrauben, einer Bodenkonstruktion aus Douglastanne, einem Gerüst aus Stahlrohr, widerstandsfähiger Verbundmembrane, Eingang und Innenwänden aus Beetle-Kill-Kiefernholz sowie Boden und Terrasse aus Bambus gebaut.

L'Autonomous Tent est décrite comme une « nouvelle forme d'architecture, élaborée comme une structure permanente mais qui peut être érigée en seulement quelques jours et "disparaître sans laisser de trace" ». Elle présente un plan au sol ouvert sous un haut plafond qui appelle la comparaison avec une yourte traditionnelle, si sa haute technicité n'était pas si visible. La tente est alimentée en énergie par ses propres panneaux solaires. On y trouve un lit king size, un foyer au gaz et une salle de bains avec douche et toilettes compostables à chasse d'eau. La membrane textile laisse pénétrer la lumière du jour et fait briller la tente dans l'obscurité lorsqu'elle est éclairée à l'intérieur. L'ensemble se compose de vis de terre en aluminium, d'une charpente en sapin de Douglas, de piquets de tente en tubes d'acier, d'une membrane composite haute performance, d'un vestibule et de murs intérieurs en déchets d'insectes mangeurs de pins, ainsi que d'un sol et d'un porche en bambou.

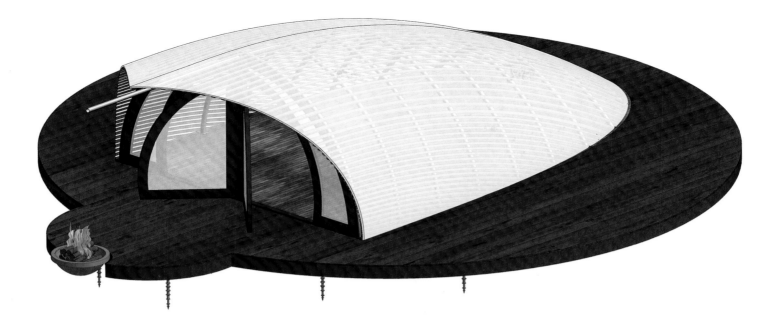

This tent is installed at Treebones, which calls itself a "glamping resort" located in South Big Sur. Described as a "giant cocoon," the tent offers a king-size bed and is powered by its own solar array.

Dieses Zelt steht in Treebones im südlichen Big Sur, das sich selbst ein „Glamping-Resort" nennt. Das als „riesiger Kokon" bezeichnete Zelt enthält ein großes Doppelbett und hat eine eigene Solarstromanlage.

La tente est installée à Treebones, un établissement qui se qualifie de « glamping », dans le sud de Big Sur. Présentée comme un « cocon géant », elle contient un lit king size et est alimentée en énergie par ses propres panneaux solaires.

The membrane structure, combined with wood fittings, serves to unite modernity and a sense of more traditional solidity.

Die Membrankonstruktion mit Holzausstattung verbindet moderne Gestaltung mit einer gewissen traditionellen Solidität.

La structure membranée associée aux accessoires en bois marie modernité et une robustesse plus traditionnelle.

BERNI DU PAYRAT
Aix-en-Provence [France] — 2017

COCOON TREE

Area: 3 meters (diameter) — Client: Glamping Technology — Cost: €6700

Cocoon Tree is a spherical, aluminum, waterproof tree-house pod. It can be assembled in less than two hours and weighs 200 kilos (empty). Rigged up with ropes and secured by nets, the structure has 12 locking points for both suspension and for lateral stability. It can hold a weight of up to 500 kilos. A large mattress (2.4 meters in diameter) and a custom-made duvet can be placed inside it, accommodating two people, or even a couple with two small children. The interior is sheltered from the elements by a robust waterproof outer skin, with fan air-conditioning and ventilation for very warm weather conditions. The designers included mosquito screens for the openings. There are different models of the Cocoon, designed according to various uses: Cocoon Tree is a tree house; Cocoon Beach is a model for beachgoers; and Cocoon Jungle, coated with synthetic fiber that imitates bamboo, offers full protection from the elements. All these can be placed on the ground with adaptable feet, fixed on a post driven into the bottom of a lake, attached to a floating ring, suspended in a tree, or floating on a platform.

Cocoon Tree ist eine kugelförmige wasserdichte Baumhauskapsel aus Aluminium. Sie kann in weniger als zwei Stunden zusammengesetzt werden und wiegt (leer) 200 kg. Die Konstruktion wird von Seilen getragen und durch Netze gesichert; sie hat zwölf Arretierungspunkte für die Aufhängung und für die Seitenstabilität. Sie kann ein Gewicht von bis zu 500 kg tragen. Auf einer großen (2,4 m im Durchmesser) Matratze mit einer speziell angefertigten Daunendecke finden zwei Personen oder sogar ein Paar mit zwei kleinen Kindern Platz. Den Innenraum schützt eine robuste Außenhaut vor den Elementen, für die Belüftung bei warmem Wetter sorgen Ventilatoren. Für die Öffnungen haben die Planer auch Fliegengitter vorgesehen. Es gibt verschiedene Ausführungen des Cocoon für unterschiedliche Nutzungen: Cocoon Tree ist ein Baumhaus, Cocoon Beach eine Version für Strandbesucher, und der mit einer Chemiefaser, die Bambus imitiert, beschichtete Cocoon Jungle bietet vollkommenen Schutz vor den Elementen. All Versionen können mit verstellbaren Füßen auf den Boden gestellt, an einen in den Grund eines Sees getriebenen Pfosten oder an einen schwimmenden Ring befestigt, in einen Baum gehängt werden oder auf einer Plattform schweben.

Cocoon Tree est une nacelle sphérique imperméable en aluminium à accrocher dans les arbres. Elle peut être assemblée en moins de deux heures et pèse 200 kilos (vide). Attachée par des cordes et sécurisée par des filets, la structure possède 12 points d'ancrage pour sa suspension et sa stabilité latérale. Elle peut contenir jusqu'à 500 kilos. Un grand matelas (2,4 mètres de diamètre) et une couette sur mesure peuvent y être installés pour recevoir deux personnes ou un couple avec deux jeunes enfants. L'intérieur est abrité par une solide enveloppe extérieure imperméable, avec ventilateur, air conditionné et aération pour les climats les plus chauds. Les créateurs ont ajouté des moustiquaires aux ouvertures. Le Cocoon existe en plusieurs modèles destinés à des usages différents : Cocoon Tree est une cabane dans les arbres, Cocoon Beach abrite les amateurs de plage et Cocoon Jungle est recouvert de fibre synthétique qui imite le bambou pour une protection complète. Tous peuvent être posés sur le sol à l'aide de pieds adaptables, fixés sur un pieu enfoncé dans le fond d'un lac, attachés à une bouée, suspendus dans un arbre ou placés sur une plate-forme flottante.

The Cocoon Tree can be mounted by three people in three hours. It has six points of suspension and six for lateral stability. It has an aluminum structure and waterproof skin.

Cocoon Tree kann von drei Personen in drei Stunden aufgebaut werden. Es hat sechs Punkte zur Aufhängung und sechs für die seitliche Stabilität sowie ein Tragwerk aus Aluminium mit einem wasserdichten Überzug.

Cocoon Tree peut être monté par trois personnes en trois heures. Le dispositif est suspendu par six points avec six autres points d'ancrage pour sa stabilité latérale. La structure est en aluminium et la toile est imperméable.

OASIS

Area: 7.4 m² — Client: Puzero Design — Cost: €4000

Oasis is a dome with a diameter and a height of four meters that was inspired by the designer's familiarity with sailing and kites. It features curtains that can be partially drawn, affording its residents a 360° view of the night sky. Vytautas Puzeras says: "I have tried houses on wheels and the houses of Svencelė called containers, but I've always come back to the thought that I don't want to return to square boxes after having spent time in the nature. I understood that I needed to find a new solution to this problem." The dome, which can be folded to fit in a small trailer, can be erected in half a day. The designer says that six people can easily fit inside the structure. "It's for city people who love nature," says Puzeras, "travellers, lovers of sport activities, a solution for a honeymoon, or just having a good time next to the lake." It is a movable and yet private space.

Oasis ist eine Kuppel mit einem Durchmesser und einer Höhe von 4 m, inspiriert von der Vorliebe des Designers für Segelboote und Drachen. Es hat Vorhänge, die zum Teil aufgezogen werden können, damit die Bewohner einen 360-Grad-Ausblick auf den Nachthimmel haben. Vytautas Puzeras sagt dazu: „Ich habe es mit Häusern auf Rädern und den Häusern von Svencelė, die man Container nennt, versucht, aber immer wieder fällt mir auf, dass ich nicht in rechteckige Kisten zurückkehren möchte, nachdem ich Zeit in der Natur verbracht habe. Mir wurde klar, dass ich eine neue Lösung für dieses Problem finden müsste." Die Kuppel kann

The Lithuanian designer Vytautas Puzeras started work on Oasis with the premise that he did not want to be in a square or rectilinear space when approaching nature, so he imagined a round and open dome.

Der litauische Designer Vytautas Puzeras begann seine Arbeit an Oasis unter der Prämisse, dass er so nahe an der Natur nicht in einem quadratischen und rechteckigen Raum sein wollte. Daher entwarf er eine runde und offene Kuppel.

Le designer lituanien Vytautas Puzeras a commencé à travailler sur Oasis en partant du principe qu'il ne voulait pas approcher la nature dans un espace carré ou rectiligne. Il a donc imaginé un dôme rond et ouvert.

zusammengefaltet werden, damit sie in einen kleinen Anhänger passt, und innerhalb eines halben Tages aufgestellt werden. Der Designer sagt, dass sechs Personen leicht darin Platz finden. „Sie ist für Stadtmenschen bestimmt, die die Natur lieben", erklärt Puzeras, „für Reisende, für Sportbegeisterte, eine Lösung für die Hochzeitsreise oder nur für eine schöne Zeit am See." Es ist ein transportabler und dennoch sehr privater Raum.

Oasis est un dôme de 4 mètres de diamètre et de hauteur qui a été inspiré au designer par sa connaissance des voiliers et des cerfs-volants. Les rideaux peuvent être en partie tirés pour offrir une vue du ciel nocturne à 360°. Vytautas Puzeras raconte : « J'ai essayé des maisons à roues et les maisons de Svencelė appelées conteneurs, mais je suis toujours revenu à l'idée que je ne voulais pas retourner dans des cubes après avoir vécu dans la nature. J'ai compris qu'il fallait que je trouve la solution à ce problème. » Le dôme, qui peut être replié et rentre dans une petite remorque, peut être monté en une demi-journée. Le designer affirme que six personnes y tiennent facilement. « Il est destiné aux citadins qui aiment la nature, dit Puzeras, aux voyageurs, aux amateurs d'activités sportives, aux couples en lune de miel ou simplement à ceux qui veulent passer un bon moment à côté du lac. » C'est un espace mobile, mais aussi intime.

The ribbed dome has high
curtains to preserve privacy,
while leaving an open view
to the sky, as seen in the image
to the right.

Die Rippenkuppel hat lange
Vorhänge, um die Privatsphäre
zu schützen, lässt aber, wie
die Abbildung rechts zeigt, den
Blick zum Himmel offen.

Le dôme nervuré est garni de
hauts rideaux qui garantissent
l'intimité de ses occupants
tout en offrant une vue dégagée
sur le ciel, comme on le voit
sur la photo à droite.

With its curtains and transparent structure, Oasis successfully combines two apparently contradictory modes—it is at once a protecting enclosure and an open stage.

Oasis verbindet mit seinen Vorhängen und der transparenten Konstruktion erfolgreich zwei scheinbar widersprüchliche Aspekte – es ist sowohl schützende Hülle als auch offene Bühne.

Avec ses rideaux et sa structure transparente, Oasis combine avec succès deux concepts apparemment contradictoires : c'est à la fois une enveloppe protectrice et une scène ouverte.

ARCHIWORKSHOP
Yang-Pyung [South Korea] — 2013

STACKING DOUGHNUT AND MODULAR FLOW

Area: 35 m² — Client: not disclosed — Cost: not disclosed

These two units are part of a "glamping" (luxurious camping) scheme—also known as Embracing Art and Architecture—imagined by the architects. They explain: "The Stacking Doughnut unit is inspired by pebble stones. The Modular Flow unit is designed as an extendable structure made by juxtaposing modular floor panels." The structures have a UV-resistant, waterproof double-layer membrane skin. Each glamping unit has a toilet with art on the walls, painted by a young Korean artist. The furniture is also designed by ArchiWorkshop and is well suited to the limited interior area. The folding furniture can be used as a sofa during the day and as a bed at night.

Diese beiden Einheiten sind Teil eines Systems für das „Glamping" (luxuriöses Campen) – von den Architekten auch als Vereinigung von Kunst und Architektur bezeichnet. Sie erläutern: „Die Einheit Stacking Doughnut wurde von Kieselsteinen angeregt. Die Einheit Modular Flow wurde als erweiterbare Konstruktion aus aneinandergestellten, modularen Bodenplatten errichtet." Die Bauten sind mit einer UV-resistenten, wasserdichten Doppelhaut versehen. Jede Glamping-Einheit hat eine Toilette mit Wandbildern eines jungen koreanischen Künstlers. Die Möbel wurden ebenfalls von ArchiWorkshop entworfen und passen gut in den begrenzten Innenraum. Das Klappsofa dient nachts als Bett.

Ces deux unités font partie d'un projet de « glamping » (camping chic) imaginé par les architectes, — également qualifié de « rencontre intime de l'art et de l'architecture ». Ils l'expliquent ainsi : « Le Stacking Doughnut s'inspire des galets. Le Modular Flow est conçu comme une structure extensible obtenue en juxtaposant des panneaux de sol modulaires. » Les deux sont revêtus d'une membrane double couche étanche et résistante aux UV. Chaque unité dispose de toilettes aux murs peints par un jeune artiste coréen. Le mobilier, également conçu par ArchiWorkshop, est adapté à l'espace intérieur réduit. Le canapé pliant peut servir de lit .

PVDF (Polyvinylidene difluoride) surface-treated membrane is used for the skin of these units that were conceived in two distinct forms.

Die mit PVDF (Polyvinyliden-fluorid) beschichtete Membran dient als Hülle dieser Einheiten, die in zwei verschiedenen Formen entworfen wurden.

L'enveloppe des deux unités aux deux formes distinctes est une membrane traitée en surface au PVDF (bifluorure de polyvinylidène).

TENTSILE
London [UK] — 2012–

TENTSILE
TREE TENTS

Area: 14.5 m² — Client: various — Cost: $300

Tentsile makes seven different types of hanging tents called Stingray (for three adults), Connect (two adults), Flite+ (2 adults), Vista (for three people), Trillium (three adults), the T-Mini (2 adults), and the Trillium XL. Images here show the Stingray, Connect, and a combination of different models being used in the same location. They are made with polyester and nylon fabrics and can be set up in less than 15 minutes. The Stingray weighs nine kilos and has a "roof" made with tear-resistant insect mesh. It can carry a maximum load of 400 kilos. The Connect weighs just seven kilos and can also carry a load of 400 kilos, or two adults plus all of their gear. Flite+ has a smaller capacity (220kg), but weighs only 3.2 kilos. Each tree tent comes with a waterproof rainfly for protection against the elements. The Trillium is an open-suspended platform with a 400-kilo capacity, supported in trees with 20 meters of automobile seatbelt material.

Tensile produziert sechs verschiedene Arten hängender Zelte namens Stingray (für drei Erwachsene), Connect (zwei Erwachsene), Flite (zwei Erwachsene), Vista (drei Personen), Trillium (drei Erwachsene) und das T-Mini (zwei Erwachsene). Diese Abbildungen zeigen Stingray, Connect und eine Kombination aus verschiedenen Modellen, die am selben Standort genutzt werden. Sie bestehen aus Polyester- und Nylongewebe und können innerhalb von 15 Minuten aufgestellt werden. Stingray wiegt 9 kg und hat ein „Dach" aus einem reißfesten Insektenschutznetz. Es kann eine Maximallast von 400 kg tragen. Connect wiegt nur 7 kg und kann ebenfalls eine Last von bis zu 400 kg oder zwei Erwachsene mit ihrer gesamten Ausrüstung tragen. Flite hat eine geringere Kapazität (220 kg), wiegt aber nur 3,2 kg. Trillium ist eine frei aufgehängte Plattform, die 400 kg tragen kann. Sie wird mit Gurten von 20 m Länge, die aus demselben Material wie Autosicherheitsgurte bestehen, in die Bäume gehängt.

Tentsile propose six modèles de tentes suspendues appelées Stingray (pour trois adultes), Connect (deux adultes), Flite (deux adultes), Vista (trois personnes), Trillium (trois adultes) et T-Mini (deux adultes). On voit ici Stingray, Connect et différents modèles au même endroit. Les tentes sont en tissu polyester et nylon et peuvent être montées en 15 minutes. Le modèle Stingray pèse 9 kilos avec une moustiquaire indéchirable en guise de « toit », et peut supporter une charge maximale de 400 kilos. Connect ne pèse que 7 kilos et peut aussi supporter une charge de 400 kilos, soit deux adultes et tout leur matériel. Flite a une capacité moindre (220 kilos) mais ne pèse que 3,2 kilos. Trillium, enfin, est une plate-forme suspendue ouverte d'une capacité de 400 kilos, accrochée aux arbres par 20 m de ceintures de sécurité automobiles.

The different Tentsile models share an unexpected design and coloring. Left, the Vista model weighs just 10 kilos and can hold up to 400 kilos.

Die unterschiedlichen Modelle von Tentsile haben alle eine ungewöhnliche Form und Farbstellung. Links: Das Modell Vista wiegt nur 10 kg und kann bis zu 400 kg tragen.

Les différents modèles Tentsile ont tous en commun un design et des couleurs originaux. À gauche, le modèle Vista ne pèse que 10 kg et peut contenir jusqu'à 400 kg.

The Flite+ is an an ultralight two-person tree tent. Flite+ can be set up even in dense tree configurations – or among rocks as is the case in the image seen here.

Das Flite+ ist ein Ultraleicht-Zweipersonenzelt für Bäume. Flite+ kann sogar in dichterem Wald installiert werden, oder zwischen Felsen, wie in der Aufnahme hier zu sehen.

Flite+ est une tente ultra-légère pour deux personnes à accrocher dans les arbres. Elle peut être montée même dans les forêts les plus denses - ou fixée à des rochers, comme on le voit ici.

TREE TENT

Area: 4 m² — Client: Tree Tents International — Cost: c. €12 000

The Tree Tent's spherical structure is made from green ash hardwood integrated into a structural aluminum airframe covered with a marine-grade fabric canopy.

Das Tragwerk des kugelförmigen Tree Tent besteht aus dem harten Holz der Grünesche, das in einen Flugzeugrahmen aus Aluminium eingearbeitet und mit einem wasserfesten Stoff bezogen ist.

La structure sphérique de la Tree Tent est en bois dur de frêne de Pennsylvanie inséré dans une cellule structurelle en aluminium et recouvert d'un auvent en tissu de qualité marine.

Tree Tents are lightweight, "hybrid aluminum and steam-bent green ash static airframes" with a cotton canvas skin. They are handmade with laths selected from the same tree. Their use has a minimal impact on trees, and they are designed with "sustainable, recyclable, recycled, and natural materials." These spherical structures are three meters in diameter and can accommodate two adults. The round form allows for even weight distribution on the wooden elements and also encourages rapid water run-off. The Tree Tent weighs 120 kilos, so can easily be transported. Thermal liners made of wool make the use of these suspended pods possible in winter. The designers refer to early zeppelin engineering and also to early lightweight aircraft design to explain their thought process. The Tree Tent concept was initially created by Jason Thawley of the design studio Luminair.

Tree Tents sind leichte, „hybride, statische Flugzeugskelette aus Aluminium und dampfgebogenem Grüneschenholz" mit einer Haut aus Baumwollgewebe. Sie sind handgefertigt mit Zweigen, die als Latten dienen und einzeln aus den Bäumen geschnitten werden, ohne sie zu schädigen. Die Zelte bestehen aus „nachhaltigen, recycelbaren, recycelten und natürlichen Materialien". Diese kugelförmigen Konstruktionen haben einen Durchmesser von 3 m und können zwei Erwachsene aufnehmen. Die runde Form verteilt das Gewicht gleichmäßig auf die hölzernen Elemente und lässt das Wasser schnell ablaufen. Das Tree Tent wiegt 120 kg und ist daher leicht zu transportieren. Durch ein Wärmefutter aus Wolle ist diese aufgehängte Kapsel auch im Winter nutzbar. Die Designer beziehen sich auf die alte Zeppelintechnik und auch auf frühe Leichtflugzeuge, um ihren Gedankengang zu erklären. Das Konzept des Tree Tent stammte ursprünglich von Jason Thawley vom Designstudio Luminair.

Ces tentes dans les arbres sont de légères « cellules fixes hybrides en aluminium et frêne de Pennsylvanie cintré à la vapeur » à revêtement en toile de coton. Produites à la main, avec des lattes issues d'un seul arbre, elles n'ont qu'un impact minimal sur les arbres et sont fabriquées avec des « matériaux durables, recyclables, recyclés et naturels ». Sphériques, elles font trois mètres de diamètre et peuvent accueillir deux adultes. La forme ronde permet une répartition égale du poids sur les éléments en bois et facilite l'écoulement de l'eau. La Tree Tent pèse 120 kilos et peut donc être facilement transportée. Des doublures thermiques en laine permettent son utilisation en hiver. Les designers se sont référés aux premiers dirigeables et aux premiers avions légers. Le concept de tente dans les arbres a été initialement inventé par Jason Thawley, du studio de design Luminair.

The tents have a quilted insulated liner that is available in a number of colors. Other options include a micro wood stove, dimmable LED lighting, skylight, desks, and folding beds.

Die Zelte haben ein gestepptes Isolierfutter, das in verschiedenen Farben lieferbar ist. Zu weiteren Optionen gehören ein kleiner Holzofen, dimmbare LED-Beleuchtung, ein Oberlicht, Tische und Klappbetten.

Les tentes possèdent une doublure capitonnée isolante disponible dans un grand nombre de coloris. Les autres options comprennent un mini-poêle à bois, un éclairage à LED à variateur, des lucarnes, des pontons et des lits pliants.

HOMES
that move

ÁBATON
Madrid [Spain] — 2013

ÁBATON PORTABLE HOME ÁPH80

Area: 27 m² — Client: not disclosed — Cost: not disclosed

The ÁPH80 series was conceived as an ideal home for two, easily transported by road and ready to be placed almost anywhere. The Portable Home includes a living room/kitchen, a full bathroom, and double bedroom. Its gabled roof has an interior height of 3.5 meters. Most of the materials used can be recycled, and the wood comes from managed forests. The exterior is covered with gray cement-wood board. The ventilated façade has 12 centimeters of thermal insulation. The timber structure is manufactured using CNC milling. The inside timber panels are made of white-dyed Spanish fir. The structure takes eight weeks to manufacture and one day to assemble.

Die Serie ÁPH80 wurde als ideales Heim für zwei Personen geplant, das einfach auf der Straße transportiert und fast überall aufgestellt werden kann. Das mobile Haus enthält einen Wohnraum mit Küche, ein voll ausgestattetes Bad und ein Schlafzimmer. Das Satteldach hat eine Innenhöhe von 3,5 m. Fast alle verwendeten Materialien sind recycelbar; das Holz stammt aus nachhaltig bewirtschafteten Wäldern. Das Haus ist außen mit grauen Holzbetonbrettern verkleidet. Die belüftete Fassade hat eine 12 cm starke Wärmedämmung. Die Holzkonstruktion ist mit CNC-Fräsen vorgefertigt. Die Holztafeln der Innenverkleidung sind aus weiß gestrichener spanischer Tanne. Die Konstruktion kann innerhalb von acht Wochen produziert und an einem Tag aufgestellt werden.

La série ÁPH80 a été conçue comme la maison idéale pour deux, facile à transporter par la route et à installer partout. Cette maison portative se compose d'un salon–cuisine, d'une salle de bains complète et d'une chambre double. Son toit à pignon lui donne une hauteur intérieure de 3,5 mètres. La plupart des matériaux utilisés sont recyclables et le bois vient de forêts gérées durablement. L'extérieur est garni de panneaux en bois et béton gris. La façade ventilée dispose de 12 centimètres d'isolation thermique. Elle est construite en bois d'œuvre par découpage à commande numérique. Les panneaux intérieurs en bois sont en sapin d'Espagne teint en blanc. Sa fabrication nécessite huit semaines et son assemblage, une journée.

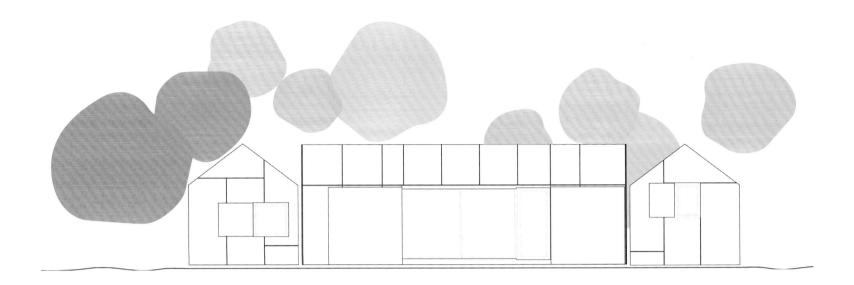

The ÁPH80 is intended to be "basically self-sufficient, transportable by road, and economically affordable."

Das ÁPH80 soll „vor allem autark, auf der Straße transportierbar und finanziell erschwinglich sein".

L'ÁPH80 est conçu pour être « fondamentalement autosuffisant, transportable par la route et économiquement abordable ».

Though the external façade of the house is severe, the interiors are friendly and livable. A plan shows the division into three basic areas.

Trotz der abweisenden Fassade des Hauses ist das Innere freundlich und wohnlich. Der Grundriss zeigt die Aufteilung in drei elementare Bereiche.

La façade de la maison est plutôt austère, mais l'intérieur est convivial et parfaitement habitable. Le plan montre la division en trois zones de base.

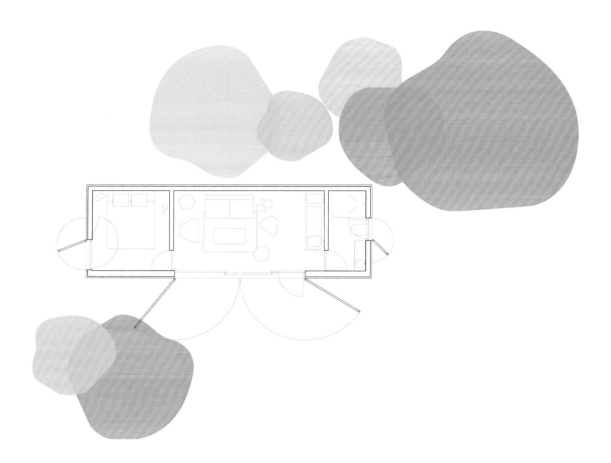

The house can be installed in one day. It is 3×9 meters in size and can readily be transported on a truck. Interiors are in white Spanish pinewood.

Das Haus kann in einem Tag aufgestellt werden. Es ist 3 × 9 m groß und kann problemlos auf einem Lkw transportiert werden. Innen ist es mit weißer spanischer Kiefer verkleidet.

La maison peut être installée en une journée. Sa taille est de 3 × 9 m et elle peut être transportée par camion. L'intérieur est en sapin d'Espagne teint en blanc.

CUBE365

Area: 12 m² — Client: Sierre Tourist Office + local sponsors
Cost: €340 000 (construction)

The Cube365 project was initiated and coordinated by Vincent Courtine, Director of the Sierre Tourist Office, in order to celebrate the 200th anniversary of the entry of the Canton of Valais into the Swiss Confederation in 1815. Imagined like a mobile hotel room, the structure was based on a standard shipping container that was moved once a week to various locations in Valais. Making use of solar panels, the structure was largely self-sufficient in terms of energy and offered a standard of luxury compared by the organizers to a 5-star hotel room. The concept is very similar to that of the Hotel Everland (2002) by the Swiss artists L/B (Sabina Lang and Daniel Baumann), which was placed on top of the Palais de Tokyo in Paris between 2007 and 2009. Containing a bathroom, double bed, and a living area, Cube365 was moved with the assistance of a crane and a truck. The sponsors of Cube365 did not claim that the idea was original, but, by moving this hotel room from one location to another for a full year, they did offer those lucky enough to be able to rent it or to be offered a stay in it a unique opportunity to see Valais from different angles. The project was entirely realized in Valais by local firms.

Das Projekt Cube365 wurde vom Direktor des Tourismusbüros in Siders (Sierre), Vincent Courtine, aus Anlass der 200-Jahr-Feier des Beitritts des Kantons Wallis zur Schweizerischen Eidgenossenschaft 1815 initiiert und koordiniert. Das als mobiles Hotelzimmer gedachte Bauwerk aus einem Standardcontainer wurde in jeder Woche an einen anderen Ort im Wallis gebracht. Es hatte dank Solarpaneelen eine weitgehend autarke Energieversorgung und bot einen Luxusstandard, den die Organisatoren mit dem eines Fünf-Sterne-Hotels verglichen. Das Konzept ähnelt dem des Hotels Everland (2002) der Schweizer Künstler L/B (Sabina Lang

The Cube365 was photographed here in Mollens, Switzerland, at an altitude of just over 1000 meters above sea level.

Der hier fotografierte Cube365 steht in Mollens in der Schweiz auf etwas mehr als 1000 m Höhe.

Cube365 est ici photographié à Mollens, en Suisse, à une altitude de presque 1 000 m.

und Daniel Baumann), das von 2007 bis 2009 auf das Pariser Palais de Tokyo gesetzt worden war. Cube365 enthielt ein Bad, ein Doppelbett und einen Wohnbereich und wurde mithilfe eines Krans und eines Lastwagens bewegt. Die Sponsoren von Cube365 erhoben nicht den Anspruch, ihre Idee sei besonders originell, aber durch die Veränderung des Standorts über ein ganzes Jahr boten sie jenen, die das Glück hatten, es mieten zu können, oder die zu einem Aufenthalt darin eingeladen wurden, die einmalige Gelegenheit, das Wallis aus verschiedenen Blickwinkeln zu sehen. Das Projekt wurde vollständig von Walliser Firmen ausgeführt.

Le projet Cube365 a été initié et coordonné par Vincent Courtine, directeur de l'office du tourisme de Sierre, pour célébrer le 200e anniversaire de l'entrée du canton du Valais dans la Confédération suisse en 1815. Conçue comme une chambre d'hôtel mobile, la structure est basée sur un conteneur maritime standard qui a changé toutes les semaines de lieu d'implantation dans le canton. Les panneaux solaires l'ont rendue largement autosuffisante sur le plan énergétique et elle a atteint un niveau de luxe que les créateurs ont comparé à une chambre d'hôtel 5 étoiles. Le concept ressemble beaucoup à celui de l'hôtel Everland (2002) des artistes suisses L/B (Sabina Lang et Daniel Baumann) qui a occupé le toit du Palais de Tokyo, à Paris, de 2007 à 2009. Cube365 contient une salle de bains, un lit double et un espace séjour ; il est transporté au moyen d'une grue et d'un camion. Les sponsors n'ont pas prétendu que l'idée était originale, mais en déplaçant leur chambre d'hôtel pendant un an, ils ont offert à ceux qui ont la chance de pouvoir le louer ou se le faire offrir un séjour et une occasion unique de voir le Valais sous différents angles. Le projet a été entièrement réalisé dans le Valais par des entreprises locales.

Inside the house, the most obvious feature is the view through the "Dragon's Eye." In the background, the rotating bed for two. At the top of the image, a glimpse of the gridshell roof.

Das auffälligste Merkmal im Inneren des Hauses ist der Blick durch das „Drachenauge". Im Hintergrund das rotierende Doppelbett. Oben: Ein Stück des Gitterschalendachs.

À l'intérieur, ce qui frappe d'emblée, c'est la vue par l'« œil du dragon ». À l'arrière-plan, le lit rotatif pour deux personnes et au-dessus, un aperçu de la toiture en gridshell.

ECOCAPSULE

Area: 6.3 m² — Client: various
Cost: not disclosed

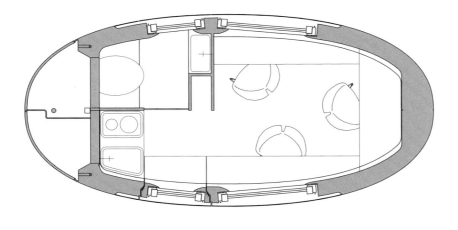

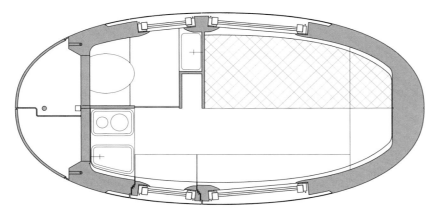

The ovoid shape of the Eco-capsule is both aesthetically pleasing and practical in terms of the maximization of the use of space.

Die ovale Form der Ecocapsule ist sowohl ästhetisch ansprechend als auch praktisch, weil sie die Nutzfläche vergrößert.

La forme ovoïde de l'Ecocapsule est à la fois esthétiquement agréable et pratique en termes d'optimisation de l'espace.

Ecocapsule is a self-sustainable intelligent micro-home that uses solar and wind energy. It allows people to live in remote places out of reach of infrastructure, while retaining a high level of living comfort. It can be used as a cottage, a pop-up hotel, caravan, or even as a charging station for electric cars. The ellipsoid shape of Ecocapsule is designed to maximize the collection of rainwater and dew. The design of the outer shell also minimizes energy loss. Hollow walls filled with highly efficient thermal insulation protect inhabitants from harsh environments and help achieve a performance almost on the level of a passive house. The Ecocapsule is optimized for easy transportation. It can fit into a standard shipping container. A specially designed trailer enables transport of the Ecocapsule with a passenger car, turning it into a fully functional caravan. In an urban environment, the small dwelling can readily be placed on a rooftop. The Ecocapsule is 4.7 meters long, 2.2 meters wide and 2.5 meters tall (5.2 meters tall with the extended wind turbine pole). The capsule weighs 1300 kilos when empty and 1700 kilos with full water tanks. The wind turbine provides approximately 750W, the solar panels on the rooftop around 600W. The battery capacity is 9 kWh. The Ecocapsule body is made of fiberglass, overlaid on a steel frame and filled with polyurethane foam insulation.

Ecocapsule ist ein autarkes, intelligentes Mikrohaus, das Solar- und Windenergie nutzt. Darin können Menschen an entlegenen Standorten leben, ohne auf hohen einen hohen Wohnkomfort verzichten zu müssen. Es kann als Hütte, als Pop-up-Hotel, als Wohnwagen, sogar als Ladestation für Elektroautos dienen. Die Kugelform von Ecocapsule soll die Aufnahme von Regen- und Tauwasser maximieren. Die Außenhaut minimiert zugleich den Energieverbrauch. Hohlwände mit hocheffizienter thermischer Isolierung schützen die Bewohner vor Kälte und tragen zu einer Leistung fast wie der eines Passivhauses bei. Die Ecocapsule ist leicht zu transportieren, sie passt in einen normalen Container. Auf einem speziell dafür entworfenen Anhänger kann die Ecocapsule von einem Personenwagen gezogen werden und wird so zu einem voll funktionsfähigen Wohnwagen. Im städtischen Umfeld kann die kleine Wohneinheit auch auf einem Dach aufgestellt werden. Die Ecocapsule ist 4,7 m lang, 2,2 m breit und 2,5 m hoch (5,2 m hoch mit ausgefahrenem Windturbinenmast). Die Kapsel wiegt leer 1300 kg und 1700 kg, wenn die Wassertanks gefüllt sind. Das Windrad liefert etwa 750 Watt, die Solarmodule auf dem Dach produzieren ungefähr 600 Watt. Die Kapazität der Batterie beträgt 9 kWh. Das Gehäuse der Ecocapsule besteht aus Glasfaser über einem Stahlskelett und ist mit einer Polyurethanschaumfüllung isoliert.

Ecocapsule est une micro-maison intelligente et autosuffisante qui exploite l'énergie solaire et éolienne. Elle permet de vivre dans les endroits les plus isolés, hors de toute infrastructure, en conservant un niveau élevé de confort. Elle peut servir de cottage, d'hôtel éphémère, de caravane, ou même de station de chargement de véhicules électriques. Sa forme sphérique a été imaginée pour optimiser la récupération de l'eau de pluie et de la rosée. De même, le design de la coque extérieure permet de minimiser les pertes d'énergie. Les murs creux remplis d'isolant thermique à efficacité élevée protègent les occupants des milieux les plus difficiles et contribuent au rendement de la structure, presque égal à celui d'une maison passive. L'Ecocapsule a également été optimisée pour un transport facile. Elle rentre dans un conteneur maritime standard. Une remorque spécialement conçue lui permet d'être tractée par un véhicule de tourisme, ce qui en fait une caravane parfaitement fonctionnelle. Dans un environnement urbain, c'est un petit logement qui peut parfaitement être placé sur un toit. L'Ecocapsule est longue de 4,7 mètres, large de 2,2 mètres et haute de 2,5 mètres (5,2 mètres avec le piquet de l'éolienne rétractable). Elle pèse 1300 kilos vide et 1700 kilos lorsque les réservoirs d'eau sont pleins. L'éolienne fournit environ 750 W, les panneaux solaires sur le toit environ 600 W. La capacité de la batterie est de 9 kWh. Le corps de l'Ecocapsule est en fibre de verre sur une structure en acier, remplie de mousse polyuréthane isolante.

KENGO KUMA
Kyoto [Japan] — 2012

HOJO-AN

Area: 9 m² — Client: not disclosed — Cost: not disclosed
Collaboration: Ejiri Structural Engineering

Kamono Chomei (1155–1216), the author of *Hojo-ki* (*An Account of My Hut*), lived in a movable house that is often described as the prototype of Japan's compact housing. This project aimed to reconstruct his house with modern ideas and methods, on the same site in the precinct of the Shimogamo Jinja Shrine. The word *hojo* implies a small cottage approximately 3 × 3 meters in size. Kengo Kuma employed ETFE sheets that can be rolled up, making the structure portable. Cedar strips combined with powerful magnets were used to create a "kind of tensegrity structure" that, when combined into a single unit, forms a "hard box."

Kamo no Chomei (1155–1216), der Autor von *Hojo-ki* (*Aufzeichnungen aus meiner Hütte*) lebte in einem beweglichen Haus, das oft als Prototyp der kompakten japanischen Wohnhäuser beschrieben wird. Dieses Projekt hatte zum Ziel, sein Haus nach modernen Vorstellungen und Methoden auf demselben Grundstück im Bezirk des Schreins Shimogamo Jinja zu rekonstruieren. Das Wort *hojo* bezeichnet eine kleine, etwa 3 × 3 m große Hütte. Kengo Kuma verwendete ETFE-Folien, die aufgerollt werden können und das Haus so tragbar machen. Aus Zedernholzlatten und starken Magneten wurde „eine Art Tensegrity-Struktur" geschaffen, die, wenn alle Teile zu einer geschlossenen Einheit verbunden werden, eine „stabile Kiste" bilden.

Kamono Chomei (1155–1216), l'auteur de *Hojo-ki* (*Notes de ma cabane de moine*), habitait une maison mobile souvent décrite comme le prototype du logement japonais compact. Le projet était de reconstruire cette maison sur le même site, dans l'enceinte du sanctuaire Shimogamo Jinja, avec des idées et des méthodes modernes. Le mot *hojo* désigne une petite maison rurale d'approximativement 3 × 3 mètres. Kengo Kuma a eu recours à des feuilles d'EFTE qui peuvent être roulées pour rendre la structure portative. Des bandes de cèdre associées à de puissants aimants créent une « structure de tenségrité » qui, assemblée en une entité unique, forme une « boîte rigide ».

A sleeping area and a tiny tea room occupy the center of the plan that also includes a study table and a small verandah.

Ein Schlafraum und ein kleiner Teeraum liegen im Zentrum des Grundrisses, der auch einen Arbeitstisch und eine kleine Veranda zeigt.

Un espace couchage et un minuscule salon occupent le centre du plan, qui comporte aussi une table de travail et une petite véranda.

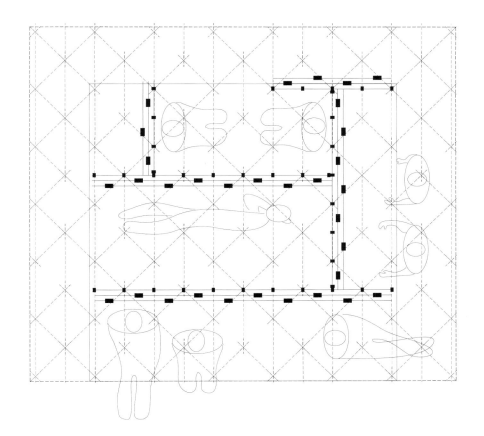

Though they appear from a distance to form a regular grid, the strips of cedar that make up the actual structure have some gaps that make its appearance even lighter.

Die Zedernholzleisten, die das eigentliche Tragwerk bilden, haben Lücken, die es noch leichter erscheinen lassen – auch wenn sie aus der Entfernung wie ein geschlossenes Gitter wirken.

Bien qu'elles semblent former un maillage régulier vues de loin, les bandes de cèdre de la structure présentent des discontinuités qui la font paraître encore plus légère.

NATIONAL AERONAUTICS AND SPACE ADMINISTRATION (NASA)
1998–2016 (ongoing)

INTERNATIONAL SPACE STATION

Mass: 419 455 kg (2015) | Length: 72.8 m | Width: 108.5 m | Collaboration: National Aeronautics and Space Administration (NASA), European Space Agency (ESA), Russian Federal Space Agency (RKA), Japanese Aerospace Exploration Agency (JAXA), and Canadian Space Agency (CSA)

Intended as an international research facility for the study of biology, chemistry, physics, astronomy, or meteorology, the ISS is by far the largest artificial satellite ever to have orbited the earth. There has been continual human presence on the ISS since October 31, 2000. The first module of the station was launched by Russia (Zarya, November 20, 1998), with the first US Space Shuttle visit occurring two weeks later. Work on the station was paused for two years due to the destruction of the Space Shuttle Columbia in 2003. By late 2016, 198 space walks had been necessary for the maintenance and assembly of the ISS. Travelling at approximately 27 750 kilometers per hour, the ISS orbits the earth 15.7 times per day. Due to the international organization required for the ISS, the obligations and rights of participants were established by the Space Station Intergovernmental Agreement (IGA, 1998). Because it is designed for the environment of outer space, the ISS has taken on a very particular form made up of modules conceived in different countries. The astronaut Jeff Williams holds the record for the longest stay on board the ISS—534 days. News about the ISS can be read on: http://www.nasa.gov/mission_pages/station/main/index.html
http://www.nasa.gov/externalflash/ISSRG/index.html

Die als internationale Forschungsstation zum Studium der Biologie, Chemie, Physik, Astronomie oder Meteorologie vorgesehene ISS ist mit Abstand der größte künstliche Satellit, der jemals die Erde umkreist hat. Seit dem 31. Oktober 2000 lebten immer wieder Menschen in ihr. Das erste Modul der Station wurde von Russland (Zarya, 20. November 1998) ins All geschickt, das erste US Space Shuttle stattete ihr zwei Wochen später einen Besuch ab. Die Arbeit der Station wurde für zwei Jahre ausgesetzt, nachdem die Raumfähre Columbia 2003 verunglückt war. Bis Ende 2016 sind 198 Weltraumspaziergänge zur Wartung und Montage der ISS erforderlich gewesen. Sie legt etwa 27 750 km/h zurück und umkreist die Erde 15,7-mal täglich. Weil internationale Organisationen für die ISS zuständig sind, wurden die Verpflichtungen und Rechte der Beteiligten im Space Station Intergovernmental Agreement (IGA, 1998) festgelegt. Die ISS wurde für den Aufenthalt im Weltraum geplant und hat daher eine ganz spezielle Form, zusammengesetzt aus Modulen, die in verschiedenen Ländern entworfen wurden. Der Astronaut Jeff Williams hält den Rekord des längsten Aufenthalts an Bord der ISS – 534 Tage.

Destinée à accueillir un centre international de recherches pour l'étude de la biologie, de la chimie, de la physique, de l'astronomie ou de la météorologie, l'ISS est de loin le plus grand satellite artificiel à avoir tourné en orbite autour de la Terre. La présence humaine y est permanente depuis le 31 octobre 2000. Le premier module de la station a été lancé par la Russie (Zarya, 20 novembre 1998) et la première visite de la navette spatiale américaine a eu lieu deux semaines plus tard. Le travail à la station a été interrompu pendant deux ans après la destruction de la navette Columbia en 2003. Fin 2016, 198 sorties dans l'espace avaient été nécessaires pour la maintenance et l'assemblage de l'ISS. Elle se déplace à environ 27 750 kilomètre à l'heure et décrit 15,7 orbites par jour autour de la Terre. En raison de l'organisation internationale que cela suppose, les droits et obligations des participants ont été fixés dans l'Accord intergouvernemental sur la station spatiale (IGA, 1998). Conçue pour le milieu spatial, la station présente une forme très particulière faite de modules réalisés dans différents pays. L'astronaute Jeff Williams détient le record du séjour le plus long à bord de l'ISS après y avoir passé 534 jours.

Left page, the ISS over the Caspian Sea on May 16, 2006, photographed by the American shuttle Discovery. Below, the partially assembled structure seen in 1998.

Linke Seite: Die ISS über dem Kaspischen Meer am 16. Mai 2000, fotografiert aus dem amerikanischen Shuttle Discovery. Unten: Die teilmontierte Konstruktion 1998.

Page de gauche, l'ISS au-dessus de la mer Caspienne le 16 mai 2006, photographiée par la navette américaine Discovery. Ci-dessous, la structure partiellement assemblée en 1998.

Above, Expedition 37 astronauts, 2013. Below, astronaut Tracy Caldwell Dyson, 2010. Left, Dan Burbank and Anton Shkaplero playing music onboard the ISS, Expedition 29, 2011.

Oben: Die Astronauten der Expedition 37, 2013. Unten: Astronautin Tracy Caldwell Dyson, 2010. Links: Dan Burbank und Anton Shkaplero machen Musik an Bord der ISS, Expedition 29, 2011.

Ci-dessus, les astronautes de l'expédition 37, 2013. Ci-dessous, l'astronaute Tracy Caldwell Dyson, 2010. À gauche, Dan Burbank et Anton Shkaplero en train de jouer de la musique à bord de l'ISS, expédition 29, 2011.

MATTHEW BUTCHER, OWAIN WILLIAMS, AND KIERAN THOMAS WARDLE
Along Hadrian's Wall, northern England [UK] — 2016

MANSIO

Area: 13 m² — Client: Hexham Book Festival and Arts&Heritage in association with Peter Sharpe, curator for Kielder Art and Architecture Program — Cost: €58 250 — Collaboration: Engineered by Structure Mode, London

The Mansio is a mobile space for writers, poets, and thinkers that toured along Hadrian's Wall, which is a World Heritage Site, in 2016. Its name references the *mansio* that were official resting places along Roman roads. According to the architects: "The design can be seen as a 'mobile ruin,' and references northern England's historic and industrial remains. It appeared like a translucent ghost among the traces of the past armies and inhabitants from all over the Roman world who occupied the trading posts, forts, and settlements of this remote border landscape." The Mansio was funded by Arts Council England Strategic Touring, Active Northumberland and contributions from partners: English Heritage, Northumberland National Park, Queen's Hall Arts, Tyne & Wear Museums, Senhouse Museum, and Vindolanda Trust. The structure was made of steel, polycarbonate, wood wool, and OSB board.

Das Mansio ist ein mobiler Wohnraum für Schriftsteller, Poeten und Denker, die 2016 den Hadrianswall, ein Weltkulturerbe, entlangreisten. Mansio hießen die offiziellen Rastplätze an römischen Straßen. Laut Erklärung der Architekten „kann man den Entwurf als ‚mobile Ruine' und als Bezugnahme auf Nordenglands historische und industrielle bauliche Überreste betrachten. Mansio erschien wie ein lichtdurchlässiger Geist auf den Spuren vergangener Armeen und Bewohner aus dem ganzen Römischen Reich, die die Handelsniederlassungen, Forts und Siedlungen dieses entlegenen Grenzlands bevölkerten." Finanziert wurde das Mansio von Arts Council England Strategic Touring, Active Northumberland und mit Beiträgen folgender Partner: English Heritage, Northumberland National Park, Queen's Hall Arts, Tyne & Wear Museums, Senhouse Museum und Vindolanda Trust. Das Gebäude bestand aus Stahl, Polykarbonat, Holzwolle und OSB-Platten.

Le Mansio est un espace mobile pour écrivains, poètes et penseurs qui s'est déplacé le long du mur d'Hadrien, site inscrit au Patrimoine mondial de l'humanité en 2016. Son nom fait référence aux *mansio*, ces relais officiels installés le long des voies romaines. Selon les architectes, « on peut en voir le design comme une "ruine mobile" qui évoque aussi les vestiges historiques et industriels du nord de l'Angleterre. Il surgit tel un fantôme translucide sur les traces des légions romaines et des habitants du monde romain qui peuplaient les comptoirs, les forts et les colonies de cette région frontalière éloignée ». Le Mansio a été financé par Arts Council England Strategic Touring, Active Northumberland et des contributions des partenaires English Heritage, Northumberland National Park, Queen's Hall Arts, Tyne & Wear Museums, Senhouse Museum et Vindolanda Trust. La structure est en acier, polycarbonate, laine de bois et panneau OSB.

Above, the structure photographed in South Shields, England. Below, an axonometric drawing of it.

Oben: Das Bauwerk, fotografiert in South Shields, England. Unten: Axonometrische Zeichnung.

Ci-dessus, la structure photographiée à South Shields, en Angleterre. Ci-dessous, schéma axonométrique.

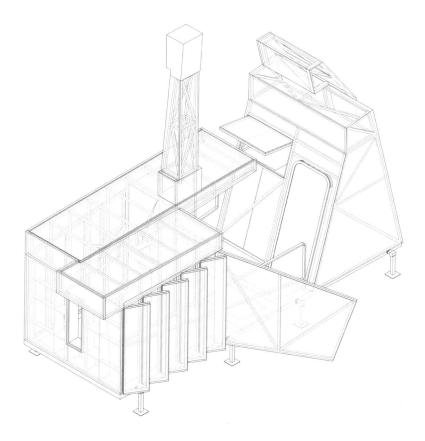

Right, two interior views of the structure with its operable openings visible. The interior is as white and "ghost-like" as the exterior.

Rechts: Zwei Innenansichten des Gebäudes zeigen, wie sich die Seiten öffnen lassen. Das Haus ist innen ebenso weiß und „gespenstisch" wie außen.

À droite, deux vues intérieures montrant les ouvertures réglables. L'intérieur est aussi blanc et « fantomatique » que l'extérieur.

MARS ONE

Area: 200 m² — Client: Mars One — Cost: $6 billion

The architecture of the Mars outpost consists of six lander modules and two elongated inflatable volumes, which will provide about 200 square meters for food production and living. The interior design of the modules is not complete, but will necessarily provide for everyday tasks and "the entire life cycle for a human being and crew." The organizers of the project state: "A great deal of flexibility has to be integrated into the interior design, making changes possible for special occasions or new situations in life. Dedicated interior areas and functionalities will be chosen for initial prototyping and evaluated during astronaut training." The organizers are quite frank about the nature of this program, saying: "There is no way to go back; going to Mars is a decision that you make for the rest of your life. The technology for a return mission does not yet exist."

Die Architektur der Mars-Außenstation besteht aus sechs Landemodulen und zwei lang gestreckten, aufblasbaren Volumen, die etwa 200 m² Fläche für die Lebensmittelproduktion und zum Wohnen bieten. Die Innenausstattung der Module ist noch nicht komplett, wird aber natürlich alles für den täglichen Ablauf und „den gesamten Lebenszyklus eines Menschen und einer Besatzung" enthalten. Die Organisatoren des Projekts erklären: „Die Innengestaltung muss sehr flexibel sein und Veränderungen im Fall besonderer Umstände oder neuer Lebenssituationen möglich machen. Für die ersten Prototypen werden bestimmte Innenbereiche und Funktionalitäten ausgewählt, die während der Ausbildung der Astronauten evaluiert werden." Die Organisatoren sprechen ganz offen über dieses Programm: „Es gibt keinen Weg zurück; die Fahrt zum Mars ist eine Entscheidung, die man für den Rest seines Lebens trifft. Eine Rückreise ist technisch nicht möglich."

L'architecture de l'avant-poste sur Mars se compose de six modules d'atterrissage et de deux volumes allongés gonflables qui offriront environ 200 mètres carrés d'espace pour produire la nourriture et vivre. L'aménagement intérieur des modules n'est pas encore achevé, mais il permettra nécessairement les travaux quotidiens et « le cycle de vie entier d'un être humain et d'un équipage ». Les concepteurs du projet l'affirment : « L'aménagement intérieur doit comporter une bonne dose de souplesse et permettre les changements dans des circonstances particulières ou en cas de situations inédites. Des espaces et fonctionnalités dédiés seront sélectionnés pour un prototype initial et testés pendant la formation des astronautes. » Ils abordent ouvertement la nature du programme : « Le retour est impossible ; aller sur Mars est une décision que vous prendrez pour le reste de votre vie. Il n'existe aucune technologie pour une mission de retour. »

Above, A rendering of Mars One's life-support modules. Below, a rendering of the exploratory Mars lander, to be built by Lockheed Martin and based in part on the 2007 NASA Phoenix mission.

Oben: Eine Darstellung der Lebenserhaltungsmodule von Mars One. Unten: So könnte die Raumsonde zur Erforschung des Mars aussehen, die von Lockheed Martin gebaut werden soll und teilweise auf der Mission Phoenix der NASA aus dem Jahr 2007 basiert.

Ci-dessus, représentation des modules de vie de Mars One. Ci-dessous, illustration de l'atterrisseur exploratoire de Mars, qui doit être construit par Lockheed Martin et basé en partie sur la mission Phoenix de la NASA en 2007.

An indoor farm for growing and harvesting foods is part of the scheme. Below, a rendering of a possible configuration of living quarters within Mars One.

Ein Indoor-Feld zum Anbau von Lebensmitteln ist Teil des Entwurfs. Unten: Darstellung einer möglichen Einrichtung des Wohnbereichs von Mars One.

Le projet comporte une ferme intérieure pour cultiver la nourriture. Ci-dessous, représentation d'une configuration possible des quartiers d'habitation de Mars One.

LOT-EK
[USA] — 2003

M.D.U. MOBILE DWELLING UNIT

Area: 46.5 m² — Client: Chris Scoates, Curator, UCSB Art Museum — Cost: not disclosed

A single standard shipping container was transformed into a Mobile Dwelling Unit by the architects. By making cuts in the metal walls of the container they created living, working, and storage volumes that can be pushed back into the basic container form during transport. The concept is intended to be used on a large scale, taking advantage of the vertical harbors that could be created in any large city. These harbors are multiple level steel racks with 2.4-meter-wide openings for the containers. Stairs, elevators, power, data, water, and sewage facilities are provided, making the harbor into a constantly changing apartment structure. The M.D.U. was exhibited at the Whitney Museum of American Art (New York), the Walker Art Center (Milwaukee), and the Art Museum UCSB (Santa Barbara).

Ein einzelner genormter Container wurde von den Architekten zu einer mobilen Wohneinheit umgebaut. Durch Einschnitte in die Metallwand des Containers schufen sie Räume zum Wohnen, Arbeiten und Lagern, die für den Transport in die Grundform zurückgeschoben werden können. Das Konzept ist zur Verwendung in großer Anzahl vorgesehen und soll vertikale Häfen nutzen, die in jeder großen Stadt angelegt werden könnten. Diese Häfen sind vielgeschossige Stahlgestelle mit 2,4 m breiten Öffnungen für die Container. Treppen, Aufzüge, Energie, Daten, Wasser und Sanitäreinrichtungen sind dort verfügbar und machen den Hafen zu einem sich ständig verändernden Wohngebäude. Die M. D. U. wurde im Whitney Museum of American Art (New York), dem Walker Art Center (Milwaukee) und dem Art Museum UCSB (Santa Barbara) ausgestellt.

Les architectes ont transformé un simple conteneur maritime en une unité mobile d'habitation. Des coupes pratiquées dans les parois métalliques ont permis de créer des volumes salon, travail et rangement qui sont repoussés à l'intérieur du conteneur pour les transports. Le concept est destiné à s'étendre à grande échelle pour tirer profit des ports verticaux qui pourraient être créés dans toutes les grandes villes et former des « étagères » en acier à niveaux multiples aux ouvertures larges de 2,4 mètres pour les conteneurs. L'ensemble dispose d'escaliers, d'ascenseurs, de branchements électriques, de systèmes de gestion des données, d'eau et d'évacuation des eaux usées, ce qui fait du port une structure d'habitat en perpétuel changement. La M.D.U a été exposée au Whitney Museum of American Art (New York), au Walker Art Center (Milwaukee) et à l'Art Museum UCSB (Santa Barbara).

Right, the M.D.U. installed in front of New York's Whitney Museum of American Art (now Met Modern). The interior is fabricated with plywood and plastic-coated plywood.

Rechts: Die M. D. U., aufgestellt vor dem Whitney Museum of American Art (jetzt Met Modern) in New York; das Innere ist mit Furnier und kunststoffbeschichtetem Sperrholz ausgestattet.

À droite, la M.D.U devant le Whitney Museum of American Art (désormais Met Modern) à New York. L'intérieur est en contreplaqué et contreplaqué recouvert de plastique.

Below, in plan and above in a general image, the kitchen is in the foreground, and the bed and shower and toilet at the far end of the image and to the right of the drawing.

Unten im Grundriss und oben als Gesamtansicht die Küche im Vordergrund sowie dahinter Bett, Dusche und Toilette (auf dem Plan rechts).

Sur le plan ci-dessous et la photo ci-dessus, la cuisine est au premier plan, le lit, la douche et les toilettes à l'autre extrémité de l'image et à droite sur le schéma.

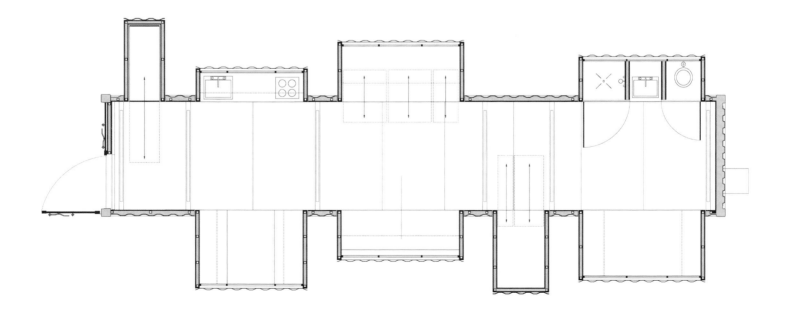

Right, shower, sink and toilet. Below, a seating area with punched-out windows. The red surfaces are in plastic-coated plywood.

Rechts: Dusche, Waschbecken und Toilette. Unten: Sitzbereich mit auskragendem Fenster. Die roten Flächen sind aus kunststoffbeschichtetem Sperrholz.

À droite, douche, lavabo et toilettes. Ci-dessous, espace assis aux fenêtres découpées. Les surfaces rouges sont en contreplaqué recouvert de plastique.

MIMA LIGHT

Area: 32 m² — Client: not disclosed — Cost: not disclosed

The architects do not hesitate to compare this transportable house to the minimalist sculpture of Don Judd, or Robert Morris. Each unit contains cooking and living areas, sleeping accommodation, and bathroom facilities. Glass façades open to allow for air circulation and electricity is distributed from a central core wall. An electric boiler functioning with solar panels can provide hot water. These homes are manufactured by Portilame in a warehouse in Viana do Castelo, before they are transported on site. MIMA Light is available in four sizes, ranging from 7.2 meters to 13.2 meters in length. The architects envisage its use as a vacation home, or temporary housing. The interiors are clad in pine with chrome details. Materials used include glulam timber, cross-laminated timber, Stacbond composite panels, and Antelio solar control glass.

Die Architekten haben keinerlei Hemmungen, dieses transportable Wohnhaus mit den minimalistischen Skulpturen von Donald Judd oder Robert Morris zu vergleichen. Jede Einheit enthält einen Wohnraum sowie Bereiche zum Kochen, Schlafen und ein Bad. Die gläsernen Fassaden können zur Belüftung geöffnet werden; die Elektrizität wird von einer zentralen Wand aus verteilt. Für Warmwasser sorgt ein Elektroboiler, der mithilfe von Solarpaneelen gespeist wird. Diese Häuser werden in einer Lagerhalle von der Firma Portilame in Viana do Castelo produziert und dann zum Standort transportiert. MIMA Light ist in vier Größen lieferbar, in Längen von 7,2 bis 13,2 m. Die Architekten sehen eine Nutzung als Ferienhaus oder als temporäre Unterkunft vor. Die Innenräume sind mit Kiefernholz verkleidet und mit Armaturen aus Chrom ausgestattet. Weitere verwendete Materialien sind Brettschichtholz, Kreuzlagenholz, Stacbond-Verbundplatten und Sonnenschutzglas von Antelio.

Les architectes n'hésitent pas à comparer leur maison transportable à la sculpture minimaliste de Donald Judd ou de Robert Morris. Chaque unité contient des espaces cuisine et séjour, un couchage et une salle de bains équipée. Les façades de verre s'ouvrent pour faire circuler l'air et l'électricité est distribuée à partir d'un mur central. Un chauffe-eau électrique couplé à des panneaux solaires fournit l'eau chaude. Les maisons sont fabriquées par Portilame dans un entrepôt de Viana do Castelo, puis transportées sur place. MIMA Light est disponible en quatre tailles, de 7,2 à 13,2 mètres. Les architectes l'envisagent comme un logement de vacances ou temporaire. L'intérieur est revêtu de pin avec des détails chromés. Différents matériaux sont utilisés, parmi lesquels le bois d'œuvre lamellé collé, le bois d'œuvre lamellé croisé, les panneaux composites Stacbond et le verre à couche de contrôle solaire Antelio.

With its mirrored base, the structure, whose design was inspired by the work of Minimalist artists like Don Judd, appears to literally float in the air above an undisturbed natural setting.

Das Bauwerk mit seiner verspiegelten Basis, angeregt vom Werk minimalistischer Künstler wie Donald Judd, scheint wirklich in der Luft über unberührter Natur zu schweben.

Avec sa base en miroirs, la structure dont le design s'inspire de l'œuvre d'artistes minimalistes comme Donald Judd semble flotter dans les airs au-dessus d'un décor naturel intact.

Photographed here in Vila Praia de Âncora in northern Portugal, the house is based on a modular concept that offers clients numerous options.

Dieses in Villa Praia de Âncora im Norden Portugals fotografierte Haus basiert auf einem modularen Konzept, das seinen Käufern viele Optionen bietet.

Photographiée à Vila Praia de Âncora, dans le nord du Portugal, la maison est basée sur un concept modulaire qui permet de multiples options.

The plan below shows the house with nine installed modules and a total area of 32.4 square meters.

Der Grundriss unten zeigt das aus neun Modulen zusammengesetzte Haus mit einer Gesamtfläche von 32,4 m².

Le plan ci-dessous montre la maison avec neuf modules installés pour une surface totale de 32,4 m².

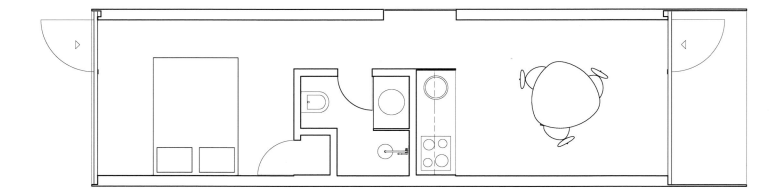

MINI LIVING – BREATHE

Area: 80 m² — Client: MINI — Cost: not disclosed

Breathe is a housing prototype "for the future living environment." The version created for the Salone del Mobile 2017 creates a living area for up to three people on an unused 50-square-meter urban plot. The prototype measures 5 × 8.25 × 10.3 meters. It has a ground-floor kitchen, with three levels of living space above. A modular metal frame forms its basic structure, and a flexible, light-permeable outer skin of light textile creates the boundary between inside and outside. This translucent skin has a special coating that filters and neutralizes the air. A total of six potential rooms and a roof garden provide space for both collective and private areas. Designed to be disassembled and reinstalled at other locations, the structure is mobile and adaptable. The fabric can be replaced to perform appropriately to a wide array of climates and environmental conditions. MINI LIVING is an initiative launched in 2016 as a creative platform for MINI to develop architectural solutions for future urban living spaces. MINI LIVING – Breathe is the third installation created as part of the initiative.

Breathe ist ein Wohnungsprototyp „für das Wohnumfeld der Zukunft". Die für den Salone del Mobile geplante Version ist ein Wohnbereich für bis zu drei Personen auf einem 50 m² großen, unbebauten städtischen Grundstück. Der Prototyp ist 5 x 8,25 x 10,3 m groß, hat eine Küche im Erdgeschoss und darüber drei Ebenen Wohnfläche. Die Grundkonstruktion ist ein Standard-Metallskelett, und eine flexible, lichtdurchlässige Außenhaut aus leichtem Gewebe bildet die Grenze zwischen innen und außen. Diese durchscheinende Haut hat eine spezielle Beschichtung, die die Luft filtert und neutralisiert. Bis zu insgesamt sechs Zimmer und ein Dachgarten bieten Raum für kollektive und private Bereiche. Das Gebäude ist mobil und anpassbar, zur Montage und Demontage an beliebigen Standorten geeignet. Das Gewebe kann auch durch andere ersetzt werden, die sich für besondere klimatische Umgebungen und Bedingungen eignen. MINI LIVING ist eine 2016 gestartete Initiative als kreative Plattform von MINI, um architektonische Lösungen für zukünftigen städtischen Wohnraum zu entwickeln. MINI LIVING – Breathe ist die dritte Installation dieser Initiative.

Breathe est un prototype d'habitation « pour un milieu de vie futur ». La version créée pour le Salone del Mobile 2017 peut loger jusqu'à trois personnes sur un terrain urbain inoccupé de 50 mètres carrés. Elle mesure 5 x 8,25 x 10,3 mètres. La cuisine, au rez-de-chaussée, est surmontée de trois niveaux d'espaces d'habitation. Un cadre métallique modulaire forme la base de la structure, tandis qu'une enveloppe extérieure en tissu léger, souple et perméable à la lumière, trace la frontière entre intérieur et extérieur. Cette « peau » translucide est couverte d'un revêtement spécifique qui filtre et neutralise l'air. Un total de six pièces potentielles et un jardin sur le toit offrent l'espace nécessaire à des usages collectifs ou privés. Conçue pour être désassemblée et réinstallée ailleurs, la structure est mobile et adaptable. Le tissu peut être remplacé pour convenir à de nombreux climats et environnements différents. L'initiative MINI LIVING a été lancée en 2016 comme une plate-forme de créativité permettant à MINI de développer des solutions architecturales pour les futurs espaces de vie urbains. MINI LIVING – Breathe est la troisième installation créée dans le cadre de cette initiative.

This installation creates a living area for up to three people on a previously unused 50-square-meter urban plot.

Diese Zusammenstellung bildet einen Wohnbereich für bis zu drei Personen auf einem vorher ungenutzten, 50 m² großen städtischen Bauplatz.

L'installation donne naissance à un espace d'habitation qui peut accueillir jusqu'à trois personnes sur une parcelle urbaine de 50 m² inutilisée auparavant.

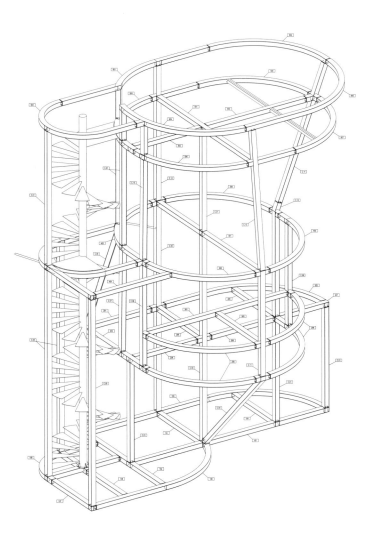

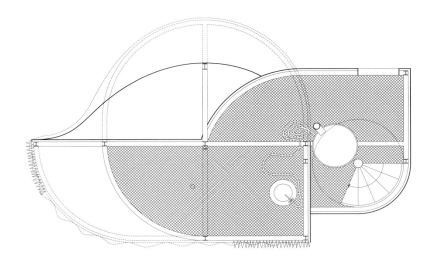

To the left, a structural diagram, and below, a plan. The house is both airy and light in conception and appearance.

Links eine Konstruktionszeichnung und unten ein Grundriss: Das Haus wirkt im Konzept und Erscheinungsbild hell und luftig.

À gauche, diagramme structurel et ci-dessous, plan. La maison est à la fois aérienne et légère dans sa conception et son apparence.

MAPA
Fazenda Catuçaba, Sãu Paulo [Brazil] — 2015

MINIMOD CATUÇABA

Area: 42 m² (per unit) — Client: Fazenda Catuçaba — Cost: not disclosed

This project, according to the architects, is "based on prefab plug & play logic." Making use of Brazilian CLT (Cross Laminated Timber), the architects built a first prototype in Porto Alegre, before going on to the Fazenda Catuçaba versions seen here. Built in a factory in an industrial town near São Paulo, they were transported as separate modules for over 150 kilometers, before being installed on site with the help of crane trucks. The two structures are located about one kilometer apart, adapting to the precise configurations of their sites. The first one is located on top of a hill, with each space of the shelter looking in a different cardinal direction. The second one is near a small pond, hidden in vegetation. Using the same number of modules but organized in a linear way, the structure remains parallel to the slope of the hill, which it integrates by using an added deck.

Dieses Projekt basiert, laut Aussage der Architekten, „auf einer vorfabrizierten Steck- und Spiellogik". Aus brasilianischem Kreuz-lagenholz bauten sie den ersten Prototypen in Porto Alegre, bevor sie die hier gezeigten Versionen der Fazenda Catuçaba entwickelten. Sie wurden in einer Industriestadt bei São Paulo in einer Fabrik produziert und dann als einzelne Module über 150 km transportiert, um vor Ort mithilfe von Kranwagen aufgestellt zu werden. Die beiden Bauten liegen etwa einen Kilometer voneinander entfernt und passen sich den Gegebenheiten ihrer Standorte bestens an. Ersterer steht auf der Kuppe eines Hügels und bietet von jedem Raum Aussicht in eine andere Himmelsrichtung. Der zweite Bau liegt in der Vegetation verborgen an einem kleinen Teich. Er besteht aus der gleichen Zahl von Einheiten, die jedoch linear angeordnet sind, und steht parallel zum Abhang, in den er durch eine zusätzliche Terrasse integriert wurde.

Pour les architectes, le projet « repose sur une logique clés en main préfabriquée ». Après avoir construit un premier prototype à Porto Alegre avec du CLT (bois lamellé croisé) brésilien, ils ont développé les versions de la Fazenda Catuçaba présentées ici. Construites en usine dans une ville industrielle proche de São Paulo, elles ont été transportées sur plus de 150 kilomètres sous forme de modules distincts avant d'être assemblées sur place à l'aide de camions-grues. Les deux structures sont distantes d'un kilomètre environ et chacune est adaptée précisément à la configuration de son site. La première occupe le sommet d'une colline et ses différents espaces ouvrent chacun vers un point cardinal différent. La seconde est située à côté d'un petit étang, dissimulée dans la végétation. Avec le même nombre de modules, mais disposés en ligne, elle reste parallèle à la pente de la colline qu'elle intègre au moyen d'un ponton ajouté.

The simple rectangular structure is extended by an outdoor deck. The two structures were built in a factory near São Paulo and transported 150 kilometers, then installed on site with crane trucks.

Das schlichte, rechteckige Gebäude wurde durch ein Außendeck erweitert. Beide Häuser wurden in einer Fabrik bei São Paulo gebaut und 150 km zu ihrem Standort transportiert, wo sie mithilfe eines Autokrans aufgestellt wurden.

La structure rectangulaire simple est prolongée par un ponton extérieur. Les deux éléments ont été construits en usine près de São Paulo et transportés sur 150 km, puis installés sur le site à l'aide de camions-grues.

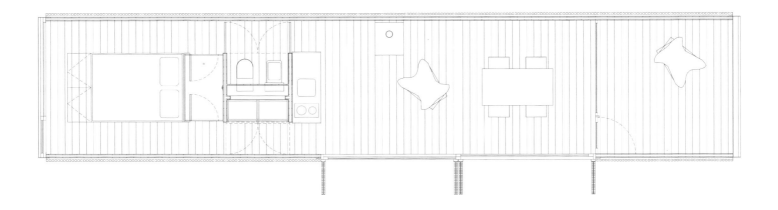

The ends of the houses are entirely open
creating a close relation with the natural site.
The stepped terrace is adapted here to the
hilly terrain.

Die Schmalseiten der Häuser sind völlig offen
und stellen eine enge Verbindung zum natürlichen Gelände her. Die gestufte Terrasse passt
sich hier dem hügeligen Gelände an.

Les extrémités des bâtiments sont entièrement
ouvertes afin de créer un lien étroit avec le site
naturel. La terrasse en escalier est ici adaptée
au terrain vallonné.

The two houses were installed near an 1850s farmhouse on a 450-hectare estate called the Fazenda Catuçaba, located between São Paulo and Rio.

Beide Häuser wurden in der Nähe eines Bauernhauses aus den 1850er-Jahren auf der 450 ha großen Fazenda Catuçaba zwischen São Paulo und Rio aufgestellt.

Les deux abris ont été installés près d'une ferme des années 1850 sur un domaine de 450 ha appelé Fazenda Catuçaba, entre São Paulo et Rio.

In this interior view, the warm wood reveals a small kitchen at the rear. A wood-burning stove provides warmth when necessary, while the large sliding glass wall offers communion with nature.

Diese Innenansicht zeigt die mit warmem Holz verkleidete Küche im Hintergrund. Ein Holzofen liefert bei Bedarf Wärme, während die große, gläserne Schiebewand die Verbindung zur Natur herstellt.

Sur cette photo l'intérieur boisé et chaleureux révèle une petite cuisine à l'arrière. Un poêle à bois fournit la chaleur nécessaire tandis que les grandes parois de verre coulissantes invitent à entrer en communion avec la nature.

TOMOKAZU HAYAKAWA
Gunma [Japan] — 2013

MUSE-ONE TIMBER CONTAINER

Area: 28 m² — Client: Muse — Cost: $50 000

This design was dictated by adherence to the rules of Japanese Industrial Standards (JIS) that prohibit the use of unaltered shipping containers except for disaster relief or the exhibition of art.

Der Plan wurde von den japanischen Vorschriften für Industriestandards (JTS) bestimmt, die die Nutzung unveränderter Container – außer bei Katastrophenfällen oder für Kunstausstellungen – verbieten.

La conception a été dictée par l'obligation de respecter les normes industrielles japonaises qui interdisent l'utilisation de conteneurs maritimes en bon état, sauf pour aider les victimes de catastrophes ou pour une exposition artistique.

The architect notes that it is difficult under Japanese law to use shipping containers for anything other than temporary art space or disaster-relief shelters. This is because the materials do not conform to Japanese industrial standards for housing. His clever solution to this problem lay in building a timber framework inside the container and declaring it to be the actual structure of the Timber Container. Using pre-cut standard timber, Tomokazu Hayakawa was able to put these interior frameworks in place in two 6.1-meter containers with three workers in half a day, opening the perspective of a more intensive use of old shipping containers in Japan. Although Muse-One was destined to a pet grooming facility, it could easily be imagined as a house.

Der Architekt betont, dass die japanischen Gesetze nur erlauben, Container für temporäre Kunstausstellungen oder als Unterkünfte im Katastrophenfall zu nutzen, weil die Materialien nicht den japanischen Industriestandards für den Wohnungsbau entsprechen. Seine clevere Lösung dieses Problems bestand in einem Holzfachwerk im Inneren des Containers, das er zum eigentlichen Tragwerk des Timber Container erklärte. Tomokazu Hayakawa verwendete vorgeschnittene, genormte Holzelemente für diese inneren Fachwerkkonstruktionen, die er mithilfe von drei Arbeitern in einem halben Tag in zwei 6,1 m große Container einbaute. Damit schuf er eine Möglichkeit zur besseren Nutzung alter Transportcontainer in Japan. Obgleich Muse-One zur Unterbringung von Haustieren vorgesehen war, könnte es durchaus auch als Wohnung dienen.

L'architecte note que la loi japonaise complique l'utilisation de conteneurs maritimes pour d'autres usages qu'un espace artistique temporaire ou des abris pour victimes de catastrophes. En effet, les matériaux des conteneurs ne sont pas conformes aux normes industrielles japonaises en matière de logement. La solution astucieuse qu'il a trouvée pour y remédier consiste à construire une charpente en bois d'œuvre à l'intérieur du conteneur qu'il a déclaré être la structure d'origine du conteneur. Tomokazu Hayakawa a pu mettre en place ces charpentes en bois standard prédécoupé dans deux conteneurs de 6,1 mètres en une demi-journée avec trois ouvriers et ouvre ainsi la perspective d'un usage plus intensif des vieux conteneurs maritimes au Japon. Muse-One était destiné à accueillir un salon de toilettage pour animaux familiers, mais elle pourrait tout à fait servir de maison.

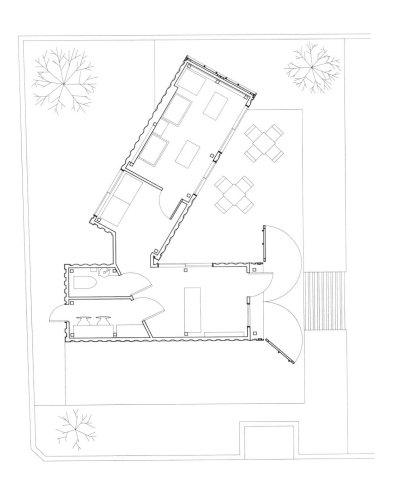

By officially declaring the interior timberwork as being the actual "building" the architect was able to obviate rules prohibiting the use of shipping containers for residence or most other purposes.

Durch eine förmliche Erklärung, dass das innere Holzwerk das eigentliche „Gebäude" sei, konnte der Architekt die Vorschriften umgehen, welche die Nutzung von Transport-containern zum Wohnen und für die meisten anderen Zwecke verbieten.

En déclarant officiellement l'intérieur en bois comme la « construction », l'architecte a pu contourner les règles interdisant l'usage de conteneurs maritimes à des fins de résidence ou pour la plupart des autres utilisations.

BONNIFAIT + GIESEN
Hangzhou [China] — 2006

PORT-A-BACH

Area: 35 m² — Client: Puke Ariki Museum, Taranaki, New Zealand
Cost: not disclosed

Built in Hangzhou, China, and shipped to New Zealand, the Port-a-Bach is part of the permanent collection of the Puke Ariki Museum in New Plymouth. It can be readily connected to solar and wind power generators and was intended as a portable holiday home that sleeps two adults and two children. The structure can be unfolded or closed to expose only its exterior steel shell. It contains a bathroom with an open shower, sink, and composting toilet. An interior fabric screen system allows the interior to be subdivided. It has bunk beds, a double bed room, dressing room, and kitchen. An exterior canvas screen covers a deck area. The 6.1-meter container has six concrete footings that allow it to be given a stable location without digging. It has wool insulation, plywood and timber linings, plywood furniture, aluminum-framed glass louvre doors and windows, and includes an electric winch to raise or lower the outside deck.

Das in Hangzhou, China, gefertigte und nach Neuseeland transportierte Port-a-Bach ist Teil der ständigen Sammlung des Puke Ariki Museum in New Plymouth. Es kann problemlos an Solar- und Windgeneratoren angeschlossen werden und wurde als transportables Ferienhaus für zwei Erwachsene und zwei Kinder geplant. Der Bau kann aufgefaltet oder geschlossen werden, sodass dann nur die stählerne Außenschale sichtbar ist. Er enthält ein Bad mit offener Dusche, Waschbecken und Komposttoilette. Ein textiles Trennsystem ermöglicht die Unterteilung des Innenraums. Dieser enthält Stockbetten, einen Doppelschlafraum, einen Ankleidebereich und eine Küche. Außen überdeckt ein textiler Schirm eine Terrasse. Der 6,1 m lange Container steht auf sechs Einzelfundamenten aus Beton, die ihm ohne Ausgrabung Stabilität verleihen. Er hat eine Isolierung aus Wolle, eine Verkleidung aus Sperrholz und Holz, Möbel aus verleimtem Holz, aluminiumgerahmte Lamellen-Glastüren und -fenster sowie eine elektrisch angetriebene Winde, um das Außendeck anzuheben oder zu senken.

Construit à Hangzhou, en Chine, et transporté par bateau jusqu'en Nouvelle-Zélande, Port-a-Bach fait partie de la collection permanente du musée Puke Ariki de New Plymouth. Facilement raccordable à des générateurs électriques solaires et éoliens, il était destiné à servir de maison de vacances portative pour deux adultes et deux enfants. Il peut être déployé ou fermé pour n'exposer que sa coque extérieure en acier. Il contient une salle de bains avec une douche à l'italienne, un lavabo et des toilettes compostables. Un ensemble de panneaux textiles permet de diviser l'intérieur qui comprend des couchettes, une chambre double, un dressing et une cuisine. Un panneau extérieur en toile recouvre le porche. Le conteneur de 6,1 mètres repose sur six pieds en béton qui le stabilisent en évitant tout creusement. Il possède une isolation en laine, des revêtements en contreplaqué et bois d'œuvre, du mobilier en contreplaqué, des portes vitrées à claire-voie avec encadrement en aluminium, ainsi qu'un treuil électrique pour lever ou baisser le pont extérieur.

Fittings include wood linings, aluminum door and window frames, and plywood furnishing.

Zur Ausstattung gehören Holzverkleidungen, Tür- und Fensterrahmen aus Aluminium und Möbel aus Sperrholz.

Les accessoires comprennent des revêtements en bois, une porte, des encadrements de fenêtre en aluminium et du mobilier en contreplaqué.

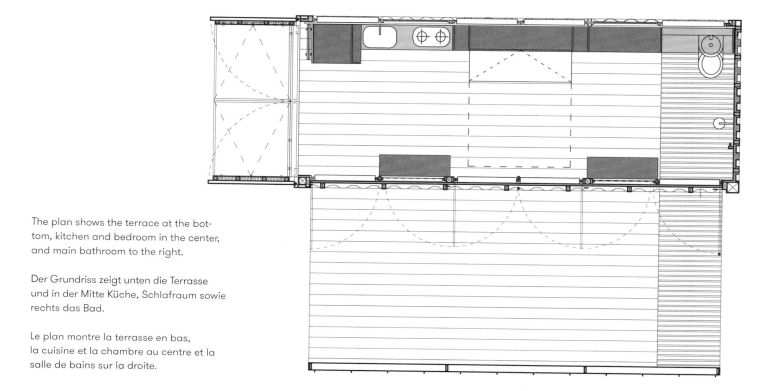

The plan shows the terrace at the bottom, kitchen and bedroom in the center, and main bathroom to the right.

Der Grundriss zeigt unten die Terrasse und in der Mitte Küche, Schlafraum sowie rechts das Bad.

Le plan montre la terrasse en bas, la cuisine et la chambre au centre et la salle de bains sur la droite.

ALEX SCHWEDER AND WARD SHELLEY

Ghent, New York [USA] — 2016

"REACTOR"

Area: 32.7 m² — Client: Art Omi — Cost: not disclosed
Collaboration: Lena Kouvela

This 15-meter-long "spinning and tilting house" was built on top of a five-meter-high concrete column at the Art Omi Center in New York State. Its motion can be influenced by the wind, but also, pointedly, by the movement of its inhabitants, who are the artists. The movable aspect of the house makes visible the kind of interaction, or reactions, of the inhabitants that form any architectural space. For its inauguration, Schweder and Shelley conducted a "five-day inhabitation performance." They write: "Inside we went about our days with reading, cooking, and just sitting on our porches watching the vista change slowly and quietly. When visitors would come by, we would chat with them about what the work might mean, how it is built, and yes… how the bathroom works."

Dieses 15 m lange, „sich drehende und neigende Haus" wurde auf eine 5 m hohe Betonsäule des Omi International Arts Center im Staat New York gesetzt. Seine Bewegung kann vom Wind beeinflusst werden, aber auch gewollt durch die Bewegung seiner Bewohner, der Künstler selbst. Dieser Aspekt der Bewegung macht die Art der Interaktion oder der Reaktion der Bewohner sichtbar, die jeden architektonischen Raum bestimmt. Zur Eröffnung führten Schweder und Shelley eine „fünftägige Wohnvorführung" durch. Sie schreiben: „Innen verbrachten wir unsere Tage mit Lesen, Kochen und nur auf unseren Veranden sitzend und still und ruhig den Wechsel der Aussicht beobachtend. Wenn Besucher vorbeikamen, sprachen wir mit ihnen über die Bedeutung des Bauwerks, wie es errichtet wurde und, ja auch …, wie das Bad funktioniert."

La « maison qui tournoie et s'incline », longue de 15 mètres, a été construite au sommet d'une colonne de béton de 5 mètres de haut érigée à l'Omi Arts Center, dans l'État de New York. Ses mouvements dépendent du vent mais aussi, visiblement, de ceux de ses habitants — les artistes eux-mêmes. Ce caractère mobile de la maison met en évidence l'interaction, ou les réactions, des habitants qui forment un espace architectural. Pour l'inauguration, Schweder et Shelley ont réalisé « une performance habitationnelle de cinq jours » qu'ils racontent ainsi : « nous avons passé nos journées à l'intérieur à lire, cuisiner et rester simplement assis sur nos vérandas à regarder la vue changer lentement et paisiblement. Lorsque des visiteurs passaient, nous discutions avec eux de ce que signifiait ce projet, de la manière dont il a été construit et, oui… du fonctionnement de la salle de bains ».

Fixed on a concrete pillar, the house spins and tilts in the wind or according to the movements of its residents.

Das auf einem Betonpfeiler befestigte Haus dreht und neigt sich im Wind oder nach den Bewegungen seiner Bewohner.

Construite sur une colonne de béton, la maison tournoie et s'incline selon le vent ou les mouvements de ses habitants.

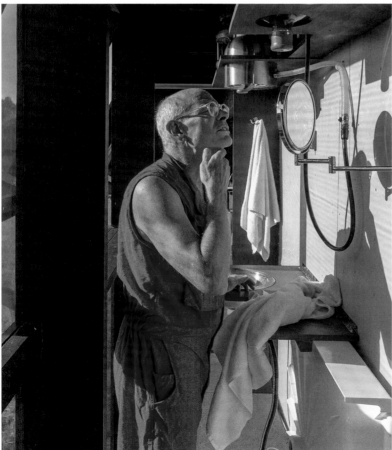

The artists occupied the house for five days in 2016, taking the term "artists in residence" in a literal fashion.

Die Künstler bewohnten 2016 fünf Tage lang das Haus, wobei sie den Begriff „artists in residence" wörtlich nahmen.

Les artistes ont occupé la maison pendant cinq jours en 2016, prenant au pied de la lettre l'expression « artistes en résidence ».

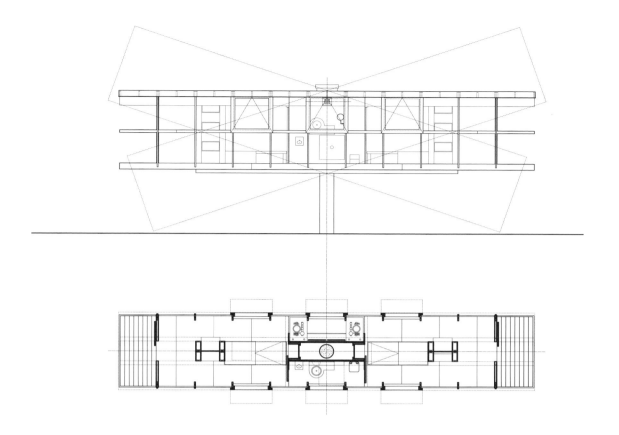

Ward Shelley stated: "It takes only the slightest breeze to set us in motion. It feels grand and processional. Always something to look at, always a new adjustment needed to stay in the shade."

Ward Shelley erklärte: „Schon die leichteste Brise setzt uns in Bewegung. Die Wirkung ist großartig und feierlich. Es gibt immer etwas zu sehen, es bedarf immer einer neuen Einstellung, um im Schatten zu bleiben."

Selon Ward Shelley, « la plus légère brise suffit à nous mettre en mouvement. C'est un sentiment de grandeur et de solennité. Il y a toujours quelque chose à voir, une nouvelle adaptation pour rester à l'ombre ».

APPLETON & DOMINGOS / JULAR

Lisbon [Portugal] — 2016

TREEHOUSE RIGA

Area: 88 m² — Client: Jular Madeiras — Cost: not disclosed

Above, the bed loft area is fitted with an integrated bed and Vipp products, such as the wall spot lights. Left, the living area has a black leather daybed and shelves, also designed by Vipp.

Oben: Das Loft zum Schlafen ist mit einem eingebauten Bett und Produkten von Vipp, wie den Wandleuchten, ausgestattet. Links: Der Wohnraum hat eine Schlafcouch aus schwarzem Leder und Regale, ebenfalls von Vipp.

Ci-dessus, l'espace couchage sous les combles est équipé d'un lit encastré et de produits Vipp comme les spots muraux. À gauche, l'espace salon comporte une banquette-lit en cuir noir et des étagères également conçues par Vipp.

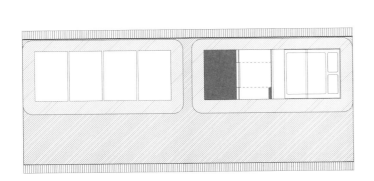

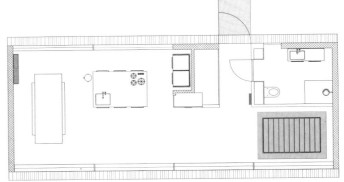

N55
Copenhagen [Denmark] — 2009–10

WALKING HOUSE

Area: 6 m² — Client: none — Cost: €50 000 — Collaboration: Sam Kronick

The WALKING HOUSE is a modular dwelling system for up to four people "that enables persons to live a peaceful nomadic life, moving slowly through the landscape or cityscape with minimal impact on the environment." It has solar cells and small windmills to generate power, a system for collecting rainwater, and a system for solar-heated hot water. A small greenhouse can be added to the basic living module to provide a substantial part of the food needed by the inhabitants. The house has a composting toilet, and a small wood-burning stove can be added as well. The framework can be made of steel, aluminum, or wood and can be covered with the same materials or with textiles. Windows are made with polycarbonate. Six legs with linear actuators are used to make the structure advance at a maximum of 60 meters an hour, but the units can also be joined together. N55 was asked by the Wysing Arts Center to collaborate with a group of travelling people in the area around Cambridge (UK). The design of the WALK-ING HOUSE was thus inspired in part by nomadic cultures and in particular by traditional Romani horse carriages from the 18th century, combined in this instance with technology and modern materials.

Das WALKING HOUSE ist ein modulares Wohnbausystem für bis zu vier Personen, „das ihnen ein friedliches nomadisches Leben ermöglicht, indem sie sich langsam, mit minimaler Auswirkung auf die Umwelt, durch das Land oder die Stadt bewegen". Es ist mit Solarzellen und kleinen Windrädern zur Stromerzeugung, einem Regenwasser-Sammelsystem und einem mit Solarenergie geheizten Warmwassersystem ausgestattet. Ein kleines Gewächshaus kann an das Grundmodul der Wohnung angefügt werden, damit die Bewohner einen Teil ihrer Nahrung selbst anbauen können. Das Haus hat eine Komposttoilette; ein kleiner Holzofen kann auch eingesetzt werden. Das Tragwerk besteht aus Stahl, Aluminium oder Holz und kann mit den gleichen Materialien oder mit Textilgewebe gedeckt werden. Die Fenster sind aus Polykarbonat. Sechs Beine mit Linearantrieb dienen zur Bewegung des Gebäudes um maximal 60 m pro Stunde, aber die Einheiten können auch miteinander verbunden werden. N55 wurden vom Wysing Arts Center zur Zusammenarbeit mit einer Gruppe fahrenden Volkes im Bereich von Cambridge in Großbritannien gebeten. So wurde der Entwurf des WALKING HOUSE teils von nomadischer Kultur und vor allem von den traditionellen Pferdewagen der Roma aus dem 18. Jahrhundert beeinflusst, in diesem Fall im Verbund mit Technologie und modernen Materialien.

La WALKING HOUSE est un habitat modulaire qui peut accueillir jusqu'à quatre personnes auxquelles il « permet une existence nomade paisible, en se déplaçant lentement dans la nature ou dans la ville avec un impact minimal sur l'environnement ». La maison est équipée de cellules solaires et de petits moulins à vent qui produisent de l'électricité, d'un système de récupération des eaux de pluie et d'un système d'eau chaude solaire. Une petite serre peut être intégrée au module de base et fournir une part substantielle de l'alimentation des habitants. La maison possède des toilettes compostables et un petit poêle à bois peut également être ajouté. La charpente est en acier, en aluminium ou en bois et peut être recouverte des mêmes matériaux ou de tissu. Les fenêtres sont en polycarbonate. Six pattes à vérins linéaires font avancer l'ensemble à une vitesse maximale de 60 mètres à l'heure, mais différentes unités peuvent aussi être regroupées. Le Wysing Arts Center ayant demandé à N55 de travailler avec un groupe de gens du voyage dans la région de Cambridge (UK), la WALKING HOUSE est donc en partie inspirée des cultures nomades, et plus particulièrement des charrettes à chevaux traditionnelles roms du XVIIIᵉ siècle, associées ici à la technologie et aux matériaux modernes.

According to the designers, the Walking House is based on a steel framework and can be covered with steel, aluminum, wood, or even semi-permeable textiles.

Laut seinen Planern basiert das Walking House auf einer Stahlkonstruktion und kann mit Stahl, Aluminium, Holz oder sogar halbdurchlässigen Textilien überzogen werden.

Les designers expliquent que la Walking House est basée sur une charpente en acier qui peut être couverte d'acier, d'aluminium, de bois, ou même de textile semi-perméable.

The Walking House surely has points in common with houseboats or even with submarines for example, as the interior image below shows. Left, three of the six legs of the house.

Das Walking House hat sicherlich Gemeinsamkeiten mit einem Hausboot oder sogar mit einem Unterseeboot, wie auf der Innenaufnahme unten zu sehen ist.

La Walking House présente certainement des points communs avec les house-boats, voire les sous-marins, comme on le voit sur la photo de l'intérieur ci-dessous. À gauche, trois des six pattes de la maison.

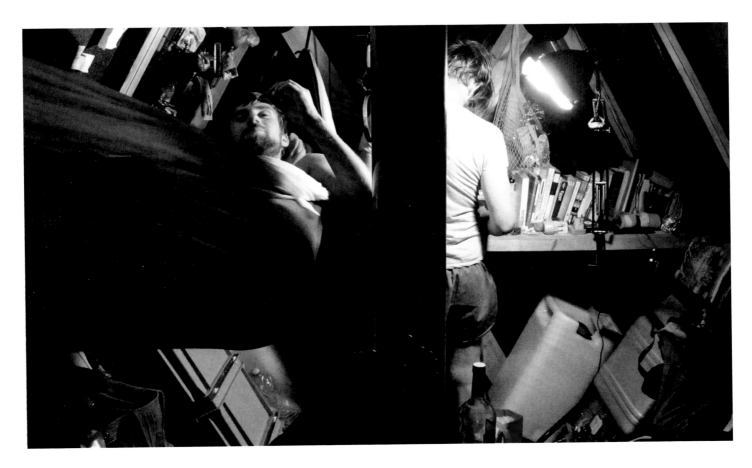

FICTION FACTORY
Amsterdam [The Netherlands] — 2016

WIKKELHOUSE

Area: 20 to 60 m² — Client: various
Cost: €40 000 to €120 000 according to size
Collaboration: Oep Schilling

The Wikkelhouse is a modular building system that uses cardboard building elements that can be assembled in a single day without creating a foundation. Interlocking cardboard segments 1.2 meters in length, each weighing 500 kilos, can be joined together to create a home or structure for any other use of the size required. Twenty-four layers of cardboard are wrapped around a patented house-shaped mold, using "environmentally friendly" glue. The rounded form of the structure makes it highly wind-resistant. The cardboard cladding is protected from the weather by waterproof foil and is finished with wooden cladding boards. Glass end façades are proposed as one alternative in the designs. The house can be expanded with a module containing a toilet, bathroom, and kitchen. It is also possible to move the house or extend it with one or more segments. All the materials employed can be recycled, but the structural models are designed to have a life of 50 years or more. It can thus be used either for temporary or for permanent housing. Although architects such as Shigeru Ban have actively used cardboard tubes as structural elements for a number of years, the combination of easily transportable modular assembly and exceptional durability proposed in the Wikkelhouse by Fiction Factory would appear to be unique.

Wikkelhouse ist ein modulares Konstruktionssystem aus Bauelementen aus Pappkarton, die innerhalb eines Tages ohne Fundament aufgestellt werden können. Die miteinander verzahnten, 1,2 m langen und jeweils 500 kg wiegenden Pappteile können zu einem Wohnhaus oder einem Gebäude für jede beliebige Nutzung verbunden werden. Unter Verwendung eines „umweltfreundlichen" Klebers werden 24 Schichten Pappkarton um eine patentierte Hausform gewickelt. Die gerundete Form des Bauwerks macht es sehr windbeständig. Die Pappverkleidung ist durch eine wasserfeste Beschichtung geschützt und zusätzlich mit Holzbrettern verkleidet. Als eine alternative Gestaltung werden gläserne Stirnfassaden vorgeschlagen. Das Haus kann erweitert werden durch ein Modul, das eine Toilette, ein Bad und eine Küche enthält. Man kann es auch versetzen oder durch ein oder mehrere Module erweitern. Alle verwendeten Materialien sind recyclebar; die Bauteile haben eine Lebensdauer von 50 und mehr Jahren. Dadurch ist das Gebäude für temporäre Nutzung und auch zum dauerhaften Bewohnen geeignet. Obgleich andere Architekten, zum Beispiel Shigeru Ban, schon seit Jahren Papprohre als Bauelemente genutzt haben, ist die Kombination von leicht transportablen, modularen Bauteilen von außergewöhnlicher Dauer, wie Fiction Factory sie mit Wikkelhouse vorschlägt, offenbar einmalig.

La Wikkelhouse est un système de construction modulaire sans fondation, faite d'éléments en carton qui peuvent être assemblés en une journée. Les segments de carton de 1,2 mètre de long pèsent chacun 500 kilos et peuvent être imbriqués et raccordés les uns aux autres pour créer une habitation ou une structure destinée à un autre usage de la taille voulue. Vingt-quatre couches de carton ont été enroulées avec de la colle « écologique » autour d'une armature brevetée en forme de maison. La forme arrondie de la structure lui permet de résister à des vents forts. Le carton est protégé des intempéries par un film imperméable avec un revêtement en bois en guise de finitions. Les extrémités aux façades vitrées sont l'une des alternatives proposées. La maison peut être agrandie avec un module contenant des toilettes, une salle de bains et une cuisine. Elle peut aussi être déplacée ou élargie avec un ou plusieurs modules supplémentaires. Tous les matériaux employés sont recyclables, mais les modèles structurels sont conçus pour une durée de vie de 50 ans ou plus. Elle peut servir de logement temporaire ou permanent. Si d'autres architectes comme Shigeru Ban ont déjà fait depuis longtemps un usage intensif des tubes de carton comme éléments de structure, l'association d'un assemblage modulaire facile à transporter et d'une longévité exceptionnelle qui est celle de la Wikkelhouse de Fiction Factory semble véritablement unique.

The modular units that make up the Wikkelhouse are visible on the left. Largely closed, they cede to full-height glazing and a large double door at one end.

Die Module des Wikkelhouse sind links zu sehen. Es ist überwiegend geschlossen, hat aber auf einer Seite geschosshohe Verglasung und eine große Doppeltür.

À gauche, les unités modulaires qui forment la Wikkelhouse. Presque entièrement closes, elles cèdent la place à un vitrage sur toute la hauteur et une grande double-porte.

The wrap-around wood panel-
ing that covers floors, walls, and
ceilings gives a feeling of modern
design to the inside the house.

Die Rundum-Holzverkleidung, die
Böden, Wände und Decken umfasst,
verleiht dem Inneren des Hauses
eine moderne Wirkung.

Le panneau de bois enroulé
qui couvre les sols, les murs et les
plafonds apporte une certaine
modernité au design intérieur de
la maison.

HOMES
for those in need

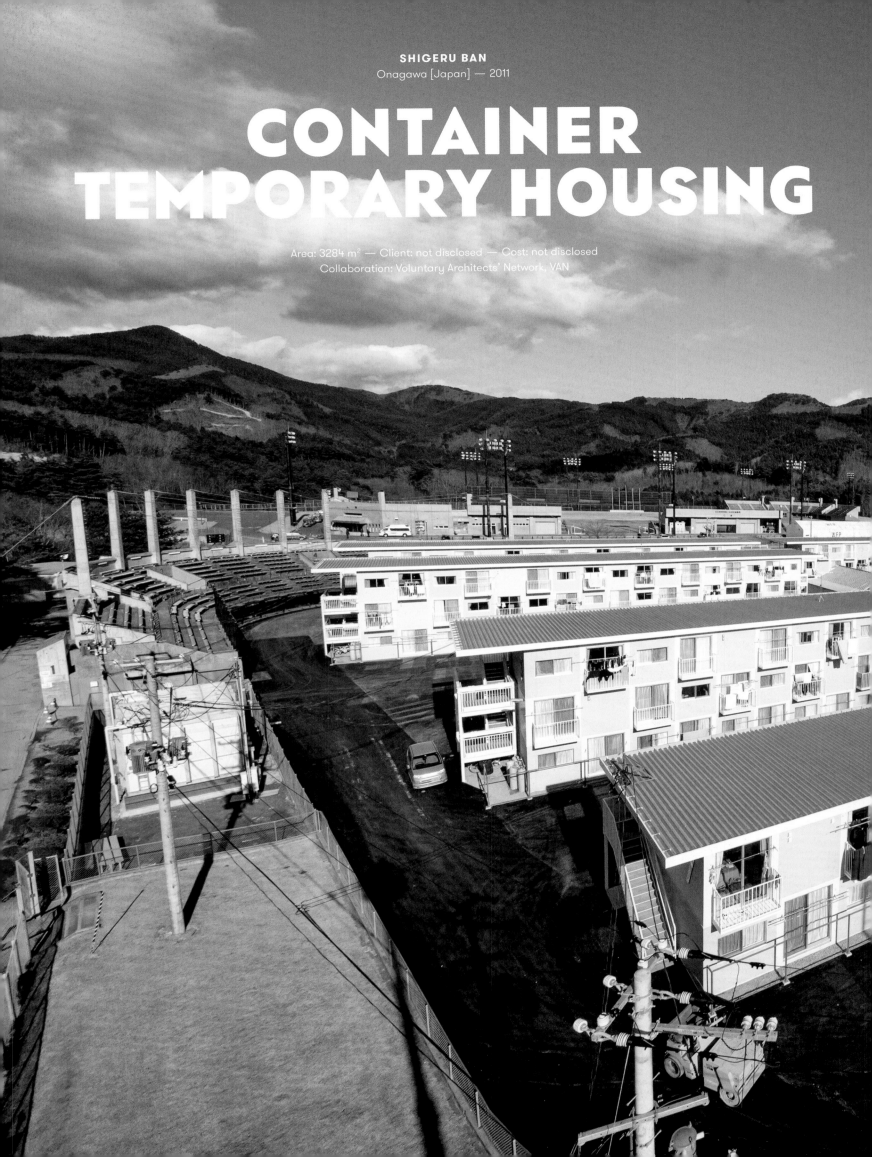

SHIGERU BAN
Onagawa [Japan] — 2011

CONTAINER TEMPORARY HOUSING

Area: 3284 m² — Client: not disclosed — Cost: not disclosed
Collaboration: Voluntary Architects' Network, VAN

Subsequent to the March 2011 earthquake and tsunami in Japan, Shigeru Ban proposed to build a three-story temporary housing structure made with 6.1-meter shipping containers in the city of Onagawa. The use of shipping containers of course speeded construction and made it easy to both assemble and eventually move the living units. Stacking units in a checkerboard pattern, this scheme generated "bright, open living spaces between the containers." The three-story configuration was used because there were few available flat pieces of land in Onagawa. As Shigeru Ban explains: "The standard temporary houses issued by the government are poorly made, and there is not enough storage space. We installed built-in closets and shelves in all of our houses with the help of volunteers and with donations." Three basic configurations were generated—with areas of 19.8 m², 29.7 m², and 39.6 m² for one to more than four residents.

Nach dem Erdbeben und Tsunami in Japan vom März 2011 schlug Shigeru Ban den Bau eines dreigeschossigen, temporären Wohnhauses in der Stadt Onagawa aus 6,1 m großen Containern vor. Die Verwendung solcher Container beschleunigte natürlich den Bau und erleichterte die Montage und danach den Transport der Wohneinheiten. Durch die Stapelung im Schachbrettsystem entstanden „helle, offene Wohnbereiche zwischen den Containern". Die dreigeschossige Aufstellung wurde gewählt, weil in Onagawa nur wenige ebene Flächen vorhanden waren. Shigeru Ban erläutert: „Die üblichen, von der Regierung zur Verfügung gestellten temporären Häuser sind von schlechter Qualität und haben nicht genug Stauraum. Wir bauten mithilfe von Freiwilligen und Spenden Schränke und Regale in alle unsere Häuser ein." Es wurden drei Grundformen entworfen – mit Nutzflächen von 19,8, 29,7 und 39,6 m² für einen bis mehr als vier Bewohner.

À la suite du tremblement de terre et du tsunami qui ont frappé le Japon en mars 2011, Shigeru Ban a proposé de construire une structure d'habitat temporaire à trois étages faite de conteneurs maritimes de 6,1 mètres dans la ville d'Onagawa. Le recours à des conteneurs a naturellement accéléré la construction et rendu les unités d'habitation faciles à assembler et éventuellement à déplacer. Empilées pour former un motif à damiers, les unités sont disposées de manière à créer « des espaces de vie clairs et ouverts entre les conteneurs ». La configuration à trois niveaux a été choisie en raison du manque de terrains plats disponibles à Onagawa. Comme l'explique Shigeru Ban, « les logements temporaires standard construits par le gouvernement sont mal faits et manquent d'espace de rangement. Avec l'aide de bénévoles et grâce aux dons, nous avons installé des placards et des étagères encastrés dans toutes nos maisons ». Trois configurations de base ont été prévues, aux surfaces respectives de 19,8 mètres carrés, 29,7 mètres carrés et 39,6 mètres carrés pour un à plus de quatre occupants.

Shigeru Ban has worked with shipping containers on a number of occasions in the past, but here he takes the stacking and assembly procedure to a larger scale.

Shigeru Ban hat in der Vergangenheit bei verschiedenen Gelegenheiten mit Transportcontainern gearbeitet, aber hier das Stapel- und Montageverfahren in größerem Maßstab angewendet.

Shigeru Ban a déjà travaillé à partir de conteneurs maritimes à de multiples occasions mais cette fois, il les empile et les assemble à plus grande échelle.

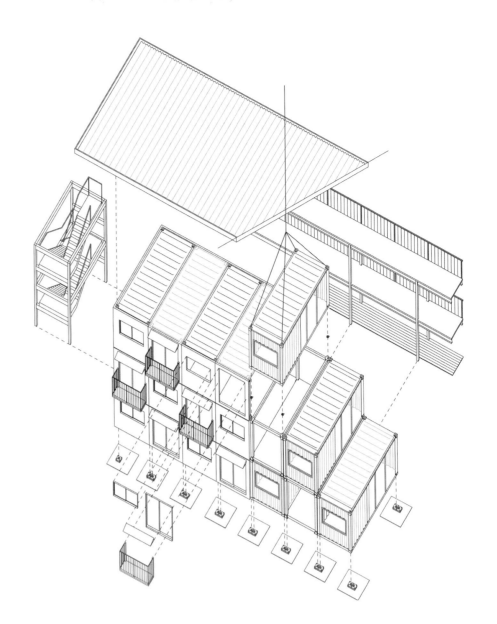

A single-slope roof atelier space is located in the central area of the complex. The interior of this space is visible on the right page, bottom.

Im zentralen Bereich der Anlage gibt es ein Atelier mit Pultdach. Die Abbildung auf der rechten Seite zeigt den Innenraum.

Un espace atelier au toit à une pente occupe le centre du complexe. On en voit l'intérieur sur la page de droite.

A community center (above) and market are located near the atelier in structures with different forms in the middle of the apartment building zone.

Ein Gemeinschaftszentrum (oben) und ein Markt in anderen Formen befinden sich nahe dem Atelier in der Mitte der Wohnbebauung.

Un centre communautaire (ci-dessus) et un marché sont situés à proximité de l'atelier dans des structures de formes différentes au milieu de la zone d'appartements.

YASUTAKA YOSHIMURA
Ishinomaki [Japan] — 2011

EX-CONTAINER

Area: 28 m² — Client: not disclosed — Cost: not disclosed

The Ex-Container is meant for emergency housing relief subsequent to natural or other disasters. Its size is the same as that of a 6.1-meter ISO shipping container. The project involves the realization of the prefabrication process that allows factory finishing of the wooden interiors of the containers so that they can be supplied in large numbers to stricken areas as required. The architect explains that the Ex-Container can readily be converted from temporary housing to permanent residences with the possibility of expanding the original structure, "therefore avoiding double investments." Two containers could thus be paired together to allow for kitchen, living room, bathroom, and bedroom spaces with a total of 60 square meters of available space. For a small site, the containers can, of course, be stacked, creating a two-story house for example.

Der Ex-Container ist als Notunterkunft nach Naturkatastrophen oder anderen Unglücksfällen vorgesehen. Seine Größe entspricht derjenigen des 6,1 m langen Transportcontainers ISO. Das Projekt beinhaltet die Ausführung der Vorfabrikation, die die fabrikmäßige Ausstattung des hölzernen Innenraums des Containers ermöglicht, sodass er bei Bedarf in großer Zahl in die betroffenen Gebiete geliefert werden kann. Die Architekten erklären, dass der Ex-Container durch Erweiterung der Originalkonstruktion problemlos von einem temporären in ein permanentes Wohnhaus umfunktioniert werden kann, wodurch „doppelte Investitionen vermieden werden". So können zwei Container zusammengestellt werden, um Küche, Wohnraum, Bad und Schlafräume mit insgesamt 60 m² Nutzfläche unterzubringen. Bei einem kleinen Bauplatz können die Container natürlich gestapelt werden, sodass zum Beispiel ein zweigeschossiges Haus entsteht.

L'Ex-container est destiné à apporter une aide d'urgence au logement après des catastrophes naturelles ou d'autre nature. Il est de même dimension qu'un conteneur maritime ISO de 6,1 mètres. Le projet comprend aussi la réalisation du processus de préfabrication qui permet de finir en usine les intérieurs en bois des conteneurs afin qu'ils puissent être fournis en grand nombre aux zones touchées. L'architecte explique que pour « éviter un investissement double », l'Ex-container est facilement transformable en résidence permanente grâce à la possibilité d'agrandir la structure d'origine. Deux conteneurs pourraient notamment être couplés pour offrir des espaces cuisine, salon, salle de bains ou chambre à coucher avec une surface totale disponible de 60 mètres carrés. Sur les terrains plus petits, les conteneurs peuvent, bien sûr, être empilés pour créer par exemple une maison à deux étages.

Left, two units can readily be joined together. Openings and interior wood finishings are prefabricated.

Links: Zwei Einheiten können einfach miteinander verbunden werden. Die Öffnungen und die hölzerne Innenausstattung sind vorgefertigt.

À gauche, deux unités peuvent facilement être couplées. Les ouvertures et les finitions intérieures en bois sont préfabriquées.

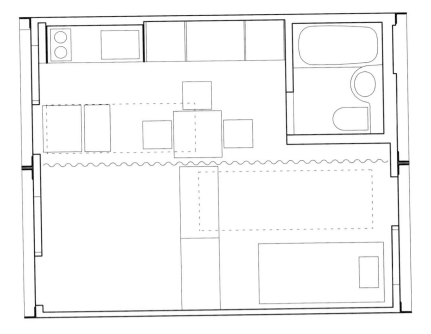

Above, a plan of a double structure with the dining and kitchen area above, together with a bathroom, and below the living and bedroom zone.

Oben: Grundriss der Doppelkonstruktion, oben Küche mit Essraum und das Bad, unten der Wohn- und Schlafbereich.

Ci-dessus, plan d'une structure double avec coin repas et cuisine en haut, ainsi qu'une salle de bains, et la partie séjour et chambre en bas.

CARTER WILLIAMSON
Sydney [Australia] — 2016

GRID

Area: 34 m² — Client: not disclosed
Cost: $37 000 — Collaboration: Linda Mathews

This project, named after the Norse goddess of peace, was originally designed subsequent to the tsunami in Banda Aceh (December 26, 2004), to be used either for disaster relief or in areas where housing poses longer-term problems. The architects describe their approach as a "prefabricated" Ikea concept "based on a 2.4-meter unit system of standard material lengths that can easily be transported by truck as flat-pack" units and assembled on site. The fully insulated steel-frame structure uses photovoltaic cells, a roof-mounted solar hot water system, and barn door windows to insure ample ventilation. A composting toilet and shower, as well as gas bottles for cooking, are located on two external perforated metal decks. The prototype house was assembled in just three and a half hours during the 2016 Sydney Architecture Festival.

Dieses nach der altnordischen Göttin des Friedens benannte Projekt wurde nach dem Tsunami in Banda Aceh (26. Dezember 2004) in Angriff genommen und ist entweder für Katastrophenfälle oder für Gebiete mit längerfristigem Wohnungsmangel bestimmt. Die Architekten beschreiben ihren Entwurf als „vorfabriziertes" Ikea-Konzept, „das auf einem System mit 2,4 m großen Einheiten aus genormten Bauelementen beruht, die als Flatpacks problemlos per Lastwagen transportiert" und vor Ort montiert werden können. Die voll isolierten Stahlkonstruktionen sind mit Fotovoltaikzellen, einem auf dem Dach angebrachten solaren Warmwassersystem und Schiebefenstern zur ausreichenden Belüftung ausgestattet. Eine Komposttoilette und Dusche sowie Gasflaschen zum Kochen sind auf zwei externen, perforierten Metalldecks untergebracht. Der Prototyp wurde beim Sydney Architectural Festival 2016 in nur dreieinhalb Stunden aufgestellt.

Le projet, qui doit son nom à la déesse nordique de la Paix, a d'abord été conçu après le tsunami de Banda Aceh (26 décembre 2004) pour servir de refuge aux victimes de la catastrophe, ou dans des zones où le logement pose problème à plus long terme. Les architectes décrivent leur démarche comme un concept Ikea « préfabriqué, reposant sur un système de 2,4 mètres d'unités aux longueurs standard qui sont faciles à transporter par camion sous forme de kits » pour être assemblées sur place. La structure parfaitement isolée à charpente d'acier possède aussi des cellules photovoltaïques, un système d'eau chaude solaire sur le toit et d'immenses fenêtres pour une ventilation suffisante. Les toilettes compostables et la douche, ainsi que les bouteilles de gaz pour la cuisine, sont placées sur deux pontons extérieurs en métal perforé. Le prototype a été assemblé en seulement trois heures et demie pendant le Festival d'architecture de Sydney en 2016.

Right, a section drawing of the structure, which can house as many as 10 people and includes a mezzanine sleeping area, seen on the left page.

Rechts: Schnitt durch das Gebäude, das bis zu zehn Personen beherbergen kann und einen Schlafbereich im Zwischengeschoss (auf der linken Seite zu sehen) enthält.

À droite, schéma en coupe de la structure qui peut loger jusqu'à 10 personnes et comprend un couchage en mezzanine qu'on voit sur la page de gauche.

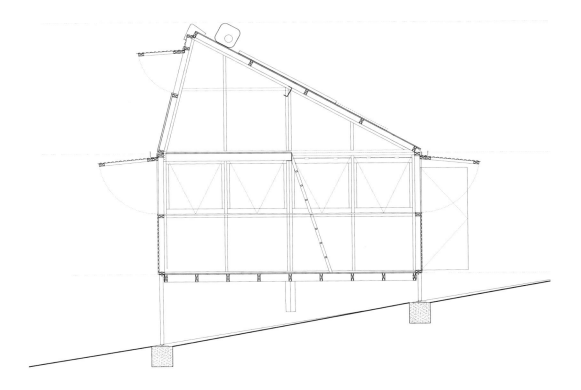

The fully insulated steel-frame structure uses photovoltaic cells and a roof-mounted solar hot-water system. Gas bottles are employed for cooking.

Die voll isolierte Stahlkonstruktion nutzt Fotovoltaikzellen und ein auf dem Dach angebrachtes solares Heißwassersystem. Gekocht wird mit Gasflaschen.

La structure parfaitement isolée à charpente d'acier possède aussi des cellules photovoltaïques et un système d'eau chaude solaire sur le toit. La cuisine fonctionne avec des bouteilles de gaz.

HEX HOUSE

Area: 47.5 m² — Client: various — Cost: $15 000

The Hex House is a project developed by Architects for Society after a collaboration with Chalmers University in Gothenburg, Sweden, aiming to develop a rapidly deployable shelter for the Syrian refugees in the Zaatari Camp in Jordan. Easily assembled by people with no construction experience, the Hex House is made with structural insulated panes for the walls, floors, and roofs, but is intended to be a flexible system allowing for substitution of available local materials. The "passive, low-tech design" is durable enough to be used for 15 to 30 years. Interior and exterior finishes can be customized, but the Hex House is designed with bamboo kitchen cabinets, ceramic tile floors in the bathroom, plywood walls, and bamboo plank floors. The hexagonal form of the house is "inherently stable" and readily used in cluster formations of various types.

Das Hex House ist ein von Architects for Society in Zusammenarbeit mit der Chalmers University of Technology im schwedischen Göteborg entwickeltes Projekt, das die Planung einer schnell einsetzbaren Unterkunft für die syrischen Flüchtlinge im Lager Zaatari in Jordanien zum Ziel hatte. Das Hex House kann problemlos von Menschen ohne Bauerfahrung aufgestellt werden. Für die Wände, Böden und Dächer verwendeten die Planer isolierte Metallplatten, aber diese können auch durch vor Ort verfügbare

Materialien ersetzt werden. Der „passive, Lowtech-Entwurf" ist für eine Nutzung von 15 bis 20 Jahren vorgesehen. Zwar kann die Innen- und Außenverkleidung verändert werden, aber ansonsten ist das Hex House mit Küchenschränken aus Bambus, Bodenfliesen aus Keramik im Bad, Gipswänden, gestrichener Metallbeschichtung und Böden aus Bambusbrettern ausgestattet. Die sechseckige Form des Hauses ist „in sich stabil" und zu unterschiedlichen Gruppierungen zusammensetzbar.

Hex House est un projet développé par Architects for Society en collaboration avec l'université Chalmers de Göteborg, en Suède, dans le but d'obtenir un abri rapide à déployer pour les réfugiés syriens du camp de Zaatari, en Jordanie. La construction est en panneaux de métal isolant faciles à trouver. Aisée à assembler même sans expérience, Hex House est en feuilles de métal ondulé, charpente métallique légère, isolation et contreplaqué pour les murs, le sol et le toit. Ce « design passif sommaire » est conçu pour durer jusqu'à 15 ou 20 ans. Les finitions intérieures et extérieures sont modifiables ; Hex House possède sinon des placards de cuisine et des planchers en bambou, un sol en carreaux de céramique dans la salle de bains, des murs en gypse et un fini métallique peint. La forme hexagonale de la maison « stable par nature » permet de former des grappes aux configurations variées.

Below, left, the plan of a two-bedroom, 40-square-meter unit. Below, right, a three or four bedroom, 80-square-meter arrangement with the kitchen and dining area at the juncture between the two hexagons.

Unten links: Grundriss einer 40 m² großen Einheit mit zwei Schlafräumen. Unten rechts: Eine Kombination von 80 m² mit drei oder vier Schlafräumen mit Küche und Essraum im Zwischenbereich der beiden Sechsecke.

En bas à gauche, plan d'une unité de 40 m² à deux chambres. En bas à droite, configuration de 80 m² à trois ou quatre chambres avec la cuisine et le coin repas à l'intersection des deux hexagones.

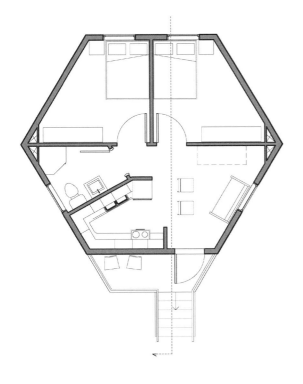

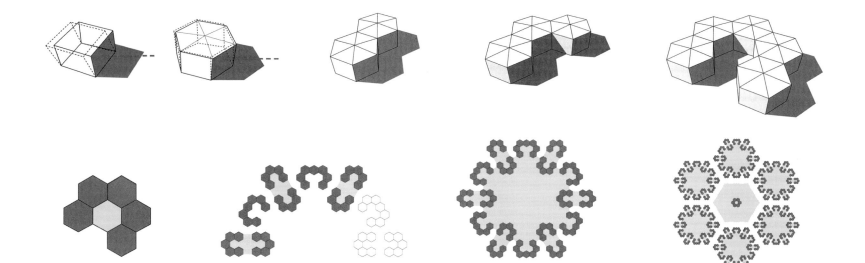

The hexagonal form is structurally more stable than a cube. The units can be combined into clusters that include shared green space. Clusters can be arranged in linear or radial patterns.

Die Sechseckform ist statisch stabiler als ein Kubus. Die Einheiten können zu Gruppen mit gemeinsam genutzter Grünfläche zusammengestellt werden. Sie können linear oder radial angeordnet werden.

La forme hexagonale présente une plus grande stabilité structurelle qu'un cube. Les unités peuvent être associées en grappes avec un espace vert commun. Les groupes d'unités peuvent être disposés en motifs linéaires ou en rayons.

A prototype unit of the New Temporary House, erected in the Philippines, is seen above. The structure of these prefabricated homes consists of wall assemblies using fiber-reinforced plastic and foam-board sandwich panels.

Oben ein auf den Philippinen errichteter Prototyp des New Temporary House; das Tragwerk dieser vorfabrizierten Häuser besteht aus Wandelementen aus faserverstärktem Kunststoff und Schaumstoff-Verbundplatten.

Ci-dessus, prototype de la New Temporary House aux Philippines. La structure de ces habitations préfabriquées est formé d'assemblages de murs en plastique renforcé par des fibres avec des panneaux-sandwich en carton-mousse.

SHIGERU BAN
Manila [Philippines] — 2013

NEW TEMPORARY HOUSE

Area: 36 m² — Client: Daiwa Lease Co., Ltd. — Cost: not disclosed

The New Temporary House is low-cost prefabricated housing, which has already been tested in the Philippines where a prototype was assembled. This project was undertaken after the 2011 earthquake in Japan when the lack of supply in temporary housing became apparent. Shigeru Ban states: "In order to avoid such a shortage during future disasters, I designed a low-cost prefabricated house that can be manufactured in developing countries such as the Philippines and India, and assembled in disaster struck zones, if the need arises." These houses have wall assemblies made with fiber-reinforced plastic (FRP) and foam-board sandwich panels. As the architect points out, the nature of this project allows the rapid creation of better quality temporary housing, and also generates local employment. Beyond disaster-relief work, these easily movable homes might improve housing in low-income areas of such countries as India and Nepal, which have expressed interest in the system.

Das New Temporary House ist ein preiswertes, vorfabriziertes Wohnhaus, das auf den Philippinen, wo ein Prototyp aufgestellt ist, bereits getestet wurde. Dieses Projekt entstand nach dem Erdbeben in Japan von 2011, als der Mangel an temporärem Wohnraum offenkundig wurde. Shigeru Ban erklärt: „Um einen solchen Zustand bei künftigen Katastrophen zu vermeiden, entwarf ich ein preiswertes, vorfabriziertes Haus, das in Entwicklungsländern wie den Philippinen und Indien produziert und bei Bedarf in den von Katastrophen betroffenen Gebieten aufgestellt werden kann." Diese Häuser bestehen aus Wandelementen aus faserverstärktem Kunststoff (FRP) und Schaumstoff-Verbundplatten. Wie der Architekt betont, ermöglicht dieses Projekt die schnelle Errichtung besserer Übergangswohnungen und schafft auch lokale Arbeitsplätze. Vom Katastropheneinsatz abgesehen, können diese einfach zu transportierenden Häuser auch den Wohnstandard in einkommensschwachen Gebieten von Ländern wie Indien oder Nepal verbessern, die bereits Interesse an diesem System angemeldet haben.

La New Temporary House consiste en logements préfabriqués à bas prix déjà testés aux Philippines où un prototype a été assemblé. Le projet remonte au tremblement de terre de 2011 au Japon, lorsque le manque de logements temporaires est devenu évident. « Pour éviter qu'une telle pénurie ne se reproduise lors des prochaines catastrophes, explique Shigeru Ban, j'ai imaginé une maison préfabriquée à bas prix qui peut être réalisée dans des pays en développement comme les Philippines ou l'Inde et assemblée dans les zones touchées en cas de besoin. » Les murs sont des assemblages de plastique renforcé par des fibres (FRP) et de panneaux-sandwich en carton-mousse. Comme le souligne l'architecte, la nature du projet permet la construction rapide de logements temporaires de meilleure qualité et crée localement de l'emploi. Au-delà de l'aide aux victimes de catastrophes, ces logements faciles à déplacer pourraient améliorer les conditions d'habitat dans les régions pauvres de pays comme l'Inde et le Népal, qui ont tous deux exprimé leur intérêt.

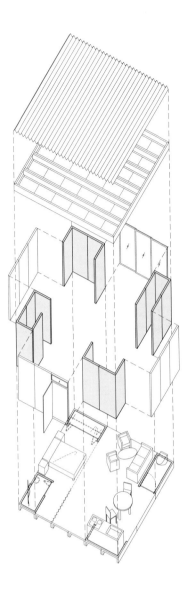

An exploded axonometric drawing shows
the different components of the house from
the floor plan to the roof.

Die axonometrische Explosionszeichnung
zeigt die verschiedenen Elemente des Hauses
vom Grundriss bis zum Dach.

Le schéma axonométrique éclaté montre
les différents éléments de la maison, du plan
au sol jusqu'au toit.

Shigeru Ban has worked for years on different ways to design dignified and easy-to-install housing systems for people in emergency situations.

Shigeru Ban hat über viele Jahre auf unterschiedliche Weise am Entwurf angemessener und einfach zu errichtender Wohnsysteme für Menschen in Notsituationen gearbeitet.

Shigeru Ban a travaillé des années à différentes conceptions d'habitat digne et facile à installer dans les situations d'urgence.

SURICATTA SYSTEMS
La Marina, Alicante [Spain] — 2016

SURI—SHELTER UNITS FOR RAPID INSTALLATION

Area: 12.6 m² — Client: Rosa Martínez — Cost: €12 000

A basic SURI unit is intended to house one person, but the units can be joined together sidewise or lengthwise to create larger shelters. The folded enclosures (above) are 15 centimeters thick and deploy to a length of 130 centimeters.

Die Grundeinheit SURI ist für eine Person bestimmt, aber die Elemente können seitlich oder der Länge nach verbunden werden. Die zusammengelegten Umhüllungen (oben) sind 15 cm dick und entfalten sich bis zu einer Länge von 130 cm.

L'unité SURI de base est conçue pour une personne, mais les unités peuvent être assemblées par le côté ou sur leur longueur pour créer de plus grands abris. Les clôtures repliées (en haut) font 15 cm d'épaisseur et se déploient sur une longueur de 130 cm.

Although it was intended mainly for disaster relief subsequent to the 2011 Lorca earthquake, the SURI shelter can also be used for temporary, seasonal, or low-cost housing, even for surfers—as seen in images reproduced here. Emergency relief efforts using the structure have been undertaken in the Sahara, Jordan, Ethiopia, and Ecuador. The system does not need a foundation. Exteriors are completed with sandbags that can be filled either with sand or other readily available local materials, thus improving the thermal performance of the shelter and its structural stability. The use of sandbags also naturally decreases transport weight for the other elements. The shelter is intended to be 100% recyclable and sustainable. All materials are reusable or biodegradable. Solar panels and a rainwater collection system can be integrated where appropriate. The SURI shelter comes as a 580-kilo flat-pack that can be assembled on site by two people without particular skills. They are made of different forms of polyethylene, wood, Plexiglas, ABS (Acrylonitrile butadiene styrene), and sand bags.

Obgleich die SURI-Unterkunft in erster Linie für den Katastropheneinsatz nach dem Erdbeben in Lorca von 2011 bestimmt war, kann sie auch als temporäre, saisonale oder Einfachwohnung, sogar für Surfer, genutzt werden – wie auf den hier gezeigten Abbildungen zu sehen ist. Einsätze des Gebäudes in Notsituationen erfolgten bereits in der Sahara, in Jordanien, Äthiopien und Ekuador. Das System benötigt kein Fundament. Die Außenwände werden aus Sandsäcken errichtet, die entweder mit Sand oder anderen verfügbaren örtlichen Materialien gefüllt werden, wodurch sich auch der Wärmeschutz und die statische Stabilität verbessern. Die Verwendung von Sandsäcken vermindert natürlich das Transportgewicht zugunsten anderer Elemente. Die Unterkunft soll 100-prozentig recycelbar und nachhaltig sein. Alle Materialien sind wiederverwendbar oder biologisch abbaubar. Solarpaneele und ein Speichersystem für Regenwasser können, falls sinnvoll, integriert werden. Die SURI-Unterkunft wird als 580 kg schwerer Flatpack geliefert und kann von zwei ungelernten Personen vor Ort aufgebaut werden. Sie besteht aus verschiedenen Arten Polyethylen, Holz, Plexiglas, Acrylnitril-Butodien-Styrol (ABS) und Sandsäcken.

Destiné essentiellement aux victimes de catastrophes et conçu après le tremblement de terre de Lorca en 2011, l'abri SURI peut aussi servir de logement temporaire, saisonnier ou à moindre frais, ou encore aux surfeurs, comme en témoignent les photos. L'abri a été utilisé dans des situations d'urgence au Sahara, en Jordanie, en Éthiopie et en Équateur. Il n'a pas besoin de fondations ; l'extérieur est complété par des sacs de sable qui peuvent aussi être remplis d'autres matériaux locaux facilement disponibles pour améliorer les performances thermiques et la stabilité structurelle de l'ensemble. Les sacs de sable réduisent aussi naturellement le poids des autres éléments à transporter. L'abri est destiné à être recyclable et durable. Tous les matériaux utilisés sont réutilisables ou biodégradables. Des panneaux solaires et un système de récupération de l'eau de pluie peuvent être ajoutés si nécessaire. L'abri SURI est livré en kit de 580 kilos et peut être assemblé sur place par deux personnes sans compétences particulières. Il est fait de différentes formes de polyéthylène, de bois, de plexiglas, d'ABS (acrylonitrile butadiène styrène) et de sacs de sable.

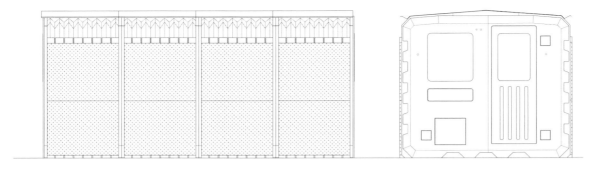

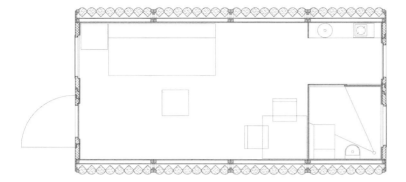

The SURI unit seen in these images is used by a surfer, but the basic intent of the structure is for humanitarian aid. The structure can be assembled by two unskilled people.

Die auf dieser Abbildung gezeigte SURI-Einheit wird von einem Surfer genutzt, aber sie ist eigentlich für humanitäre Hilfsaktionen bestimmt. Die Konstruktion kann von zwei ungelernten Personen montiert werden.

Si l'abri SURI qu'on voit ici est utilisé par un surfeur, sa destination première est l'aide humanitaire. La structure peut être assemblée par deux personnes sans compétences particulières.

WEARABLE SHELTER

Area: n/a — Client: Royal College of Art — Cost: not disclosed

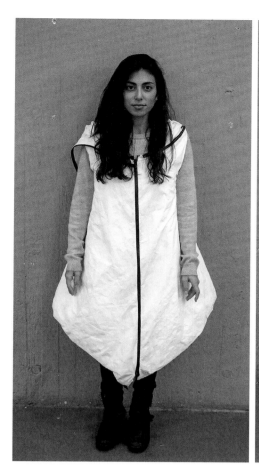  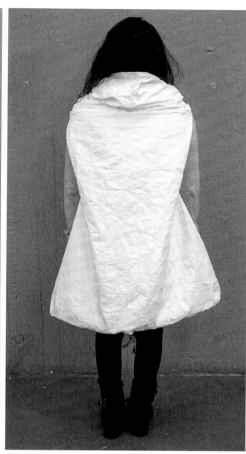

The Refugee Wearable Shelter was developed by Gabriella Geagea and Anne-Sophie Geay, working with other students under Professor Graeme Brooker, Head of the M.A. Interior Design program at the RCA, and Dr. Harriet Harriss, who is a Senior Tutor in Interior Design and Architecture at the RCA. The students developed this project for an innovative and multifunctional wearable dwelling "in direct response to the Syrian refugee crisis." The garment is designed to convert from a jacket with large storage pockets into a sleeping bag and also a tent. Although the students have now graduated, Sophie-Anne Geay and Gabriella Geagea are continuing to develop the project as a not-for-profit social enterprise, with a view to mass-producing the garment next year through crowd-funding and distributing them through established aid agencies already working in the area. Graeme Brooker says: "We are very keen to explore the way in which Interior Design can exemplify a commitment to social change. The Wearable Shelter will not solve this crisis but in a small way it may provide some help and also act as a catalyst for more assistance in this tragic situation." This garment is made of Tyvek, a protective barrier made by DuPont and used for building envelopes, sterile packaging, cargo covers, and protective apparel, among other applications.

Der Refugee Wearable Shelter wurde von Gabriella Geagea und Anne-Sophie Geay entwickelt, die mit weiteren Studierenden unter der Leitung von Professor Graeme Brooker, dem Leiter des Programms M. A. Interior Design am Royal College of Art, und Dr. Harriett Harriss, Senior Tutor für Innenarchitektur und Architektur am RCA, zusammenarbeiteten. Die Studierenden entwickelten dieses Projekt einer innovativen und multifunktionalen, tragbaren Unterkunft „als unmittelbare Reaktion auf die syrische Flüchtlingskrise". Das Kleidungsstück lässt sich von einer Jacke mit großen Aufbewahrungstaschen zu einem Schlafsack und auch zu einem Zelt umfunktionieren. Obgleich Anne-Sophie Geay und Gabriella Geagea ihr Studium inzwischen abgeschlossen haben, entwickeln sie ihr Projekt als soziales Non-Profit-Unternehmen weiter mit der Aussicht, das Kleidungsstück aufgrund von Spendeneinnahmen im nächsten Jahr in Serie zu produzieren und es durch angesehene, bereits in dem Gebiet tätige Hilfsorganisationen verteilen zu lassen. Graeme Brooker sagt: „Wir wollen unbedingt herausfinden, wie Innenarchitektur ein Beispiel für ein Engagement für den sozialen Wandel sein kann. Der Wearable Shelter wird diese Krise nicht lösen, aber im kleinen Bereich kann er Hilfe leisten und auch als Katalysator für mehr Hilfsbereitschaft in dieser tragischen Situation dienen." Dieses Kleidungsstück ist aus Tyvek, einem Vliesstoff mit hoher Dichte, der von DuPont hergestellt und unter anderem als Umhüllung von Bauten, für sterile Verpackungen, Cargo-Abdeckungen und Schutzbekleidung verwendet wird.

Cet abri portatif pour réfugiés a été développé par Gabriella Geagea et Anne-Sophie Geay avec d'autres étudiants du professeur Graeme Brooker, qui dirige le M.A. Architecture intérieure au Royal College of Art (RCA), et Harriet Harriss, directrice d'études en architecture intérieure et architecture au RCA. Les étudiants ont créé ce projet d'« habitat » portatif innovant et multifonction, « en réponse directe à la crise des réfugiés en Syrie ». Le vêtement est conçu pour se transformer, d'une veste aux larges poches en sac de couchage et tente. Les étudiants sont aujourd'hui diplômés, mais Anne-Sophie Geay et Gabriella Geagea travaillent encore au projet sous forme d'entreprise sociale à but non lucratif dans l'idée d'en commencer la production de masse l'année prochaine grâce à un financement participatif et la distribution par l'intermédiaire d'organisations caritatives qui travaillent déjà dans la région. « Nous tenons à explorer la manière dont l'architecture intérieure peut illustrer un engagement en faveur du progrès social, explique Graeme Brooker. L'abri portatif ne résoudra pas la crise, mais il peut modestement aider et jouer un rôle déclencheur pour favoriser l'aide dans cette situation dramatique. » Le vêtement est en Tyvek, une barrière de protection fabriquée par DuPont et utilisée notamment pour les enveloppes de constructions, les emballages stériles, les cache-bagages et les vêtements de protection.

+31 ARCHITECTS

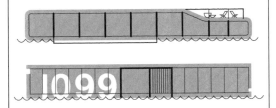

+31 Architects
Veemarkt 191
1019 CH Amsterdam
The Netherlands

Tel: +31 624 67 16 31
E-mail: info@plus31architects.com
Web: www.plus31architects.com

Jasper Suasso de Lima de Prado was born in 1975 in Laren, the Netherlands. He was an exchange student at the École d'Architecture de Montpellier (France, 1998) and worked from 1998 to 1999 at Marc Prosman Architects, Amsterdam. In 2001, he graduated from Delft University of Technology, and again worked with Marc Prosman from 2001 to 2005. He cofounded +31 Architects in Amsterdam in 2005. Jorrit Houwert was born in Dornach (Switzerland) in 1974. He worked with Architects PT Gunawan Cipta Arsindo (Jakarta, Indonesia, 1997) and then at Neutelings Riedijk Architects (Rotterdam, 1999), graduating from Delft University of Technology in 2001. He was also employed from 2002 to 2005 by Marc Prosman Architects in Amsterdam, before cofounding +31 Architects. Their work includes Watervilla Omval (Amsterdam, 2010) and Watervilla Weesperzijde (Amsterdam, 2014), both published here (**see pp. 150, 154**).

ÁBATON

Ábaton Arquitectura
Calle Ciudad Real 28
28223 Pozuelo de Alarcón
Madrid | Spain

Tel: +34 91 352 1616
E-mail: info@abaton.es
Web: www.abaton.es

Camino Alonso was born in 1965. She received her training as an architect at the ETSAM (Madrid) and is a Partner and Creative Manager of Ábaton, which she founded with the architect Ignacio Lechón and the industrial engineer Carlos Alonso in 1998. Realizing the importance of construction, they immediately created their own firm in that area as well. Ábaton has built more than 200 houses, hotels, offices, and restaurants, as well as carrying out 80 refurbishments in Spain and abroad. Their work includes Las Mariàs, a series of eight semidetached residences (Torrelodones, Madrid, 2009); an estate in Extremadura (2012); Ábaton Portable Home ÁPH80 (Madrid, 2013; **see p. 194**); Ed Office (refurbishment, Madrid, 2015); the L House (refurbishment, Pozuelo de Alarcón,

Madrid, 2015); and Camino de la Huerta (La Moraleja, Madrid, 2016). Current work includes the expansion of the CVNE Wineries (La Rioja, under construction) and the Atlanterra Beach House (Cadiz, under construction).

APPLETON & DOMINGOS / JULAR

Appleton & Domingos-Arquitectos
Rua do Centro Cultural 10 – 1o andar
1700–107 Lisbon | Portugal

Tel: +351 218 48 66 58
E-mail: geral@appletondomingos.pt
Web: www.appletondomingos.pt

Jular Madeiras, SA
Quinta de Santa Rosa – Apt. 1042
2681–901 Camarate Loures, Lisbon
Portugal

Tel: +351 219 48 40 00
E-mail: mail@jular.pt
Web: www.jular.pt

Both born in 1971, João Appleton and Isabel Domingos graduated from FAUTL (Faculdade de Arquitectura da UTL, Lisbon) in 1992 and received their Master's in Construction Systems from the IST (Instituto Superior Técnico, Lisbon) in 2000. They have worked together since 1995. In 1999, they founded Appleton & Domingos Architects. Their main projects include the City Hall (Odivelas, 2000–04); Calçada do Combro Car Parking (Lisbon, 2003–04); the Frei Aleixo Neighborhood (Évora, 1999–2007); the Rehabilitation of the Padre António Macedo High School (Vila Nova de Santo André, 2008–10); the Rehabilitation of Santa Maria High School (Sintra, 2008–10); the House in San Pedro de Sintra (2011–13), all in Portugal; and the Treehouse System for Jular (various locations, 2005–16; **see p. 272**).

ARCHITECTS FOR SOCIETY

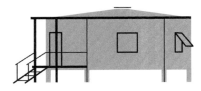

Architects for Society
Studio 439, 1500 Jackson Street N.E. #175
Minneapolis, MN 55435 | USA

Tel: +1 612 425 8391
E-mail: info@architectsforsociety.org
Web: www.architectsforsociety.org

Architects for Society is an international non-profit design organization based in the United States. Amro Sallam (American architect born in Cairo) is the Executive Director and one of the main founders of Architects for Society. He worked for

Skidmore, Owings & Merrill in Chicago, and Herzog & de Meuron in Basel (2012–15). He received a BS in Architecture from the University of Illinois (Urbana-Champaign, 1995) and an M.Arch from SCI-Arc (Los Angeles, 1998). Born in Riyadh, Saudi Arabia, in 1984, Yousef Oqleh is the Chairman of Architects for Society. He worked in the office of Herzog & de Meuron (Basel, 2013–15) and is presently with Gensler in Abu Dhabi. Altaf Engineer is a founding member and Communications Director of Architects for Society. He was born in 1979 in Mumbai and obtained his Master's (2005) and Ph.D. (2015) in Architecture from the University of Illinois at Urbana-Champaign. They are among those—with David Dwars, Taru Niskanen, Mourad Bendjennet, David Koch, Stephan Wedrich, Adam Whipple, Dan Clark, Klass Elsinga, Luca Marchetti, and Sonal Mithal—who created the NGO in 2015 with the aim of "enhancing the built environment of disadvantaged communities through innovative architecture and design." Published here is Hex House (Zaatari Refugee Camp, Mafraq, Jordan, 2015; **see p. 314**).

ARCHIWORKSHOP

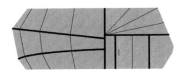

ArchiWorkshop
26 Juheung 1-gil, Seocho-gu
06543 Seoul | South Korea

Tel: +82 2 542 3947
E-mail: office@archiworkshop.kr
Web: www.archiworkshop.kr

ArchiWorkshop was founded by Hee-Jun Sim and Su-Jeong Park. Hee-Jun Sim participated in an exchange program at the ETH (Zurich) and graduated from the University of Stuttgart (Germany). He has worked at RPBW (Paris), Herzog & de Meuron (Basel), and Rasch & Bradatsch (Stuttgart). Su-Jeong Park graduated from Kwangwoon University in Architecture. She participated in the Erasmus program at the Delft University of Technology and obtained her Diploma in Architecture from the University of Stuttgart. She has worked with Behnisch Architekten (Stuttgart), and Mecanoo Architects (Delft). As well as Stacking Doughnut and Modular Flow (also called Embracing Art and Architecture) of 2013 (**see p. 176**), their work includes Membrane Pavilion (Mobile Library; Seoul, 2015); Attached Block Pavilion (Mobile Library; Seoul, 2015); Pipe Pavilion (Seoul, 2015); CampTong Island project (Chung-Pyeong, 2016); and Glamping on the Rock (2016).

AUTONOMOUS TENT

Autonomous Tent Co. LLC
615 E. 7th Avenue #A
Denver, CO 80203 | USA

Tel: +1 303 898 9161
E-mail: info@autonomoustent.com
Web: www.autonomoustent.com

Autonomous Tent Co. was founded in 2013 to "design the world's first transportable 5-star boutique hotel that would be located in secluded natural locations for a season at a time." Powered by the sun and wind, using advanced water filtration and composting technology, the structure was billed as being fully ecological. A prototype of the Autonomous Tent that was developed on the basis of this project was installed during the summer of 2015 on the West Bijou Bison Ranch, which is run by the Prairie Conservation Center in Aurora, Colorado. The Treebones Resort in California has been renting out an Autonomous Tent since April 2016 (**see p. 164**). The founder of Autonomous Tent, Phil Parr, worked for 23 years in technology businesses and, in 2012, he asked the noted California architect Harry Gesner to help in the transportable hotel project. Gesner, born in 1925, was self-taught as an architect and is known for his environmental consciousness.

SHIGERU BAN

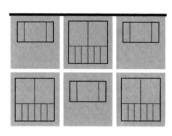

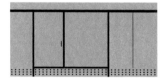

Shigeru Ban Architects
5-2-4 Matsubara
Setagaya-ku
Tokyo 156-0043
Japan

Tel: +81 3 3324 6760
E-mail: tokyo@shigerubanarchitects.com
Web: www.shigerubanarchitects.com

Born in 1957 in Tokyo, Shigeru Ban studied at SCI-Arc from 1977 to 1980. He then attended the Cooper Union School of Architecture, where he studied under John Hejduk (1980–82), returning to graduate in 1984, after working in the office of Arata Isozaki for a year. He then founded his own firm in Tokyo in 1985. He designed the Japanese Pavilion at Expo 2000 in Hanover. His work includes Maison E (Fukushima, 2005–06); the disaster-relief Post-Tsunami Rehabilitation Houses (Kirinda, Hambantota, Sri Lanka, 2006–07); the Nicolas G. Hayek Center (Tokyo, 2007); Haesley Nine Bridges Golf Clubhouse (Yeoju, South Korea, 2010); and the Metal Shutter House on West 19th Street in New York (2010). He installed his Paper Temporary Studio on top of the Pompidou Center in Paris to work on the new Pompidou-Metz Center (Metz, France, 2010). Recent work includes L'Aquila Temporary Concert Hall (Italy, 2011); Container

Temporary Housing, disaster-relief project for the east Japan earthquake and tsunami (Onagawa, Miyagi, 2011; **see p. 300**); Tamedia (Zurich, 2011–13); the Cardboard Cathedral (Christchurch, New Zealand, 2013); New Temporary House (Manila, Philippines, 2013; **see p. 320**); Aspen Art Museum (Aspen, Colorado, 2014); Oita Prefectural Art Museum (Oita, Japan, 2015); the Cast Iron House (New York, 2013–17); La Seine Musicale (Île Seguin, Boulogne-Billancourt, France, 2017); and the Swatch Group Headquarters and Production Facility (Bienne, Switzerland, 2012–).

BONNIFAIT + GIESEN

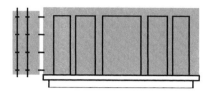

Bonnifait + Giesen
Atelierworkshop
43 Haining Street
Wellington 6011
Aotearoa | New Zealand

Tel: +64 4384 6688
E-mail: enquiry@atelierworkshop.com
Web: www.atelierworkshop.com

Cécile Bonnifait was born in France in 1971. She studied and worked in Bordeaux from 1989 to 1995, where she obtained her architecture degree, and in Helsinki in 1996, before moving to Wellington, New Zealand, in 2000. She founded Bonnifait + Giesen with William Giesen in 2001. After beginning his architectural studies at Victoria University in Wellington, William Giesen travelled to France in 1997 to play rugby and to pursue his architectural studies at the Bordeaux School of Architecture and Landscape Design (1998–99). Their work includes the Lloyd Holiday House (Paekakariki, Kapiti Coast, 2011); the Jumpstart Pre-School (New Plymouth, 2014); White Hart Hotel Precinct (New Plymouth, 2015); Werry House (Paekakariki, Kapiti Coast, 2015); Robertson House (Te Awanga, Hawkes Bay, 2016) and the upcoming Streamline Training Pool (New Plymouth, 2017), all in New Zealand. Their Port-a-Bach (2006; **see p. 262**) was built in Hangzhou, China.

BUREAU DES MÉTIERS

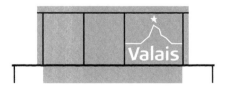

Bureau des Métiers
Rue de la Dixence 20
1950 Sion
Switzerland

Tel: +41 27 327 51 11
E-mail: info@bureaudesmetiers.ch
Web: www.cube365.ch /
www.bureaudesmetiers.ch

The Bureau des Métiers is an association of local artisans in the area of construction grouped together under that name for the first time in 1938. It has been directed since 2005 by Gabriel Décaillet. The Bureau des Métiers was one of the significant sponsors of the Cube365 project (**see p. 198**), and its member organizations were in good part responsible for the realization of the actual structure. The total cost of the project, including transport, was approximately €785 000, divided among a prestigious group of sponsors representing the Canton in this celebration of its history. The Cube365 was placed in many symbolic locations of Valais, including the Aletsch Glacier, and ski resorts like Saas-Fee or Verbier. After its use during 2015, Cube365 became the property of the Bureau des Métiers, which had guaranteed the financial aspects of the operation. Put up for sale, the structure had inspired queries coming from as far afield as Kazakhstan and Qatar.

MATTHEW BUTCHER, OWAIN WILLIAMS, AND KIERAN THOMAS WARDLE

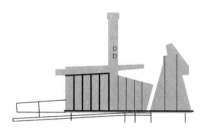

Matthew Butcher was born in London in 1977. He graduated from the Bartlett School of Architecture, and has worked in the offices of Sauerbruch Hutton (Berlin), and Arup Engineers in London. Owain Williams was born in 1988 in Pontypridd, Wales. He also graduated from the Bartlett, and is presently an architect and urban designer at Publica Associates, London. Kieran Thomas Wardle was born in 1988 in Liverpool. He studied at the Liverpool School of Architecture and the Universidad Europea de Madrid, before graduating from the Bartlett in 2013. He has worked as an architect at alma-nac and Ian Ritchie Architects in London. Mansio (2016; **see p. 224**) was designed by Matthew Butcher, Owain Williams, and Kieran Thomas Wardle. Their design team was assembled principally for the Mansio project.

BRIAN & JONI BUZARDE

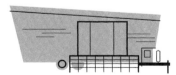

Brian Buzarde
Topos Homes LLC
1955 Marble Village Drive
Marble, CO 81623 | USA

Tel: +1 970 497 0925
E-mail: brian@toposhomes.com
Web: www.toposhomes.com /
www.landarkrv.com

Topos Architecture LLC was created by Brian Buzarde, born in 1984 in Wheatridge, Colorado, and is currently owned and operated by him. Previously Buzarde worked with Bldg Seed Architects, Rowland+Broughton Architecture and Urban Design, BWM Group, and Lake Flato Architects. Joni Roberson Buzarde was born in 1983 in Lubbock, Texas. She has a background in marketing and project management, and worked with her husband on launching Land Ark RV, of which Woody (2011–12; see p. 82) is a prototype. Brian Buzarde explains that the couple's other projects, including another residence, are under development.

CARTER WILLIAMSON

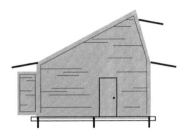

Carter Williamson Architects
1/142 Smith Street
2130 Summer Hill, NSW
Australia

Tel: +61 97 99 4472
E-mail: mail@carterwilliamson.com
Web: www.carterwilliamson.com

Carter Williamson Architects was established in 2004 by Shaun Carter, who studied architecture and engineering in Sydney. The firm's built work includes the Brise Soleil Residence (Balmain, 2008); Blues Point Hotel (McMahons Point, 2008); Cowshed House (Glebe, 2011); Light Cannon House (Annandale, 2013); and the Spiegel Hause (Alexandra, 2014), all in Sydney, as well as Grid published here, a transportable disaster-relief project originally designed in 2005 and seen in prototype form at the Sydney Architecture Festival (2012, 2016; see p. 310).

DUBLDOM / BIO ARCHITECTS

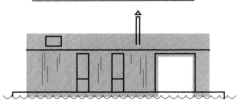

BIO Architects
DublDom
Zhukovka Village, DublDom Factory
117393 Moscow
Russia

Tel: +7 495 118 2723
E-mail: com@dubldom.com
Web: www.dubldom.com

Ivan Ovchinnikov was born in Moscow in 1980. In 2003 He graduated from the Moscow Architectural Institute 2003, and then worked for four years as a Senior Architect in the Asadov Architectural Studio (Moscow). In 2005, together with Andrey Asadov, he organized the Goroda Architectural Festival, which continued until 2013. From 2011 to 2013 he directed ArchFarm, a "country art residence." Beginning in 2013, he developed and organized the production of the serial modular house DublDom. In 2014, he became the co-founder and a member of the Club of Industrial Designers (KPD, Moscow). His work includes the ArchShelter (Tygatchev Mountain Ski Club, Moscow Oblast, 2011); and the DublDom Houseboat (Kalyazin, Tver Region, Russia, 2015; see p. 90); and he has been involved in the DublDomClub network of country hotels with rooms made using the DublDom modular houses.

ECOCAPSULE

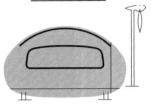

Ecocapsule
Zlta 22/G
85107 Bratislava
Slovakia

Tel: +421 904 67 25 30
E-mail: info@ecocapsule.sk;
info@nicearchitects.sk
Web: www.ecocapsule.sk;
www.niceandwise.sk

Founded in 2015, Ecocapsule is a company led by the architects Tomáš Žáček (1980) and Soňa Pohlová, formerly of Nice Architects (Nice&Wise, Bratislava). Working with Žáček's brother Igor (1982) and designer Matej Pospisil (1985), in late 2009 they created the concept of the Ecocapsule (see p. 212), a self-sustainable micro-home, dubbed the Rolling Stones capsule, which they entered into a competition sponsored by the Andes Sprouts Society, a non-profit arts organization located on farmland near Highway 28 in the Delaware County Catskills region of New York. The competition called for the creation of a sustainable studio or living unit. Tomáš Žáček explains: "They wanted a mobile house, almost like a hotel room that could operate off-grid." The idea of Ecocapsule became a reality with the first prototype in 2015. Beginning as a start-up, Ecocapsule was transformed into a full-fledged company in early 2017.

AXEL ENTHOVEN

Axel Enthoven
Yellow Window N.V.
Mechelsesteenweg 64 Box 701
2018 Antwerp
Belgium

Tel: +32 3 203 53 00
E-mail: info@yellowwindow.com
Web: www.yellowwindow.com

Born in 1947 in Antwerp, Axel Enthoven founded both Enthoven Associates and Yellow Window. He was educated at the Design Academy in Eindhoven, the Salesian Polytechnic (Tokyo), and at the GE Research Center (Cleveland, Ohio). He has been Dean of the Mobility Department at the Design Academy in Eindhoven and a professor at the Antwerp Design University. He has been the Worldwide Design Consultant for the Ideal and American Standard sanitary firms. His mobile work includes the MIVB Tram (Brussels, 2005); Opera, Your Suite in Nature (2009; see p. 64); the Qatar Education City Avenio People Mover (Siemens, 2012); the Halo First Class Suite (Zodiac Aerospace, 2014); and the Alstom tramway for Jerusalem and Rio (2016).

FICTION FACTORY

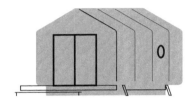

Fiction Factory
Back-Upstraat 1
1033 NX Amsterdam
Netherlands

Tel: +31 20 635 24 24
E-mail: hello@wikkelhouse.com
Web: www.wikkelhouse.com;
www.fictionfactory.nl

Fiction Factory was founded in 1989 as a theatre décor company, under the name Schilling & De Nijs. This two-man business has since become a professional construction studio with 45 full-time craftsmen. They still manufacture stage settings, but also stands for trade fairs throughout Europe, as well as office and shop interiors for international fashion labels. Fiction Factory also markets a number of the objects they have designed, including FF022 Leather Case, FF007 and FF029 standing lamps, the FF017 desk, FF029 round table, and even FF037 socks. The firm has branched out further with the creation of the modular Wikkelhouse (Wrap House; see p. 292) that can be readily transported and reassembled on different sites and for different uses including residence.

FRANCIS & ARNETT

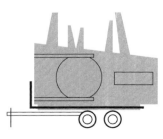

Francis & Arnett
4 Plender Street
NW1 0JT London | UK

Tel: +44 75 47 06 78 68
E-mail: info@francisandarnett.com
Web: www.francisandarnett.com;
www.epicretreats.wales

The Welsh government backed this scheme to create the first "pop-up boutique hotel" in the country in the context of their "Visit Wales 2017 Year of Legends" program. Organized by Epic Retreats, a partnership between Best of Wales, Cambria Tours, George + Tomos Architects, and the Welsh Government's Tourism Product Innovation Fund, a competition selected eight mobile structures, each designed by a different architect, to be installed in two sites in North and South Wales during the summer of 2017. The cabins had to make use of Welsh materials and be suitable for transportation on a 2.7-meter-wide, 5.7-meter-long, and 3.4-meter-high chassis. The cabins also include a shower, compost toilet, king-sized bed and mattress, basin, seating area, and wood burning stove. A separate communal eating and food preparation area provides a fridge and barbeque. The selected architects are Miller Kendrick, Waind Gohil + Potter, Rural Office for Architecture, Francis & Arnett, How About Studio, Carwyn Lloyd Jones, Barton Wilmore, and Trias Studio. Francis & Arnett, the office responsible for the Animated Forest project (see p. 46), is based in London and was founded by Rania Francis (born in 1991 in Derynia, Cyprus) and Mike Arnett (born in 1990 in Coventry, UK). According to their own description: "Francis & Arnett is a design studio based on providing unique objects, spaces, and experiences... We explore the boundary between function and pleasure with a focus on the bespoke. Our designs seek to be enjoyable and memorable while retaining a sensitivity to their context and purpose."

FRIDAY / FERNANDO SEABRA SANTOS

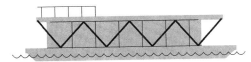

Friday, Ciência e Engenharia do Lazer, SA
Instituto Pedro Nunes, Edifício C,
Rua Pedro Nunes
3030–199 Coimbra
Portugal

Tel: +351 239 78 00 82
E-mail: info@gofriday.eu
Web: www.gofriday.eu

Fernando Seabra Santos was born in Coimbra, Portugal, in 1955. He graduated in Civil Engineering from the University of Coimbra in 1977. In 1982, he obtained a DEA degree from the Institut National Polytechnique de Grenoble, in the area of industrial fluid mechanics. In 1985, in the same institution, he obtained a Ph.D. in Oceanography. Since 1998, he has been a tenured Professor in the Department of Civil Engineering of the Faculty of Science and Technology at the University of Coimbra. Between 1980 and 2000 he participated in more than 20 scientific research projects. In 2012, he created the company Friday, Ciência e Engenharia do Lazer. He is currently Chairman of the company, which is now publicly

traded and which conceives, designs, and builds nautical projects, including floating houses and small submarines for pleasure and research for two or three people. FloatWing® (2015; see p. 116) is "a new floating house concept," and is the company's first major project.

MIKAEL GENBERG

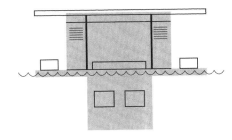

E-mail: info@mikaelgenberg.com
Web: www.mikaelgenberg.com

Mikael Genberg, born in 1963, is a Swedish artist who has become well known for proposing alternative living environments. His works include the Otter Inn (an underwater hotel located in Västerås, Sweden, three meters under the surface of Lake Mälaren); Café Koala; Klosette Kameleont (Chameleon Toilet); and the Hackspett Hotel (Woodpecker Hotel) tree house. The form of this hotel recalls an earlier project by Genberg, his 1999 idea to put a little red house on the moon "to symbolize people's faith in the ability to make changes." He went on to design a house that would automatically open once it had been delivered to the surface of the moon by an unmanned lunar module. The Café Koala has five-meter-high chairs that "give a coffee break a new meaning." There is a Café Koala in both Västerås and Rio de Janeiro. The Västerås café is located on the island of Elba in Lake Mälaren and has a view of the Otter Inn. The Klosette Kameleont is an outdoor toilet that is built with one-way mirrored glass "that completely changes the feeling of one of our most private moments." The Manta Underwater Room (Pemba Island, Tanzania, 2013; see p. 124) is clearly related in its concept to the earlier Otter Inn.

GÜTE

Güte
348050 4th Line
Maxwell, Ontario N0C 1J0
Canada

Tel: +1 519 377 3190
E-mail: dylan@gute.ca
Web: www.gute.ca

Born in Germany, Thomas Güte grew up in Ontario and trained for seven years with a German master-builder, Art Kuebler. He founded Constellation Homes and built custom homes in south-

ern Ontario for a period of 30 years. Dylan Güte studied at McMaster University (Hamilton, Ontario), before creating the current firm, Güte, with his father. The Shepherd Huts they design—2.3 meters wide and 4.6 meters long—are fitted with their own modular furniture designs that are created in their workshop in solid wood. This includes kitchenettes, desks, and beds, as well as the electric composting toilets or a ventless ethanol fireplace that can be installed in them. Published here is the Collingwood Shepherd Hut of 2015 (see p. 52).

TOMOKAZU HAYAKAWA

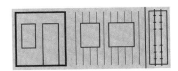

Tomokazu Hayakawa Architects
13–16 Nampeidaicho
1500036 Shibuya, Tokyo
Japan

Tel: +81 3 6416 9736
E-mail: info@thykw.com
Web: www.thykw.com

Tomokazu Hayakawa was born in Gifu Prefecture in 1975. He received a Master's degree in Engineering from Keio University (Tokyo, 2003), and worked in the office of Kengo Kuma in Tokyo (2005), before creating his own firm in 2010. Aside from the Muse-One Timber Container (Gunma, 2013) published here (see p. 258), he has completed the H-House, a three-story, 130-square-meter residence in Tokyo (2016); and Steel Box the Roof House (Kansai, 2016). His earlier Timber Container CC4441 (Tokyo, 2014) makes use of the same ideas as the Muse-One Timber Container by stacking two shipping containers on top of each other that can be opened and closed.

HOFMANN ARCHITECTURE / HOFARC

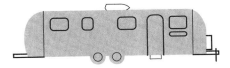

Hofmann Architecture / HofArc
519 N Quarantina Street
Santa Barbara, CA 93103 | USA

Tel: +1 805 618 2461
E-mail: info@hofarc.com
Web: www.hofarc.com

Created by a father and son team, Matthew and Wally Hofmann, Hofmann Architecture is specialized in "small space mobile design and build services." Matthew Hofmann, Chairman and founder of the firm, graduated from California Polytechnic State University with a B.Sc. in Architecture and then worked with DesignARC Architects in Santa Barbara. He is licensed to practice architecture in California and is a US Green Building Council LEED Accredited Professional. Wally, who is the President of the firm, graduated from Pacific Union College, in the Napa Valley, with a Bachelor's degree in Design. Their work includes a number of refitting projects based on Airstream campers, such as Elizabeth and Michelle, the former published here (see p. 38). These campers serve as offices, recreational vehicles, or food service facilities.

HRISTINA HRISTOVA

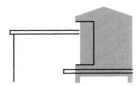

Hristina Hristova
Koleliba
41 Borovo Street
1000 Sofia
Bulgaria

Tel: +359 886 63 38 42
E-mail: info@koleliba.com
Web: www.koleliba.com

Hristina Hristova received her Bachelor's degree from the University of Architecture and Civil Engineering in Sofia (2009–13) and is working on her Master's in Architecture with a focus on historic preservation from the same institution (2015–present). She worked as an intern with Simon Gill Architects (London, 2013–15) before creating her own office, Koleliba, in 2015. Koleliba is also the name of the project published here (2015; see p. 56), a "made up word meaning a hut with wheels." Aside from Koleliba, Hristina Hristova has worked on projects for a mobile classroom for 15 children, a mobile museum on biodiversity for 15 children, a seaside mobile house for a young couple of artists, and a mobile live-work unit for a couple, all still in the planning phase.

CARWYN LLOYD JONES

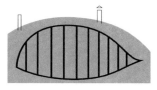

Carwyn Lloyd Jones
Timber Design Wales
Maes Awelon, Pen Y Garn, Bow Street
SY24 5BQ Aberystwhyth, Ceredigion
Wales
UK

Tel: +44 197 082 00 27
E-mail: carwynljones@aol.com
Web: www.timberdesignwales.co.uk

Carwyn Lloyd Jones, born in 1973 in Aberystwyth, Wales, is an expert in timber framing. He attended Ceredigion College (Cardigan), and has been the main tutor for a "Build a Tiny House" course featured in *The Guardian* newspaper and organized by the Welsh Centre for Alternative Technology (CAT, Machynlleth, Powys). He is also a tutor in advanced timber-frame joints and DIY furniture. He is the designer and builder of the Dragon's Eye, published here (Wales, 2017; see p. 206). In 2015, he created a surprising mobile home from an old caravan bought on EBay for just £720 that he covered with 4000 reclaimed CDs. He also designed a building for a biomass boiler at CAT in 2016. He says: "I tend to build smaller buildings and structures as they are more achievable. Working on my own, which means I can and will do everything, I really enjoy designing and building, creating."

KENGO KUMA

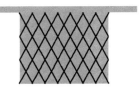

Kengo Kuma & Associates
2-24-8 Minami Aoyama
Minato-ku
Tokyo 107-0062
Japan

Tel: +81 3 3401 7721
E-mail: kuma@ba2.so-net.ne.jp
Web: www.kkaa.co.jp

Born in 1954 in Kanagawa, Japan, Kengo Kuma graduated in 1979 from the University of Tokyo with an M.Arch degree. In 1987, he established the Spatial Design Studio, and in 1991 he created Kengo Kuma & Associates. His recent work includes the Great (Bamboo) Wall Guesthouse (Beijing, China, 2002); One Omotesando (Tokyo, 2003); LVMH Osaka (Osaka, 2004); the Nagasaki Prefectural Art Museum (Nagasaki, 2005); Zhongtai Box, Z58 building (Shanghai, 2003–06); Steel House (Bunkyo-ku, Tokyo, 2005–07); Tiffany Ginza (Tokyo, 2008); Nezu Museum (Tokyo, 2007–09); Museum of Kanayama (Ota City, Gunma, 2009); Glass Wood House (New Canaan, Connecticut, 2007–10); Yusuhara Marche (Yusuhara, Kochi, 2009–10); and the Yusuhara Wooden Bridge Museum (Yusuhara-cho, Takaoka-gun, Kochi, 2010), all in Japan unless stated otherwise. Two recent small projects (Même Experimental House, Hokkaido, 2011–12; and Hojo-an (Kyoto, 2012; see p. 216) demonstrate the architect's attachment to innovative structures, often based on historic precedents. The architect has also begun to work extensively in Europe: FRAC PACA (Marseille, France, 2011–13); the Conservatory of Music, Dance, and Theater (Aix-en-Provence, France, 2011–13); and the ArtLab (EPFL, Lausanne, Switzerland, 2014–16).

LOT-EK

LOT-EK
181 Chrystie Street #2
New York, NY 10002
USA

Tel: +1 212 255 9326
E-mail: info@lot-ek.com
Web: www.lot-ek.com

Ada Tolla was born in 1964 in Potenza, Italy. She received her M.Arch from the Architecture Faculty of the "Federico II" University (Naples, 1982–89) and did postgraduate studies at Columbia University (New York, 1990–91). She is one of the two founding Partners of LOT-EK, created in Naples, Italy, in 1993 and in New York in 1995. The other cofounder is Giuseppe Lignano, who was born in Naples in 1963. He also received his M.Arch degree from the "Federico II" University (1982–89) and did postgraduate studies at Columbia at the same time as Ada Tolla. Their work includes the Guzman Penthouse (New York, 1996); M.D.U. Mobile Dwelling Unit (2003; see p. 232); UNIQLO Container Stores (New York, 2006); Theater for One (Princeton University, Princeton, New Jersey, 2007); PUMACity (Alicante, Spain, and Boston, Massachusetts, 2008); Weiner Townhouse (New York, 2008); PUMA DDSU (South Street Seaport, New York, 2010); APAP OpenSchool (Anyang, South Korea, 2010); and Van Alen Books (New York, 2011). More recent projects include the Whitney Studio (New York, 2012); Pier 57 (New York, 2011–13); and Band of Outsiders (Tokyo, 2012–13). Their current work includes Drivelines, residential building (Maboneng, Johannesburg, South Africa, 2014–16); Qiyun Mountain Camp, entry pavilion, retail, service and activity facilities (Qiyun, China, 2015–17); and the West Collection, art and retail center (Philadelphia), all in the USA unless stated otherwise.

MAPA

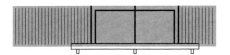

MAPA Architects
Rua Padre Chagas 67, 303
CP 90570-080 Porto Allegre, RS
Brazil

Tel: +55 51 3312 6574
E-mail: portoalegre@mapaarq.com
Web: www.mapaarq.com

MAPA Architects
Luis Alberto de Herrera 1042, 001
CP 11300, Montevideo
Uruguay

Tel: +598 2624 0530
E-mail: montevideo@mapaarq.com
Web: www.mapaarq.com

MAPA Architects is a bi-national collective that works in Brazil and Uruguay. Luciano Andrades was born in Porto Alegre in 1972 and graduated from ULBRA (São José, Canoas, RS, 2002). Matías Carballal was born in Montevideo in 1979 and graduated from the Universidad de la República

Uruguay in 2009. Rochelle Castro was born in Porto Alegre in 1978 and graduated from ULBRA in 2002. Andrés Gobba was born in Montevideo in 1978 and established the office MAAM in Montevideo in 2002. Mauricio López was also born in Montevideo in 1978, graduating from the Universidad de la República in 2009. Silvio Machado was born in Porto Alegre in 1977 and graduated from UniRitter (Porto Alegre) in 2004. They collectively established MAPA in 2013. Their work includes the Retreat in Finca Aguy (Pueblo Edén, Maldonado, Uruguay, 2014–15); MINIMOD Catuçaba (Fazenda Catuçaba, São Paulo, Brazil, 2015; see p. 248); a retreat in José Ignacio (José Ignacio, Maldonado, Uruguay, 2015); and Sacromonte Landscape Hotel (Maldonado, Uruguay, 2016–).

MARS ONE

Web: www.mars-one.com

Mars One was cofounded by Bas Lansdorp, who is the firm's CEO, with the intention of creating a permanent human settlement on Mars. Mars One consists of the non-profit Stichting Mars One (Mars One Foundation) based in the Netherlands and the publicly traded Swiss firm Mars One Ventures AG. Lansdorp explains: "Looking at images of the Mars surface by the Sojourner rover in 1997 as a young student made me want to go to Mars myself. As I explored the idea in the years that followed in my spare time with friends and colleagues, each piece of the puzzle seemed to fall in place. When I solved the last piece of the puzzle, I sold part of my shares in my previous company to finance the start-up of Mars One, and started working full time on the plan in March 2011." The goal of Mars One is to create a self-sustaining colony on Mars (see p. 228). The first phase calls for four people to travel there, with four more joining them every two years. They are convinced that the technology required to "keep a growing colony alive and thriving already exists." They plan to extract water from Martian ice in the soil, while a life-support system will extract nitrogen from the Martian atmosphere to make breathable air inside the modules. In 2016, a group of 200 000 candidates was reduced to 100 potential astronauts.

MIMA HOUSING

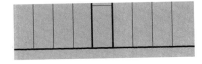

MIMA Housing
Caminho do Telheiro, no 338
Afife
4900–012 Viana do Castelo
Portugal

Tel: +351 913 04 58 35
E-mail: info@mimahousing.pt
Web: www.mimahousing.com

MIMA Housing is a multidisciplinary design office that seeks to "carry forward the Modernist dream of prefabrication, of integrated design, of architectural democratization." Simply put, the focus on readily transportable prefabricated housing. Marta Brandão is an architect who studied at the FAUP in Porto and at the EPFL in Lausanne. Between 2008 and 2012 she worked in the office of Herzog & de Meuron (Basel). A Partner and Art Director of the firm, she is responsible for the design and development of new projects, the supervision of construction as well as public relations. Màrio Sousa also studied architecture at the FAULP. He worked in Lausanne with Richter Dahl Rocha from 2007 to 2011, when he cofounded MIMA. A Partner of the firm, he conceives the new projects of MIMA Housing. Aside from MIMA Light (2015; see p. 236), they have designed the larger MIMA House, MIMA Essential, and MIMA Mass residences.

NILS HOLGER MOORMANN

Nils Holger Moormann GmbH
An der Festhalle 2
83229 Aschau im Chiemgau
Germany

Tel: +49 8052 904 50
E-mail: info@moormann.de
Web: www.moormann.de

Nils Holger Moormann was born in 1953 in Stuttgart, and began work as a transporter of furniture. He began to produce and sell the furniture of emerging designers, such as Konstantin Grcic and Axel Kufus, in 1982. He met success with the shelf Gespanntes Regal, a work by Wolfgang Laubersheimer, and has focused on objects with what is called a "reduced formal language," or "minimalist design and authentic materials." In 1984, Moormann founded his own company, which moved to Aschgau im Chiemgau in southern Bavaria in 1992. Six years later, he converted a former horseback-riding hall into a design workshop. He has 50 employees, including four designers working for him. Among those who have designed for Nils Holger Moormann are Takashi Sato, Tom Fischer, Neuland Industriedesign, and Katharina Ploog. The converted VW Minibus (Moorman's New Standard Class, 2016; see p. 60) shows his sense of combining practical features with interesting materials and technologically oriented solutions.

MORPHOSIS

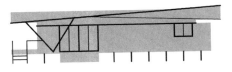

Morphosis
3440 Wesley Street
Culver City, CA 90232 | USA

Tel: +1 424 258 6200
E-mail: studio@morphosis.net
Web: www.morphosis.com

Morphosis Design Director Thom Mayne, born in Connecticut in 1944, received his B.Arch in 1968 from the University of Southern California, Los Angeles, and his M.Arch degree from Harvard in 1978. He founded Morphosis in 1972. He has taught at UCLA, Harvard, Yale, and SCI-Arc, of which he was a founding Board Member. Thom Mayne was the winner of the 2005 Pritzker Prize as well as the 2013 AIA Gold Medal. Some of the main early buildings by Morphosis are Cedar's Sinai Comprehensive Cancer Care Center (Los Angeles, 1987–88); Crawford Residence (Montecito, 1988–90); and the International Elementary School (Long Beach, 1998–99). More recent work includes the NOAA Satellite Operation Facility in Suitland (Maryland, 2001–05); San Francisco Federal Building (San Francisco, 2000–07); 41 Cooper Square (New York, 2006–09); the Float House (New Orleans, 2008–09; see p. 96); and the Giant Interactive Group Corporate Headquarters (Shanghai, China, 2006–10). They have also completed the Perot Museum of Nature and Science (Dallas, 2010–12). Ongoing work at the time of publication included the Casablanca Finance City Tower (Morocco, 2014–17); Hanking Center Tower (Shenzhen, China, 2014–17); and the Bloomberg Center at Cornell University (Ithaca, New York, 2015–17).

N55

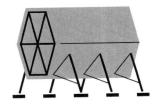

N55
Burmeistergade 10
1429 KBH K Copenhagen | Denmark

Tel: +45 20 66 40 89
E-mail: n55@n55.dk
Web: www.n55.dk

Ion Sørvin cofounded N55 in 1996, with the late Ingvil Aarbakke (1970–2005). He received a Master's degree at the Royal Danish Academy of Fine Arts (Copenhagen, 1991–98). His main collaborators at present are the architect Anne Romme and Tim Wolfer, who is a "designer, artist and activist." N55 has been involved in a large number of exhibitions, notably in Europe and the United States since 1996. Aside from the WALKING HOUSE (Copenhagen, 2009–10; see p. 286), N55 has created XYZ SPACEFRAME VEHICLES in collaboration with Till Wolfer, thus allowing people to build their own vehicles. The plans for the XYZ ONESEATER are available as open-source under Creative Commons <https://creativecommons.org/licenses/by-nc-sa/3.0/>. Other projects include SHOP, a system that "enables persons to exchange things without the use of money"; N55 SPACEFRAME, a "low-cost, movable, lightweight" structure that can be used as a living space for three to four people; and the SNAIL SHELL SYSTEM, a low-cost cylindrical polyethylene tank that is mobile both on land and water. According to the designer: "One person can move it slowly, either by pushing it like a wheel, or by walking inside it or on top of it."

NATIONAL AERONAUTICS AND SPACE ADMINISTRATION (NASA)

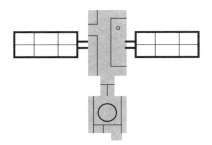

National Aeronautics and Space
Administration (NASA)
Public Communications Office

NASA Headquarters
Suite 5K39

Washington, DC 20546-0001 | USA

Tel: +1 202 358 0001
Web: www.nasa.gov

The National Aeronautics and Space Administration (NASA) runs the space, aeronautics, and aerospace research of the United States government. Created in 1958, NASA was responsible for the Apollo missions to the moon, or, more recently, the Space Shuttle. At present it supports the International Space Station as part of its goal to "pioneer the future in space exploration, scientific discovery, and aeronautics research." The agency currently employs about 18 000 people and has an annual budget in the range of $17.5 billion. Previously, President George W. Bush declared that NASA should lead an effort to return to the moon and possibly go on to Mars, an ambition confirmed by the Administrator of NASA in 2007, who said the goal would be to reach Mars by 2037. However, former President Barack Obama sought to limit this plan and asked that NASA should place its focus on "space taxis" limited to trips to orbital stations such as the ISS (see p. 220). The current Administrator of NASA is Robert M. Lightfoot Jr.

NINEBARK

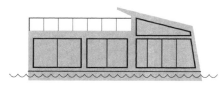

Ninebark Design Build LLC
3021 16th Avenue South
Seattle, WA 98144 | USA

Tel: +1 206 391 8736
E-mail: info@ninebarkstudio.com
Web: www.ninebarkstudio.com

Ryan Mankoski was born in Sacramento, California, in 1976. He is the owner, principal designer, and Managing Director of Ninebark Design Build

LLC. He received a BSD in Architecture from Arizona State University (1999). Founded in 2008, his company is involved in the design, production, and promotion of sustainable structures. His completed work includes the Portage Bay Floating Home (Seattle, Washington, 2009–10; see p. 128).

BERNI DU PAYRAT

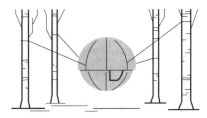

Berni du Payrat
Long Sun Corporation
268 Des Voeux Road, Central
Hong Kong, China

Tel: +336 1583 6813
E-mail: bernidupayrat@cocoontree.com
Web: www.cocoontree.com

The Cocoon Tree (Aix en Provence, France, 2017; see p. 168) was designed by Berni du Payrat, who is the owner of the brand name. A former creative director of advertising agencies in Paris, Du Payrat asked Long Sun Corporation in Hong Kong to manage the Cocoon Tree brand worldwide and Glamping Technology to take care of the manufacturing in Portugal.

PEOPLE'S INDUSTRIAL DESIGN OFFICE

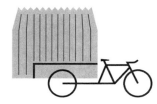

People's Industrial Design Office
37 Tiaozhou Hutong, Yard No.37
Xi Cheng District
Beijing 100051 | China

Tel: + 86 10 6523 8106
E-mail: office@peoples-products.com
Web: www.peoples-products.com

Zang Feng was born in Lanzhou, Gansu Province, and obtained an M.Arch degree at the Graduate Center of Architecture at Beijing University. He worked at Ateler FCJZ (founded Yung Ho Chang and Lijia Liu) from 2006 to 2010, when he cofounded People's Architecture Office and People's Industrial Design Office (PIDO) with He Zhe and James Shen. He Zhe was born in Jinua, Zhejiang Province. He obtained a B.Arch and Master of Urbanism degree from Xi'an University of Architecture and Technology. He also worked at FCJZ before cofounding PIDO. James Shen, a product designer, was born in Los Angeles, California, and received his M.Arch degree from MIT in 2007. He worked as a project architect for Atelier FCJZ prior to 2010. Aside from architectural projects and the Tricycle

House (Beijing, 2012; see p. 76), their work includes the 3D Copypod (2016) a 3D scan booth that can instantly digitize subjects of a wide range of sizes.

VYTAUTAS PUZERAS

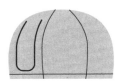

Puzero Design
Elnių 27–62
08101 Vilnius | Lithuania

Tel: +370 68 60 90 09
E-mail: order@oasisdome.eu
Web: www.oasisdome.eu

Born in 1976, Vytautas Puzeras created Puzero Design in Vilnius in 2000. He received a Bachelor's degree in Design from the Vilnius Art Academy in 1998 and a Master's from the same institution in 2000. He began work in advertising design even before his graduation. Since that time he has focused on social projects, interiors, furniture, lighting, landscape, and architecture. He created the Oasis tent in 2015 (see p. 172). Other work includes the furnishings for the main office of Swedbank (Vilnius, 2010); a public revitalization project called Upes Korys (Vilnius, 2010); the interior of the Aero Club (Kyviskes, 2011); the Eggy Easy Chair (2013); furniture and interior design for the Lithuanian Presidency of the European Union to equip NDG premises in Vilnius (2013); the interior identity design of the Lithuanian Delegation in the European Union Council building (Brussels, 2017); and ideas for the interior of the permanent delegation of the Republic of Lithuania to NATO (2017).

RENZO PIANO BUILDING WORKSHOP

Renzo Piano Building Workshop
Via P. Paolo Rubens 29
16158 Genoa | Italy

Tel: +39 01 06 17 11
E-mail: italy@rpbw.com
Web: www.rpbw.com

Renzo Piano was born in 1937 in Genoa, Italy. He studied at the University of Florence and at Milan's Polytechnic Institute (1964). He formed his own practice (Studio Piano) in 1965, associated with Richard Rogers (Piano & Rogers, 1971–78)—completing the Pompidou Center in Paris in 1977—and then worked with Peter Rice (Piano & Rice Associates, 1978–80), before creating the Renzo Piano Building Workshop in 1981 in Genoa and Paris. Piano received the RIBA Gold Medal in 1989 and the Pritzker Prize in 1998. Built work after 2000 includes the Maison Hermès (Tokyo, 1998–2001); Rome Auditorium (1994–2002); conversion of the Lingotto Factory Complex (Turin, 1983–2003); Woodruff Arts Center expansion (Atlanta, 1999–2005); renovation and expansion of the Morgan Library (New York, 2000–06); and the New York Times Building (New York, 2005–07). Other recently completed work includes the Broad Contemporary Art Museum (LACMA, Los Angeles, 2003–08); California Academy of Sciences (San Francisco, 2008); the Modern Wing of the Art Institute of Chicago (2005–09); Ronchamp Gatehouse and Monastery (France, 2006–11); London Bridge Tower (London, 2009–12); Kimbell Art Museum Expansion (Fort Worth, 2010–13); Diogene (Weil am Rhein, 2011–13; see p. 202); and the Whitney Museum at Gansevoort (New York, 2007–15). Very recent and current work includes the Valletta City Gate (Malta, 2008–15); the Stavros Niarchos Foundation Cultural Center (Athens, 2008–16); and the Botín Art Center (Santander, Spain, 2010–17).

ROYAL COLLEGE OF ART

Royal College of Art
Interior Design, Darwin Building
Kensington Gore
London SW7 2EU | UK

Tel: +44 20 75 90 42 75
E-mail: interior-design@rca.ac.uk
Web: www.rca.ac.uk

Gabriella Geagea was born in 1991 in Paris. She has French, British, and Lebanese nationalities. She studied Architecture at the EPFL (Lausanne, 2009–11), received a B.A. degree in Interior and Spatial Design from the Chelsea College of Art (London, 2011–14), and an M.A. in Interior Design from the Royal College of Art (London, 2014–16). Anne-Sophie Geay was born in Paris in 1990. She received an M.A. in Interior Architecture and Product Design from the École Camondo (Paris (2008–14), and an M.A. in Interior Design from the Royal College of Art (London, 2014–16). The Wearable Shelter (2015; see p. 330) was part of their work at the Royal College of Art for their M.A. in Interior Design program.

ALEX SCHWEDER AND WARD SHELLEY

323 W 39th Street #503
New York, NY 10018 | USA

Tel: +1 917 940 1731
E-mail: alex@alexschweder.com
Web: www.alexschweder.com /
www.wardshelley.com

Alex Schweder (1970, New York City) attended the Pratt Institute (B.Arch, Brooklyn, 1988–93), the Princeton School of Architecture (M.Arch, 1996–98), and the University of Cambridge (Ph.D., UK, 2012–16). Ward Shelley (1950, New York City) obtained a Bachelor of Fine Arts degree from Eckerd College (St. Petersburg, Florida) and a Master of Art degree from New York University. They met in 2005 while they were fellows of Architecture and Fine Arts respectively at the American Academy in Rome on year-long Rome Prize fellowships. They describe their collaborative practice as "performance architecture" to characterize the buildings that they construct and occupy as a performance, as they seek to define "how people and the environments they occupy construct one another." Since 2007 they have completed five such buildings: *Flatland* (New York, 2007); *Stability* (Seattle, 2009); *Counterweight Roommate* (Basel, 2011); *In Orbit* (New York, 2014); and *ReActor* (New York, 2016; see p. 266). Their work has been exhibited at the Museum of Modern Art (New York).

SKIDMORE, OWINGS & MERRILL

Skidmore, Owings & Merrill LLP
224 South Michigan Avenue
Chicago, IL 60604 | USA

Tel: +1 312 554 9090
E-mail: somchicago@som.com
Web: www.som.com

Skidmore, Owings & Merrill LLP (SOM) is one of the largest architecture firms in the United States. Founded in Chicago in 1936 by Louis Skidmore and Nathaniel Owings (John Merrill joined the firm in 1939), they have worked on some of the best-known skyscrapers in the US, including Lever House (New York, 1952); John Hancock Center (Chicago, 1969); the Willis (formerly Sears) Tower (Chicago, 1973); and the Burj Khalifa (Dubai, 2010). Some of the firm's most prolific partners include Gordon Bunshaft, Bruce Graham, and more recently David Childs, who took over the One World Trade Center project from Daniel Libeskind on the Ground Zero site in lower Manhattan, New York, and Adrian Smith, lead designer of the Burj Khalifa Tower (Dubai, 2004–10). Other work includes the 420-meter Jin Mao Tower in Pudong (Shanghai, 1998); Time Warner Center at Columbus Circle in New York (2003); and Terminal 3 at Ben Gurion Airport (Tel Aviv, 2004, in association with Moshe Safdie). More recently, the firm has completed the OKO Tower (Moscow, 2015); the NATO Headquarters (Brussels, 2017); and the New United States Courthouse in Los Angeles. Aside from AMIE (Knoxville, Tennessee, 2015; see p. 42), SOM has been involved in other research projects, such as the design for the Digital Manufacturing and Design Innovation Institute developed by UI

Labs, a Chicago-based organization that forges partnerships to solve difficult problems; and the carbon-sequestering Timber Tower. The firm states: "Each of these projects demonstrate the power of multi-sector collaborations, and their ability to transform the architectural marketplace."

CHRISTOPHER SMITH

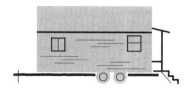

Christopher Smith
Speak Thunder Films
1928 Taft Avenue
Los Angeles, CA 90068 | USA

Tel: +1 720 937 4977
E-mail: speakthunderfilms@gmail.com
Web: www.tiny-themovie.com

Christopher Smith was born in 1981 in Bad Tölz, Germany. He received a B.A. in Philosophy (University of Colorado, Boulder) and an M.P.A. degree in Public Administration (University of Colorado, Denver). He is a documentary filmmaker and "simple living advocate." His first feature documentary, *TINY: A Story About Living Small*, about the small house movement and illustrating the house published here, premiered at SXSW (South by Southwest Conference, Austin, Texas, 2013; see p. 72) and has screened at more than 40 film festivals around the world, and was aired on Al Jazeera America. He is currently producing two new features, *American Espionage*, and *Barang*. Christopher Smith also "produces branded content for nonprofits and causes."

SO – IL

SO – IL
320 Livingston Street
Brooklyn, NY 11217 | USA

Tel: +1 718 624 6666
E-mail: office@so-il.org
Web: www.so-il.org

SO – IL was founded in 2008 by Florian Idenburg and Jing Liu, and since 2013 has been led together with Ilias Papageorgiou. Florian Idenburg was born in 1975 in Heemstede, the Netherlands. He received an M.Sc. degree in Architectural Engineering from the Technical University of Delft (1999), and worked with SANAA in Tokyo from

2000 to 2007. Jing Liu was born in 1980 in Nanjing, China. She received her M.Arch II degree from Tulane University (2004) and worked from 2004 to 2007 with KPF in New York. lias Papageorgiou was born in 1980 in Athens, Greece, and holds a degree in Architecture form the Aristotle University in Greece and an M.Arch from the Harvard GSD (2008). The work of SO – IL includes the "Pole Dance" installation (PS1, New York, 2010); "Tri-Colonnade" (Shenzhen, 2011); Kukje Gallery (Seoul, 2009–12); Frieze Art Fair (New York, 2012); Logan offices (New York, 2012); "Passage" installation for the inaugural Chicago Architecture Biennial (Illinois, 2015); Tina Kim Gallery (New York, 2015); "Blueprint" installation at the Storefront for Art and Architecture (New York, 2015); Site Verrier de Meisenthal (competition first prize, 2015; expected completion 2022); the Manetti Shrem Museum of Art at the University of California (Davis, California, 2016); and MINI LIVING—Breathe (Salone del Mobile, Milan, 2016–17; **see p. 242**).

DANIEL STRAUB

Daniel Straub
Sealander GmbH
Bollhörnkai 1
24103 Kiel | Germany

Tel: +49 431 55 68 63 60
E-mail: info@sealander.de
Web: www.sealander.de

Daniel Straub was born in Siegburg, Germany, in 1981. He received a degree in Industrial Design from Muthesius Art University (Kiel, 2010). He worked on the design and development of Sealander prototypes between 2010 and 2012 and also did fund-raising to back up his project. In 2012, he founded Sealander GmbH in Kiel, but in 2011 he had already sold his first Sealander (**see p. 138**). He is presently the Managing Director of the firm, which started series production and sales in 2015. Aside from the original concept and design work, he has also been involved in marketing, sales and, distribution, now on an international scale.

SURICATTA SYSTEMS

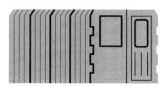

Suricatta Systems
Belando 22, Bajo
03004 Alicante | Spain

Tel: +34 636 47 76 70
E-mail: info@suricattasystems.com
Web: www.suricattasystems.com

Suricatta Systems was created by the R&D department of Urbana IDR, a repair, maintenance, and construction company based in Alicante, Spain. Their SURI project (**see p. 324**) was conceived for humanitarian use but has numerous other applications. Pedro Sáez, the head of Urbana IDR, and founder of Suricatta Systems, was born in Alicante in 1974 and has a degree in Technical Architecture from Superior Polytechnic Institute of Alicante (1998). Rafael Rodriguez was born in Alicante in 1974. He has a Certificate of Higher Education in Construction and Civil Engineering and is the R&D Manager of Suricatta Systems. Carmen García was born in Elda in 1983. She studied Architecture at the Polytechnic institute of Valencia, ETSAV (2012) and at the School of Architecture, Design, and Civil Engineering in Winterthur (ZHAW, 2009).

TENTSILE

Tentsile LTD
Suite 507, 1 Alie Street
E1 8DE London | UK

Tel: +44 20 83 61 92 20
E-mail: info@tentsile.com
Web: www.tentsile.com

Tentsile was created in 2012 by Alex Shirley-Smith and product designer Kirk Kirchev. In collaboration with WeForest, Eden Projects, and Arbor Day foundation, Tentsile supports the planting of three trees for every tent purchased. Their first tent, called the Stingray, was marketed in 2013. They conceive their products as "portable tree houses." Very light, these tents are made with polyester and nylon fabrics, and are designed to be easily suspended from trees, no matter what the underlying terrain (**see p. 180**). The designers explain: "Our range of Tree Tents combines the versatility of a hammock with the comfort and security of a tent, allowing you and your friends to experience a new way to connect with the natural world. The tents leave no footprint at all, meaning that both the tree and the ground around it remain completely unharmed. Tentsile's unique designs create a comfortable camp, for all seasons, no matter what the ground conditions, and provides increased separation from lumps, bumps, water, mud, insects—even snakes and other predators for more exotic locations."

TREE TENTS INTERNATIONAL / JASON THAWLEY

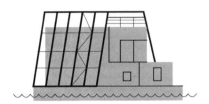
Tree Tents International
Brickyard Farm, Town Littleworth Road
BN8 4TD Barcombe, East Sussex | UK

Tel: +44 1273 40 00 94
E-mail: info@treetents.co.uk
Web: www.treetents.co.uk

Jason Thawley worked as an engineer for Land Rover and Lola cars, before obtaining his degree in Mechanical Engineering in the late 1990s. He has been part of a design team for a group of audio companies working on groundbreaking professional amplifier and control products, developing his skills in electromechanical, thermal, and ergonomic design (Soundcraft Studer, 1998–2004). In 2004, Thawley created his own firm, Luminair, focusing on lighting design, but he has also worked on architecture, including an eco-house and the Tree Tent published here (2012; **see p. 186**). He has been the Design and Innovation Director of Tree Tents International since May 2016.

CARL TURNER

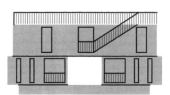

Carl Turner Architects CTA
Unit 61, Regent Studios
8 Andrews Road
London E8 4QN | UK

Tel: +44 020 38 46 18 90
E-mail: info@ct-architects.co.uk
Web: www.ct-architects.co.uk

Carl Turner Architects was founded in 2006 by Carl Turner, who graduated from the Royal College of Art and was an inaugural Research Associate at the Helen Hamlyn Research Center at the RCA. He founded Turner Castle with Cassion Castle in 1999. He is presently the Director of his own firm, CTA. Aside from the planned Floating House (UK, 2016; **see p. 102**) published here, CTA has designed the Frame House (London, 2011); Designer's House (London, 2006); Slip House (London, 2012)—winner of the Manser Medal and a RIBA National Award; and A House for London, a prefabricated structure made from two shipping containers for the 2015 London Design Festival which was placed outside the Building Center (London).

URBAN RIGGER / BIG

Urban Rigger Office
Strandvejen 337
2930 Klampenborg
Denmark

E-mail: info@urbanrigger.com
Tel: +45 27 11 42 42
Web: www.urbanrigger.com

BIG-Bjarke Ingels Group
Kløverbladsgade 56
2500 Valby, Copenhagen
Denmark

Tel: +45 72 21 72 27
E-mail: big@big.dk
Web: www.big.dk

Urban Rigger was founded in Copenhagen in 2013 by the entrepreneur Kim Loudrup. "The idea," states the founder and CEO of the firm, "was to develop a revolutionary and innovative floating dwelling system that will have a positive impact on the housing situation for students in Europe, as well as completing an attractive untapped and geographically independent niche in the market: the water ways—thousands of kilometers of unused quay's across the harbor, canal, and river intensive cities across the world." Loudrup teamed up with Bjarke Ingels Group (BIG). Bjarke Ingels, Jakob Sand, Jakob Lange, and Finn Nørkjær are the Partners-in-Charge of Urban Rigger. The first full-scale result of their collaboration was delivered in 2016 (see p. 142). The concept was nominated for the 2017 Edison Awards (among others), which commented: "Urban Rigger is the first floating, carbon neutral student housing constructed from up-cycled shipping containers and designed for mass production, with the goal of creating an affordable alternative to the rising housing prices in major cities. Multiple units can be configured to fit any port organization, allowing for maximum flexibility."

VIPP

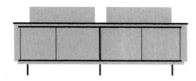

Vipp
Snorresgade 22
2300 Copenhagen
Denmark

Tel: +45 45 88 88 00
E-mail: info@vipp.com
Web: www.vipp.com

Vipp was created in 1939 in Copenhagen when the artisan Holger Nielsen created a pedal bin for his wife's hair salon. The Vipp pedal bin is still the firm's most famous product and is considered a worldwide design classic. In fact the name of the firm is derived from the Danish word meaning to tilt (vippe), like the cover of the waste bin. Vipp is still a Danish industrial-design company and still in the hands of the family, remaining totally independent. At the death of Holger Nielsen in 1992, his daughter Jette Egelund took over the firm. Today they make kitchens, a lamp series, and many types of kitchen and bathroom products. The 38-year-old chief designer Morten Bo Jensen, who has been with the firm for 11 years, is responsible for most of the new designs. He was educated as

an industrial designer in Denmark and had worked previously for Biomega. Kasper Egelund, the CEO of Vipp, says that when he lived in New York, he dreamed of a getaway that he could have without building it himself—this was the origin of the Vipp Shelter (Immeln, Sweden, 2014; see p. 278).

WATERSTUDIO.NL

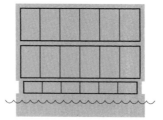

Waterstudio.NL
Generaal Berenschotlaan 211
2283 JM Rijswijk
The Netherlands

Tel: +31 70 394 42 34
E-mail: info@waterstudio.nl
Web: www.waterstudio.nl

Koen Olthuis was born in 1971, and studied Architecture and Industrial Design at the Delft University of Technology. In 2002, he created Waterstudio.NL with Rolf Peters, apparently "the first architecture firm in the world exclusively dedicated to living on water." In 2007, he was on Time magazine's list of the most influential people due to the increasing interest in development on water. In 2011, the French magazine Terra Eco selected him as one of the 100 "green people" who will change the world. Olthuis also participates in Dutch Docklands with Paul van de Camp, "a developer of large-scale water projects worldwide." His City Apps are floating urban components that add a certain function to the existing static grid of a city. He states: "Using existing urban water as building ground offers space for new density, offering worldwide opportunities for cities to respond flexibly to climate change and urbanization." The first city in which this vision is being developed is The Westland, near The Hague in Holland. This project incorporates floating social housing, floating islands, and floating apartment buildings. Realized projects by Waterstudio.NL include the two Villa IJburg Floating Villas published here (Amsterdam, 2008; see pp. 108, 112).

WILLIAM WINKELMAN

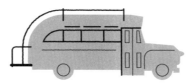

Winkelman Architecture
41 Union Wharf, Suite 4
Portland, ME 04101 | USA

Tel: +1 207 699 2998
E-mail: will@winkarch.com
Web: www.winkarch.com

William Winkleman was born in Memphis, Tennessee, in 1958. He graduated from the University of Houston (Texas) with a Bachelor of Architecture degree in 1982. He worked with Goduti/Thomas Architects (Portland, Maine, 1984–90) and with Whitten Architects (Portland, Maine, 1991–2006), before founding Winkelman Architecture in 2007, which he describes as "a highly collaborative design and craft driven service exclusively for residential clients." The work of the firm includes three houses currently under construction—Burke (Raymond, Maine); West (Standish, Maine); and Drexel (Mount Desert Island, Maine)—as well as the 2009 project published here, the 1958 Chevy Viking Short-Bus Retro (see p. 32).

YASUTAKA YOSHIMURA

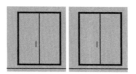

Yasutaka Yoshimura Architects
3-13-20-503, Sendagaya, Shibuya-ku
151-0051 Tokyo
Japan

Tel: +81 3 6434 0386
E-mail: mail@ysmr.com
Web: www.ysmr.com

Yasutaka Yoshimura was born in Toyota, Aichi, in 1972. He received a Bachelor's degree from the Faculty of Science and Engineering of Waseda University (Tokyo, 1995), and a Master's degree from the Graduate School of Science and Engineering at the same university (1997). From 1999 to 2001, he worked with MVRDV in Rotterdam. He founded his own firm in Tokyo in 2005. His built work includes a hostel in Kyonan (Chiba, 2012); Window House (Kanagawa, 2013), Lattice House (Toyama, 2016) and the Fukumasu Kindergarten Annex (Chiba, 2016). He also designed the Ex-Container (Ishinomaki, 2012; see p. 306).

RUSS GRAY

is a designer/illustrator based in Salt Lake City, Utah, running his own creative studio, Russ Gray Design. He has been creative-director and senior designer at several agencies working for worldwide brands such as Disney Publishing, Google, Franklin Mill, Chapters/Indigo, and *New Scientist Magazine*.

Illustrations: Russ Gray, Salt Lake City, Utah
Design: Benjamin Wolbergs, Berlin
Project management: Florian Kobler, Berlin
Collaboration: Harriet Graham, Turin
Production: Ute Wachendorf, Cologne
German translation: Nora von Mühlendahl, Ludwigsburg
French translation: Claire Debard, Freiburg

Cover: Brian & Joni Buzarde, Woody, Land Ark Prototype, Marble, Colorado, USA

Printed in Slovakia

ISBN 978-3-8365-6233-1

© 2017 TASCHEN GmbH
Hohenzollernring 53
D-50672 Cologne
www.taschen.com